T0331117

Seasonal Stock Market Trends

Founded in 1807, John Wiley & Sons is the oldest independent publishing company in the United States. With offices in North America, Europe, Australia, and Asia, Wiley is globally committed to developing and marketing print and electronic products and services for our customers' professional and personal knowledge and understanding.

The Wiley Trading series features books by traders who have survived the market's ever changing temperament and have prospered—some by reinventing systems, others by getting back to basics. Whether a novice trader, professional, or somewhere in-between, these books will provide the advice and strategies needed to prosper today and well into the future.

For a list of available titles, visit our web site at www.WileyFinance.com.

Seasonal Stock Market Trends

The Definitive Guide to Calendar-Based Stock Market Trading

JAY KAEPPEL

WILEY

John Wiley & Sons, Inc.

Copyright © 2009 by Jay Kaeppel. All rights reserved.

Published by John Wiley & Sons, Inc., Hoboken, New Jersey.
Published simultaneously in Canada.

No part of this publication may be reproduced, stored in a retrieval system, or transmitted in any form or by any means, electronic, mechanical, photocopying, recording, scanning, or otherwise, except as permitted under Section 107 or 108 of the 1976 United States Copyright Act, without either the prior written permission of the Publisher, or authorization through payment of the appropriate per-copy fee to the Copyright Clearance Center, Inc., 222 Rosewood Drive, Danvers, MA 01923, (978) 750-8400, fax (978) 646-8600, or on the web at www.copyright.com. Requests to the Publisher for permission should be addressed to the Permissions Department, John Wiley & Sons, Inc., 111 River Street, Hoboken, NJ 07030, (201) 748-6011, fax (201) 748-6008, or online at http://www.wiley.com/go/permissions.

Limit of Liability/Disclaimer of Warranty: While the publisher and author have used their best efforts in preparing this book, they make no representations or warranties with respect to the accuracy or completeness of the contents of this book and specifically disclaim any implied warranties of merchantability or fitness for a particular purpose. No warranty may be created or extended by sales representatives or written sales materials. The advice and strategies contained herein may not be suitable for your situation. You should consult with a professional where appropriate. Neither the publisher nor author shall be liable for any loss of profit or any other commercial damages, including but not limited to special, incidental, consequential, or other damages.

For general information on our other products and services or for technical support, please contact our Customer Care Department within the United States at (800) 762-2974, outside the United States at (317) 572-3993 or fax (317) 572-4002.

Wiley also publishes its books in a variety of electronic formats. Some content that appears in print may not be available in electronic books. For more information about Wiley products, visit our web site at www.wiley.com.

Library of Congress Cataloging-in-Publication Data:

Kaeppel, Jay.
    Seasonal stock market trends : the definitive guide to calendar-based stock market trading / Jay Kaeppel.
        p. cm.
    Includes index.
    ISBN 978-0-470-27043-1 (pbk.)
    1. Stocks–Charts, diagrams, etc.   2. Investment analysis.   3. Investments.   I. Title.
    HG4638.K34 2009
    332.63'22–dc22

                                                                                    2008036344

10   9   8   7   6   5   4   3   2   1

To Maggie, Jenny, and Jimmy

Contents

Preface

I t was just about the dumbest thing I'd ever heard. And I remember it as plain as day. Like a lot of ideas that have come and gone over the years, I don't even remember the source, sadly. But the message was simple— the stock market was soon to embark on a major bull market, rising to new all-time highs in the process. It was a preposterous notion.

The time was April 1982. For the previous 16 years, the Dow Jones Industrial Average had fluctuated in a wide range between 1,051 on the upside and 578 on the downside. The Dow had approached or exceeded the magical 1,000 level on five occasions, always to be turned back. There had also been a series of painful bear markets during this 16-year stretch. The bear market of 1966 ended with the Dow plunging 969 to 744, down 23 percent in a little more than nine months. The 1969–1970 bear market was a near replay, with the Dow shedding 36 percent from its bull market high. The 1973–1974 bear market was the worst since the Great Depression. From peak to valley, the Dow fell a staggering 45 percent, and the combination of high inflation and deflated stock prices—not to mention the Watergate scandal—took a powerful toll on investors' psyches. Following a 75 percent advance from the December 1974 low to the September 1976 high, the Dow experienced another decline of 27 percent between September 1976 and February 1978. Over the next 38 months, the Dow again advanced back above 1,000, peaking at 1,024 in April 1981. And, as investors had come to expect, the rally failed to hold. By March 1982, the Dow was back under 800, 22 percent off of the April 1981 high.

So there I was, a neophyte in the market, learning the lessons of the market. The conventional wisdom at the time was pretty straightforward:

- The Dow trades in a range between roughly 600 and 1,050.
- Whenever it approaches 1,000, it is time to keep an eye on the exits, because the stock market *always* tops out when it nears that level.
- It is a given that the stock market declines during a post–presidential election year. Within the 16-year trading range, the Dow lost ground in 1969 (15 percent), 1973 (16 percent), 1977 (17 percent), and 1981

(9 percent). So looking ahead, it was pretty much a sure thing that 1985 would be a bad year for stocks.
- The good news of the day was that the stock market always makes a low every four years. The years of 1962, 1966, 1970, 1974, and 1978 had all witnessed a meaningful multiyear low.

So, sitting there in April 1982, with the Dow roughly 20 percent off of its April 1981 high, investors might have felt confident that a multiyear low was in the offing. Unfortunately, at the time, everyone knew that things were different this time around. Ronald Reagan had been in office a little more than a year, and despite the fact that he had promised to lower inflation and get the economy going, inflation and interest rates were still high (albeit declining), the economy was still struggling, and some of the leading stock market advisers of the day were extremely bearish. In fact, Joe Granville, who had called the 1981 top almost exactly—clearly a man with his finger on the pulse of the market—was forecasting another economic depression. So, when I stumbled upon a tidbit of cyclical stock market history, I almost had to laugh.

As I mentioned earlier, I don't recall where I read it. But, wherever it came from, this piece pointed out that the stock market had staged strong rallies between the end of June of years ending in 2 and the end of December of years ending in 5—get this—every other decade. In other words, we were supposed to care that between June 1902 and December 1905, the Dow had rallied 50 percent and that, 20 years later, between June 1922 and December 1925, the Dow had rallied 69 percent. And, it was supposed to hold some historical significance that between June 1942 and December 1945, the Dow had advanced 87 percent and that, another 20 years later, the Dow had rallied 73 percent between June 1962 and December 1965.

In a nutshell, we were supposed to believe that what had happened in the stock market 20, 40, 60, and 80 years prior somehow mattered a hoot in the present day. What a hoot, indeed. And we were also to ignore the fact that this trend from June of years ending in 2 through December of years ending in 5 only worked every other decade. In other words, this pattern did not necessarily work from 1912 to 1915, from 1932 to 1935, from 1952 to 1955, and from 1972 to 1975. To put it mildly, I did not put much faith in this little nugget of stock market history, especially with a leading expert like Joe Granville predicting a depression. Nevertheless, because I was still learning the ropes in the stock market, I tried to keep track of as many market tools as possible. With a chuckle, I wrote, "Every 20 years between June of year 2 and December of year 5 indicator" into my log of stock market tools. Then I quickly turned my attention back to more useful tools, like economic and earnings forecasts.

On June 30, 1982, after the stock market closed, I wrote down the level of the Dow: 811.93. This was just 2 percent above its recent low of 796, achieved a few months earlier during March. By August 12, 1982, the Dow had drifted lower to 776.92, its lowest level in more than 28 months. With the weight of negative economic and market forecasts still hanging heavy, this new low appeared to be a strong confirmation that investors needed to brace themselves for a continuing stock market decline. Then something strange happened.

Over the subsequent two days, the Dow staged a respectable 2 percent gain. Then, on August 16, 1982, something inexplicable happened. The stock market rallied 4.9 percent, in one day. And from there, it never looked back. About a month later, the Dow stood 20 percent above its August low. Some investors leaped aboard the soaring rocket ship that the stock market had suddenly become. Most others stood by with their collective jaws on the floor, unable to pull the trigger in the face of a market reality completely at odds with the conventional wisdom, or such as it was just a month prior.

On June 30, 1982 (i.e., at the end of June of year 2 of an even-numbered decade), the Dow stood at 811.93. And 36 months later, on December 31, 1985 (i.e., at the end of December of year 5 of an even-numbered decade), the Dow stood at 1,546.67. This represented a gain of 99 percent in just two and a half years. By that time, a cyclical analyst had been born.

Over the past 25 years, I have examined in great detail a wide range of seasonal and cyclical trends as they relate to the stock market. Much of the best of what I have learned is contained in the following pages. The cycle marking June of year 2 through December of year 5 has been refined somewhat and appears in Chapter 5 as the cycle of October of year 2 through December of year 5. I have written in the past about some of the discoveries I have made. In many cases, those discoveries amount to things that other analysts have already learned and made public. Some of the pioneers of seasonal stock market analysis are noted in Chapter 1 and throughout the book as the ones who deserve credit for a particular finding. In *Technical Analysis* magazine, I have published articles such as, "The January Barometer: Myth or Reality" (discussed in Chapter 2), "The 40-Week Cycle in the Stock Market" (discussed in Chapter 6), and "The Stock Market, the Calendar, and You," which incorporated a variety of seasonal trends into one comprehensive market-timing model.

Numerous studies have shown that the greatest influence on the price action of any given stock is the action of the overall stock market. A rising tide lifts all boats. In the stock market, it is a similar story. Whereas a bullish stock market in no way ensures that all stocks will participate, it is easier to make money in stocks when the overall market is rising than when it is falling. Likewise, it is often best to invest defensively, or perhaps even raise some cash, if the prospect for an overall decline in stock prices is great. The material presented throughout this book is designed to help investors weigh the likelihood of an overall stock market advance or decline during a particular time frame.

The most important thing that you can do in analyzing and considering the research presented in this book is to read with an open mind. As I described at the outset, the easiest thing to do is to laugh off ideas that seem to have no foundation in fundamental analysis, be they related to earnings and sales or supply and demand. What people think about what the stock market will do next and why has no real bearing on what the stock market ends up doing. The methods and tools presented herein provide a very useful road map for investors who seek to maximize their long-term profitability by using all tools at their disposal.

JAY KAEPPEL

Seasonal Stock Market Trends

CHAPTER 1

Introduction to Seasonality in the Stock Market

Within nature there exists an undeniable ebb and flow. The sun unfailingly rises in the east and then sets in the west. The moon revolves around the earth. The earth revolves around the sun. Trees grow leaves in the spring. The leaves turn bright colors in the fall and by winter they have fallen to the ground. The following spring the same routine starts anew. Most people go to bed at night and rise in the morning. What happens in nature affects humans, not only physically, but also emotionally and psychologically. Thunderstorms instill fear and a desire to seek shelter. A blizzard triggers an urge in people to hunker down and cocoon at home under a blanket. A dark, dreary day has an undeniable tendency to cause many people to experience—for lack of a better word—a funk, a state of mind in which virtually nothing feels right. But, ah, a warm, sunshine-filled day can all by itself suddenly make everything feel right. For millennia, the human race was a slave to the sun. And, to this day, people are drawn to bask in its glow. To better understand this phenomenon, picture opening the drapes first thing in the morning on a cloudless, sunny day following three days of dreary weather. Suddenly, almost magically, the darkest of moods seem to melt away.

So, what does any of this have to do with the stock market? The heart of the matter comes down to the fact that humans are a creature of habit and repetition, and that many, many things in life happen on a cyclical basis. And these cycles can greatly affect the way a person thinks or feels. Let's first consider the concept of seasons.

THE CONCEPT OF SEASONS AND SEASONALITY

Virtually everyone is familiar with the concept of a season. We can start with winter, spring, summer, and fall. Add in hunting season, football season, mating season, hurricane season, holiday season, and so on. Factor in "a season for all things," "now is the season of our discontent," "the seasons changed and so did I," and you start to get the idea.

In a nutshell, in many aspects of life things occur in a repetitive pattern. Spring follows winter, then summer, fall, and then winter again. Things do in fact change over time. Yet, the basic underlying idea of seasons and seasonality is that although things do change, they often return to a particular state over and over again—often in a very cyclic and predictable way. Over time, the human mind comes to understand the cyclic or seasonal nature of certain occurrences and begins to adapt. In the old days in cold-weather climates—before the advent of heat and running water—humans used to gather up provisions as the fall progressed to ensure that there would be enough food to last the winter. Nowadays, many individuals in cold-weather climates use the beginning of baseball spring training in February as something to latch onto to help get them through the remaining cold months of winter and to remind them that better (or at the very least, warmer) days are certainly ahead. Today, many people living along the Atlantic Ocean or the Gulf of Mexico make preemptive plans regarding the potential for hurricanes during the late summer and fall months.

So what, you might ask, does any of this have to do with the stock market? I mean, certainly, one might be willing to grant the notion that weather-related seasonal trends could have an impact on commodities and grains. Things that grow in the ground or that eat the things that grow in the ground clearly can be affected if the ground is too wet or too dry (or covered with three feet of snow) and does not allow for the normal planting process to proceed. But the stock market is primarily based on financial assets, not physical assets. As long as the New York Stock Exchange has electricity, the nature of the weather outside is seemingly irrelevant. And the Nasdaq market doesn't even operate a physical exchange. So, here too, the vagaries of weather and seasons would at first blush seem to be quite irrelevant. But the reality is that there is more to cyclicity, seasons, and seasonality than mere weather.

In many cases, seasons become a state of mind. As I have already described, in many instances, people prepare for certain recurring events, proceed as planned during the period in question, and then relax and redirect their energies in different directions once the anticipated cyclic or seasonal period or event has passed. In summary, human emotion becomes intertwined with cyclical trends.

So, to sum up so far, we all accept the fact that many things in life are seasonal in nature, or cyclic. Most of us recognize and accept the notion that people's thoughts, attitudes, and emotions can change with the seasons. This is an important connection, because the stock market can be thought of as the ultimate arbiter of human emotion as it relates to all things financial.

It can be argued that the stock market experiences seasons or cycles. At the very least, one can make the case that there are bull seasons, when the stock market advances, and bear seasons, when the stock market declines. In addition, one could argue that there are at least two or three other seasons in the stock market:

- A pullback in a longer-term bull market.
- A rally in a longer-term bear market.
- An extended trendless period.

Although none of these seasons are related to weather and although bull markets and bear markets certainly cannot be counted on to always begin and end on the same dates each year, the fact remains that these seasons are a fact of life for stock market investors. As such, most investors ultimately have to learn to deal with the inevitable change of seasons in the stock market.

Whereas many individuals try to deal with these seasons as objectively as possible, ultimately, much of the decision-making process comes down to emotion. As a result, the gyrations of the stock market have a direct relationship with human emotion that is deeply intertwined. At times, the fluctuations of the stock market can cause mass changes in the overall emotional state of market participants. Likewise, at other times, the emotional state of market participants as a whole can exert a direct effect on the direction of stock prices. In essence, what happens over time is that the season for investors moves from greed to complacency to fear, and then the process repeats. To better understand this change of seasons, let's consider a typical stock market cycle and how it affects investors' thinking and vice versa.

The initial stages of a bear market are generally marked by denial, as investors who have become used to making money can't bring themselves to believe that the good times have come to an end. As the bear market unfolds, more and more investors eventually bail out—often swearing never to risk their hard-earned money again—whereas others cling to every countertrend rally, hoping that it is the start of the next bull market. As the bear market reaches its low, fear typically ramps up and ever more people decide they can't stand the pain of losing money anymore. At a major stock market bottom, there is typically great despair among investors. And, at about this time, the season changes. The stock market no longer continues to make new lows but, in fact, may stage a strong rally off of a low. With human nature being what it is, many investors refuse to believe that the bottom is in. And, they refuse to be sucked into the market once again in fear that another plunge is in the offing. But, even as these former investors stand aside and get left behind, the season is changing back from bearish to bullish. As the bull market continues, optimism grows and investors flock back to the market, looking to make their money grow. Eventually, concerns of downside risk give way to fears of missing out, and money pours into stocks of all stripes and colors. As optimism and complacency reach their peak, the stock market tops out once again. It is often said that the masses are right in the middle and wrong at the extremes. In other words, the majority of investors are typically too bullish at the top and too bearish at the bottom. And, in my experience, this adage has proved to be true.

One of the key factors that drives emotion when it comes to investing is the fact that it involves the potential increase—or decrease—in one's hard-earned money. Making or losing a lot of money quickly tends to have strange effects on people. For example, in most instances, people prefer to buy something when the price is lower. If an item cost $20 yesterday and today costs only $18, most people will be more attracted to that item today on the basis that it now represents a better value than it did yesterday. When that item comes to the stock market, however, this is not always the case. This is partly because no one can ever be sure how low is low. In other words, it is possible for the stock of a given company to go to zero if the company goes bankrupt or out of business. The fear of this potential outcome always lingers in the back of investors' minds. And, as a result, a decline in the price of a stock more often is likely to persuade someone to sell that stock than it is to persuade someone to buy it. In other words, the thinking eventually changes along the following lines.

I bought it at $22 because I thought it was a value. At $20 I figured it must be an even better value so I bought some more. At $18 I started to wonder whether maybe my analysis was a bit early in selecting this stock as a value. At $16 I started to think seriously about cutting my losses. By the time the stock reached $14, I couldn't take it anymore and decided to bail out. As the stock hit $10 a share, I realized that it was one of the biggest dog companies to ever exist so I decided to sell it short. Three days later, it was back over $14 and I finally realized that I had no idea what I was doing.

And, so it goes. In some ways, buying a stock can be viewed along the lines of finding a mate. Investors first identify and become involved with an attractive stock. But, as happens sometimes, things go south. As the price of the stock declines, investors first attempt to remain convinced that the stock is attractive. Eventually, investors realize that this mate is trying to take them for all they are worth. Painfully, investors accept the fact that they were wrong and that they must terminate the relationship. After that comes the remorse and recriminations. Now, clearly this cycle does not play out just this way with every stock purchase (nor, thankfully, with every relationship). Still, it only takes one or two of these types of experiences for the pain associated with them to be permanently seared into an investor's psyche. And, this memory can strongly affect the way one looks at other future relationships.

Investors who suffer a loss beyond what they had expected will typically be gun shy for a good long while into the future, as they do not wish to repeat this unpleasant experience. They may find themselves bailing out of positions at the first sign of trouble, only to then find themselves on the sidelines when the rally starts in earnest. Likewise, investors who achieved a quick profit and then watched it vanish, never to return, may be very quick to take profits in the future. These are just two simple examples of how the market can affect an investor's thinking, and how that thinking can affect the actions that take place in the stock market. Clearly, investors' moods and outlooks change as the investment season changes. And, just as clearly, changes in the moods and outlooks of the majority of investors can affect the investment season.

So is it that much of a stretch to believe that the stock market could have seasons? That is the question that this book will attempt to answer.

WHAT IS SEASONALITY?

The Merriam-Webster online dictionary defines the words "season" and "seasonal" as follows:

> **Season**: a period characterized by or associated with a particular activity or phenomenon.
>
> **Seasonal**: of, relating to, or varying in occurrence according to the season.

For our purposes, we will use the word "seasonality" to define any number of seasonal trends that seem to exist in the stock market. We will define the phrase "seasonal trend" as a recurrent period characterized by certain occurrences—most notably, a tendency for the stock market to rise (or fall) in price. The seasonal trends that I will detail in this book will be outlined in a moment. For now, let's define what seasonality is not.

You must accept the fact that seasonality in the stock market is not a magic formula. Throughout this book we will be looking at a variety of seasonal trends, each with specific buy and sell dates. And, as you will see, the results for many of these seasonal trends have accumulated an extremely impressive track record. And, to some individuals, it might seem to make sense to use these trends on a systematic basis. But that is a determination that each investor must make on his or her own. In the end, the goal of this book is to convince you that seasonality has a place in your investment strategy. However, the goal is not necessarily to try to convince you that you should rely solely on seasonal tendencies to the exclusion of all other analyses.

The best analogy that I have heard for describing the proper way to look at seasonal trends in the financial markets came from Michael Santoli in his *Barron's Financial Weekly* "Streetwise" column from November 26, 2007. In that particular column he stated the following:

"Seasonality is climate, not weather."

Although this comment may not make intuitive sense to everyone, it very accurately sums up the proper perspective that an investor should have when considering incorporating seasonal trends into an investment strategy. Just because it is December in Chicago does not necessarily mean that the temperature will be extremely cold. On an unseasonably warm day, the high in Chicago can reach above 50 degrees even during what is considered a winter month. Seasonality tells us that it should be cold, or more accurately, that it is more likely than not to be cold on a December day in Chicago, but the weather outside can vary widely. As we will see, the same is true regarding seasonal trends in the stock market. If a given time of year has been up 60 times in the past 70 years, we would intuitively look for that period to be bullish again this year. But whether this year ultimately falls into the normal bullish category or joins that smaller number of bearish aberrations cannot be accurately predicted in advance.

So the bottom line is that seasonality in the stock market should not be thought of as an exact science. Nevertheless, the other key piece of the equation is to recognize from the data presented throughout this book the powerful trends that seasonal patterns can help you to identify in the stock market, and the fact that seasonal trends should not be ignored simply because they are not based on hard fundamental data such as earnings or on a price-based technical indicator. In essence, a given seasonal trend is a form of a psychological or sentimental indicator, as each seasonal trend is a measure of the tendency of the investment masses to act in a certain way in a certain repetitive form. Before jumping into the details of the actual seasonal trends themselves, let's first take a moment to recognize some of the pioneers in the area of seasonally related research.

THE PIONEERS OF STOCK MARKET SEASONALITY

Whereas some individuals will look questioningly upon the notion of seasonality in the stock market, the fact remains that some of the best minds in the business have spent countless hours, and even years, conducting a great deal of research in the area of seasonal trends in the stock market. In the following text, I would like to give mention to a few of the early pioneers in the area of seasonal stock market research.

Yale Hirsch

It might be appropriate to refer to Yale Hirsch as the "founding father" of seasonal trend analysis in the stock market. He was the original editor and publisher of *The Stock Trader's Almanac* (www. stocktradersalmanac.com), which has been published annually since 1967. As a result of countless hours of groundbreaking research, Hirsch became the leading analyst in the area of historical stock market behavior and cycles in different political and economic environments.

His most notable contribution to the area of seasonality is the much renowned January barometer. The premise underlying the January barometer is simply that as the month of January goes, so goes the entire stock market year. This method is discussed in-depth in Chapter 2 along with several variations. Other indicators that Hirsch has developed or popularized over the years are the Santa Claus rally (Chapter 4) and the best six consecutive months of the year (Chapter 8). In summary, Hirsch's research over the years has helped many astute investors to profit in the stock market and has effectively served to legitimize the analysis of seasonal trends in the stock market.

It should also be noted that Yale Hirsch's son Jeffrey Hirsch has followed in his father's footsteps and become another major player in the area of research of seasonal market trends. Jeffrey is now the publisher of *The Stock Trader's Almanac* and authored *The Almanac Investor: Profit from Market History and Seasonal Trends* (Wiley, 2005).

Norman Fosback

Norman Fosback authored the classic stock market book *Stock Market Logic* in 1976. Fosback was and is a serious student of the market and gained prominence in the 1970s and 1980s for implementing econometrics in his stock market analysis. He edited a newsletter titled *Market Logic* from 1975 until 1995. He also founded and was editor-in-chief of *Mutual*

Funds Magazine, one of the most widely read personal investment publications ever produced. But for our purposes, Fosback's most prominent contribution was in the area of stock market seasonality. It was from a research project that lasted from 1971 into 1975 that he developed his "seasonality switching system."

Much of what he discovered in his testing and incorporated into that original switching system is used throughout the pages of this book. The heart of Fosback's original research was the recognition that the period comprising the last trading day of the month and the first four trading days of the next month was by far the most favorable time of the month to invest in the stock market (Chapter 4). Over the years, the original system evolved and some of the rules became a bit more arcane (e.g., Fosback's Rule 5 states, "Do not own equities on the second day before a holiday closing if that day happens also to be the first trading day of the week"; Fosback's Rule 6 states, "Continue to own equities on the first day after a market holiday closing if that day is also the last trading day of the week"). Nevertheless, despite the seemingly arcane nature of some of the updated rules, the bottom line is that these changes may in fact result in better performance over the long run.

One ironic note: Although Fosback did do some research on individual stocks, the real heart of his analysis was based on the overall stock market itself. Unfortunately for him, virtually no index funds existed back in the 1970s and they became a viable investment choice only in the 1990s. Thus, whenever Fosback's methods generated a buy signal, he was faced with the task of building a portfolio or buying a stock mutual fund that would hopefully closely track the overall stock market averages. Nowadays, investors have an important advantage in that they can buy an index fund and instantly own a position that will accurately track the performance of a given stock index.

Dick Stoken

Dick Stoken authored a book titled *Strategic Investment Timing in the 90s* in 1990. In that book, he discussed something he referred to as the "investment climate." He claimed that this investment climate turned favorable on October 1 two years before the next presidential election, and that this favorable period extended through the end of the following (or preelection) year. This claim will be examined in much greater detail in Chapter 7, "Election Cycle Investing." For now, suffice it to say that Stoken did indeed speak the truth, and that this 15-month period has consistently provided investors with an above-average climate for investing in stocks.

Peter Eliades

Peter Eliades is a stock market analyst who gained prominence in the 1980s as the editor of an advisory letter titled *Stock Market Cycles*. As the name of his advisory service implies, Eliades has done a great deal of work in the area of identifying meaningful cycles in the stock market. One of his primary contributions to seasonal analysis that we will look at in this book is the 212-week cycle, which is discussed in Chapter 6, "Repetitive Time Cycles of Note."

Much of what appears in this book is either taken whole or derived from the works of pioneers such as those individuals whom we have just discussed. As a self-admitted graduate from the School of Whatever Works, I greatly appreciate the fact that so many respected analysts have refused the initial urge to scoff at seasonality in the stock market and, in fact, have not only embraced the concept but also taken the time to do research in an area that some might consider arcane. Last, they were willing to share their findings so that the rest of us might benefit also.

MEASURING MARKET PERFORMANCE THROUGHOUT THIS BOOK

This book is dedicated to the idea of highlighting a wide variety of seasonal trends in the stock market. One great thing about the stock market is that ultimately the success or failure of any idea can be quantified simply by running the numbers. If you can establish objective buy and sell rules for virtually any method you choose, you can then apply those rules and identify specific buy and sell points. From there you can simply compare the selling price to the buying price and determine whether a given trade generated a profit or a loss. You can also total and analyze for risk and reward characteristics the cumulative total of profits for all trades made according to a given method.

For the purposes of this book, we will use the performance of the Dow Jones Industrial Average (hereafter referred to as "the Dow") in almost all cases to measure the performance of each given seasonal trend. Some will argue that this index is among the most narrowly based of all, as it consists of only 30 large-cap stocks and can at times differ significantly in performance from the performance of the average stock. But, for our purposes, this is acceptable. The benefits of using the Dow as our benchmark are severalfold. First off, there are well more than 100 years of history available for analysis. Nothing is ever guaranteed to work forever. Still, if a given trend or method tests well more than a century of data, it is fair to ask,

What more do you want? In other words, if 100-plus years of strong performance are not enough to convince you that a given method or trend is viable, then you are awfully tough to please.

In some ways investors today have it far better than those of just a few short years or decades ago. For example, in the discussion of Norman Fosback's analysis of seasonal historical trends, I mentioned the fact that prior to a certain time there was essentially no such animal as an index fund. Also, among the few that existed, there were some severe limitations regarding how often an investor could switch in or out of them. As a result, investors who wanted to take advantage of market movement had little choice but to buy a group of stocks that they felt would closely track the movement of the index they hoped to track. Sometimes this approach worked out fine, and other times it did not. In this scenario, it was possible to be exactly correct about one's expectation for the overall market, yet still lose money because the purchased stocks underperformed the index that one was trying to emulate.

Fortunately, for investors nowadays, it is a relatively easy task to replicate the performance of an index such as the S&P 500. This objective can be accomplished by simply buying an index fund, an exchange-traded fund, or a futures contract that tracks that particular index. Other choices include the Dow, the Nasdaq 100, and the small-cap Russell 2000 index.

One other thing that should be pointed out up front regarding the performance numbers that appear in this book is that we will use different starting points for different methods. There are two approaches that we can choose from. We can use the same starting date for each test of each different method, or we can start each test at a point where the method in question actually begins to start working. In other words, some methods might test well more than 100 years of data, whereas others might not have been of much use prior to, say, 1950. So, if we start the test for both methods 100 years ago, the first method will likely end up looking like the most effective over the entire test period. However, it is possible that the second method might have outperformed significantly over the most recent 50 years.

In a nutshell, a strong argument can be made either way regarding whether to start all tests for all methods at the earliest possible date or to choose different starting dates to test different methods. For the purposes of this book I have chosen the latter. Individuals who believe that methods tested over a shorter test period—and/or did not work particularly well prior to the chosen starting date—are less valid than other methods tested over a longer time frame are free to make their own determination regarding the reliability of the results that appear in this book.

HOW TO TRADE THE DOW

As I just mentioned, we will primarily be using the Dow as our benchmark for virtually all of the stock market performance testing to be done in this book. As I also mentioned, it is now possible to replicate almost exactly the performance of the Dow using an index fund. There are several choices, which I will detail next. It should also be pointed out that there may be times when an investor might wish to attempt to maximize his or her profitability by using leverage. Leverage simply means that your investment will fluctuate more than 1 percent based on a 1 percent price movement by the Dow itself. This can also be accomplished now using leveraged index funds. An index fund with a leverage factor of 2-to-1 will gain roughly 2 percent if the Dow rises 1 percent and will lose 2 percent if the Dow declines by 1 percent. Last, investors should also be aware that there are now inverse and leveraged inverse index funds available. The available funds for trading the Dow are listed in Table 1.1.

Investors who wish to branch out a bit more may consider using an index fund or exchange-traded fund that tracks the performance of the S&P 500 rather than the Dow. As you might guess, the S&P 500 Index is made up of 500 stocks, essentially all of the same large-cap variety as those that constitute the Dow. The correlation of the performance of these two

TABLE 1.1 Vehicles for Trading the Dow (Long, Short, and with Leverage)

Fund	Ticker Symbol	Type	Objective
Diamonds	DIA	Exchange-traded fund	Long the Dow; no leverage
Rydex Dynamic Dow	RYCVX	Open-ended mutual fund	Long the Dow*2
Profunds UltraDow	UDPIX	Open-ended mutual fund	Long the Dow*2
ProShares UltraDow	DDM	Exchange-traded fund	Long the Dow*2
ProShares Short Dow30	DOG	Exchange-traded fund	Short the Dow; no leverage
Rydex Inverse Dow x 2	RYCWX	Open-ended mutual fund	Short the Dow*2
Profunds UltraShort Dow	UWPIX	Open-ended mutual fund	Short the Dow*2
ProShares UltraShort Dow 30	DXD	Exchange-traded fund	Short the Dow*2

TABLE 1.2   Vehicles for Trading the S&P 500 Index (Long, Short, and with Leverage)

Fund	Ticker Symbol	Type	Objective
Spyder	SPY	Exchange-traded fund	Long the S&P 500
iShares S&P 500 Index Fund	IVV	Exchange-traded fund	Long the S&P 500
Rydex S&P 500	RYSPX	Open-ended mutual fund	Long the S&P 500
Profunds Bull	BLPIX	Open-ended mutual fund	Long the S&P 500
Rydex S&P 500 2x	RYTNX	Open-ended mutual fund	Long the S&P 500*2
Profunds UltraBull	ULPIX	Open-ended mutual fund	Long the S&P 500*2
ProShares UltraS&P 500	SSO	Exchange-traded fund	Long the S&P 500*2
Rydex Inverse S&P 500	RYURX	Exchange-traded fund	Short the S&P 500
Profunds Bear	BRPIX	Open-ended mutual fund	Short the S&P 500
ProShares S&P 500	SH	Exchange-traded fund	Short the S&P 500
Rydex Inverse S&P 500 2x	RYTPX	Open-ended mutual fund	Short the S&P 500*2
Profunds UltraShort Dow	URPIX	Open-ended mutual fund	Short the S&P 500*2
ProShares UltraShort S&P 500	SDS	Exchange-traded fund	Short the S&P 500*2

indexes over the years is sufficiently close enough that an investor who did not want to focus solely on the 30 stocks in the Dow index could generate similar results using the S&P 500. Just remember that at times the Dow will generate better results than the S&P 500 and at other times the S&P 500 will outperform the Dow. The key, then, is to pick an index and stick with it rather than chase the one that has performed the best over the past year, month, week, or hour. Table 1.2 displays a variety of index funds that an investor could use to trade the S&P 500 Index.

As you can see in Tables 1.1 and 1.2, there are many choices available to investors who want to trade these two large-cap indexes. In fact, there are possibly too many choices. But, ultimately, it comes down to three decisions:

Decision 1: Do you want to trade an open-ended mutual fund—typically through the mutual fund company itself—or would you prefer to trade an exchange-traded fund that you can trade through a regular brokerage account?

Decision 2: Do you want to play only the long side of the market—in other words, attempt to buy low and sell high when you think the market will rise and switch to cash when you expect the market to decline? Or do you also want to play the short side of the market, whereby you attempt to profit from a decline in stock prices?

Decision 3: Do you wish to use leverage any or all of the time? In other words, are you confident enough in your timing methods and risk-control procedures that you are willing to leverage your investment?

There are pros and cons associated with all of these choices. Exchange-traded funds offer you the convenience of being able to trade them anytime during the day, and they can be traded through a typical brokerage account just like any other stock. The downside is that you will likely pay a commission each time you buy or sell. Buying and selling through an open-ended mutual fund can typically be done with no transaction fees.

Being willing to trade the short side of the market opens up a number of additional moneymaking opportunities beyond those available to those who trade only the long side of the market. During a major bear market, the investor willing to trade the short side can actually accumulate greater profits than can the only-long trader, whose best hope is to be in cash and earn interest as prices decline. The risk, of course, is that the investor may be short in the market while the market stages a surprisingly strong rally.

Last, leverage is indeed a double-edged sword. On the one hand, if you have a method that consistently outperforms over the long run, then the use of leverage can help you to compound your returns exponentially and can generate vastly superior returns over the long run. The downside is that during those periods when losses occur, losses will be twice as great as they would have been if you had not used leverage. And the bottom line is that every investor has an uncle point, a point at which he or she feels compelled to act to eliminate the risk of losing more money altogether. The use of leverage can cause this point to come twice as quickly. So, typically, leverage is best used only when you are highly confident about your outlook and after you have carefully assessed the risks associated with what might happen if things move in the opposite direction of what you had expected. Nevertheless, the judicious use of leverage under favorable conditions can greatly enhance your long-term returns.

Clearly, any investor who ultimately decides to trade an index fund, to use any of the methods detailed in this book, you will ultimately have several important decisions to make. I encourage you to take your time and choose the vehicle that you feel best suits your objectives and tolerance for risk.

SEASONAL TRENDS TO CONSIDER

It is common for an individual approaching the topic of seasonal trends in the financial markets for the first time to be skeptical. And this is understandable. Still, what may surprise many readers is the sheer number of identifiable trends. In the following seven chapters, we will delve into and analyze a wide array of seasonal stock market trends. In each case, we will strive to identify specific and objective rules for using each trend. In other words, for virtually every trend we discuss, there will be a specific day of the week, month, or year designated as a buy date and another specific date designated as a specific sell date. The beauty of designating specific dates in this manner is that this process enables us to track the performance of a given strategy on a consistent and objective basis. This, in turn, enables us to make intelligent decisions about the potential usefulness of any particular seasonal trend and to compare the strength and consistency of performance for any given trends. The subsequent sections introduce the topics that we will discuss in the following chapters.

January

In 1971, seasonal analysis pioneer Yale Hirsch first detailed the famed January barometer. The basic theory underlying this method is that the performance of the stock market during the month of January acts as a harbinger of the action for the rest of the year. In Chapter 2, "The Month of January," I will examine the performance of the original January barometer over 70-plus years of history and will clearly detail the ways in which this storied tool is useful and not useful. I will also add a few new wrinkles to fine-tune our analysis of the month of January in ways that may help to maximize our profitability. To achieve this goal, we will look at several intramonth periods as further clues to the underlying strength or weakness of the stock market during this key month. Last, I will introduce something I call the "JayNewary barometer," which incorporates all of the key January measures and has demonstrated an accuracy rate of better than 90 percent in forecasting the performance of the stock market over the subsequent February through December period.

Holidays

Norman Fosback's original seasonality switching system first recognized the fact that the stock market tended to perform on a better-than-average basis during trading days that lead up to major stock market holidays. Since that time, many analysts have taken a closer look at the performance of the stock market both before and after each holiday. One of the most comprehensive and useful guides was incorporated in Martin Zweig's 1986 book *Winning on Wall Street*. In that book, he looked at the performance of both the S&P 500 Index and a much broader unweighted average that more closely reflected the performance of the average stock. This was important at the time because, even then, most investors did not have a way to actually buy an index and had to resort to buying a group of stocks that they felt would closely track the movement of the overall market. Nowadays, an investor can easily replicate the performance of an index such as the Dow or the S&P 500 by simply buying an index fund, exchange-traded fund, or futures contract that tracks that particular index. Other choices include the Nasdaq 1000 and the small-cap Russell 2000 index.

In Chapter 3, "Holiday Seasonal Trends," we will look at the performance of the stock market around the major stock market holidays. We will first look at the day before each holiday and then at the combined performance of the two days prior to each holiday. Last, we will expand the test and consider the three trading days before and after each holiday. In subsequent chapters, we will combine this holiday trading information with other seasonal timing methods to create enhanced trading methods.

Monthly Trends

In Chapter 4, we will look at a variety of intramonth market trends. The objective will be to break down the trading month as much as possible into favorable and unfavorable trading days. Specifically, we will examine the data to determine whether there are certain days or blocks of contiguous days of the month that tend to perform better than others on a consistent basis. Also, in addition to identifying the single best trading day of the month, we will build on Norman Fosback's work and zero in on the most powerful times of the month to be invested in the stock market. Finally, we will examine the Santa Claus rally, and then incorporate all of the most powerful, consistent trends into one comprehensive model. The results are sure to surprise a great many individuals.

Yearly Trends

In Chapter 5, "Yearly Seasonal Trends," we will break the performance of the stock market down on the basis of yearly performance. Specifically, we will identify where each years falls within a given decade and then examine the data to determine whether there are any general trends based on year-of-decade proximity that can be useful to investors. Then we will look a little more closely at something known as the "decennial road map." This road map depicts the typical performance of the stock market over the course of the average decade during the past century. As you will see, there are some definite repetitive trends that investors should look for as each decade progresses. Specifically, there are four separate trends that tend to play out within each given decade. We will examine the performance of the stock market on a decade-by-decade basis to highlight each of these trends and to identify how often each trend has occurred. We will then highlight how investors can use this information to maximize their profitability as each decade unfolds. Last, we will highlight three specific intradecade periods that have consistently been accompanied by great stock market strength. What we will ultimately find is that, by following the decennial road map and by investing aggressively during the favorable intradecade periods, an investor could have participated in the bulk of major bull markets over the past century while avoiding a great deal of the bearish activity over that same time frame.

Time Cycles of Note

In Chapter 6, "Time Cycles of Note," we will focus on the performance of the stock market in relation to three specific and repetitive time cycles. We will first look at each cycle individually. As you will see, there are ways to use each cycle to identify favorable times to be in the stock market, as well as unfavorable times when an investor may do best to be out of the market. One thing to note regarding these cycles is that, as they are presented in this chapter, each cycle is of an exact length with no exceptions. This is noteworthy in that, nowadays, it is not uncommon to hear market analysts say things like, "The ten-week cycle is due to bottom out in the next several days." In other words, it is suggested that there is something that is supposedly a ten-week cycle that may start anew in ten weeks, or ten weeks and one day, or ten weeks and two days, and so on. This type of analysis can become very subjective very quickly. So, what I want to accomplish in this book is to provide you with information on as many fully objective seasonal methods as possible and then allow you to judge them on their own merits using the data. At the end of Chapter 6, we will combine these three cycles into one comprehensive model and examine how we can use them in combination to generate some surprisingly profitable results.

There is one other important point that should be made regarding cycles such as those detailed in Chapter 6. Whatever the performance results may be for a given method, the goal is not to try to find the single best method and then use that method to the exclusivity of all others. Rather, the goal is to find a variety of methods that can be combined and that by so doing will give an investor the greatest likelihood of maximizing his or her profitability over the long run. The results in Chapter 6 will demonstrate one example of combining indicators that should not necessarily be used as stand-alone systems, which when combined together can generate some very powerful and useful results.

Election Cycle Investing

Over the years, much analysis has been done and much has been written about the tendency for the stock market to make a major bottom. In addition, it has often been suggested that this cyclical tendency revolves around the presidential election that occurs once every four years in the United States. In Chapter 7, "Election Cycle Investing," we will examine this phenomenon in great detail. We will start by looking at each of the four years that constitute the election cycle—postelection, midterm, preelection, and election year—separately to identify whether there are any broad trends that may give us clues as to where to search for the most favorable times to be in (and out of) the market. From there, we will build on the work of Dick Stoken, as mentioned earlier, and try to identify specific time periods within the 48-month election cycle that have consistently witnessed superior stock market performance. As it turns out, we are able to narrow down his original finding of a 15-month bullish phase just a bit (to 14 months) and then add another favorable 7-month period to identify 21 favorable months for investors within the context of each election cycle. As we will detail in Chapter 7, this 21-month favorable period within each election cycle has outperformed the 27 remaining months of each election cycle during 16 of the past 17 four-year election cycles. Investors who wish to invest aggressively when the odds are most in their favor will certainly want to be aware at all times of where the market is within this cycle.

In Chapter 7, we will also look at two much narrower time frames within the favorable periods that have tended to witness especially bullish market action over the years. And last, we will combine all of the information detailed throughout the chapter into one comprehensive model, the ultimate election cycle system.

Sell in May and Go Away

The title of Chapter 8—"Sell in May and Go Away"—has been a popular adage among stock market participants for many years. The notion that the stock market has performed much better during the six-month period starting in November versus the six months starting in May was first popularized by seasonal analysis founding father Yale Hirsch. In Chapter 8, we will analyze and update this theory in great detail. The idea of having a set time of each year to be in the market and a set time to be out of the market is an alluring one to many investors. If it were possible to maximize our profitability by simply making one round-turn trade every year—and to make more money in the process than we might by using a simple buy-and-hold approach—this would, in theory, relieve a lot of concerns and would greatly reduce the amount of time, effort, and energy that we might otherwise feel compelled to exert on stock market analysis. So, is it really that simple? I will leave you to read Chapter 8 to decide for yourself.

In any event, after we thoroughly analyze the advantages and disadvantages of breaking the year into two six-month periods for investment purposes, we will then look at another method that has greatly improved on those initial results. This method involves applying a relatively simple market-timing method to the November to May method, as first popularized in *The Stock Trader's Almanac*. This is one of the few techniques detailed in this book that will actually require something more than a calendar to follow. However, because this minor modification has increased the profit generated during this time frame by a factor of 2.5 to 1 since 1950, it certainly appears to be worth the effort.

One other departure in Chapter 8 from the data that is analyzed throughout most of this book is an analysis of the action of the Nasdaq market from October through the following June. This time frame has tended to witness some very favorable price action—with several notable exceptions. So, we will take a closer look at the Nasdaq price action during this time frame and try to identify the potential benefits as well as the inherent risks. We will also apply the same simple market-timing method I mentioned a moment ago to this period of October to June in the Nasdaq method and measure the impact on the overall trading results there.

Last, in Chapter 8 we will also look at what I call the "dead zones." In this chapter we will try to identify whether there are certain periods within the May through October period that are most likely to experience negative price action. Knowing when not to be in the market can sometimes be almost as useful as knowing when to be in the market, as this can allow an alert investor to act in advance to preserve capital until such time that the market turns favorable once again. We will examine the once-vaunted summer rally and take a very close look at both the action of the stock market during the month of September and an interesting—and potentially important—anomaly regarding the month of October.

SUMMING UP

The primary request that must be made of you, the reader, is that you consider the information contained in this book with an open mind. There is something in human nature that tends to cause people to be skeptical of anything that involves their money. Even more than that, there is also something in human nature that makes people skeptical of things that they do not understand or that cannot be explained logically. The fact of the matter is that the majority of the trends, methods, cycles, and ideas contained in this book will likely fall into this category—hence the need for an open mind. Please remember that no one is going to try to convince you to adopt anything from this book and use it to the exclusion of all other methods. Probably the best way to get the most out of the material in this book is to approach it with the idea of trying to find ways to enhance and improve whatever investment methods you are presently using or are considering.

Ultimately, this book is about market timing. Market timing is another topic that elicits a great deal of skepticism among investors. However, there are two things to keep in mind here:

1. If your idea of market timing is picking tops and bottoms with uncanny accuracy, then you are right to be skeptical, because this simply does not happen. Regardless of the many claims to the contrary, no one always picks the tops and bottoms.

2. However, if your idea of market timing is trying to identify periods when the probabilities suggest that the stock market is more likely to advance than not, then you may eventually find the material in this book to be extremely useful.

Some of the techniques detailed in this book can be explained (at least to some extent), but many cannot. Therefore, you may find yourself at times facing a bit of a conundrum. On the one hand, you will find that some of the techniques detailed in this book have amazingly consistent track records. And the temptation to implement them in your own investment strategy may be great. At the same time, because there is no logical, rational explanation as to why some of these trends seem to exist and persist, there will also be doubt. No one ever set out with the goal of becoming a purely seasonal trader. Still, some of the seasonal trends that have existed over most or all of the past century are quite compelling. As a result, I am a strong proponent of using seasonal trends as part of an overall investment strategy.

All that being said, there is one caveat that I am compelled to mention—and that I will repeat often. Simply put, there is no guarantee that any of the seasonal trends detailed in this book will continue to work as well—or even at all—in the future as they have in the past. The purpose of writing this book is not to tell you what you should do, to reveal the hidden order in the stock market, or anything of the sort. The sole purpose is to enlighten you and to make you aware of some trends that you might not have been aware of up until now. I encourage you to take the time to absorb the information, review it, and then come to your own conclusions regarding its usefulness.

CHAPTER 2

The Month of January

L et's start at the beginning—of the year, that is. It is, in fact, an interesting quirk of human nature to note that most people actually do view the start of a new calendar as the beginning of something truly new. In reality, changing from December 31 to January 1 is no different from changing from March 31 to April 1 or from July 31 to August 1. One day simply passes to the next. Without a calendar, none of this would have any real significance. But, over the course of time, people have developed the interesting habit of viewing the change to a new calendar year as a new start—hence the long lists of New Year's resolutions, a ritual whereby individuals vow to change or adapt some current situation in their lives or personal behavior for the better. It should be noted that the person who writes down his or her New Year's resolutions on December 27 could just as easily begin implementing them on December 28. But how many people ever do that? Probably none. In the minds of the people who make these lists, these are not resolutions; these are New Year's resolutions. So they wait for January 1 to enact these supposedly life-altering changes, believing apparently in some sort of cosmic significance of a year that is new. And thus, under the category of "perception is reality," the stock market—that ultimate arbiter of human emotion in regard to money and investing—also has developed a tendency to view the start of each calendar year as a meaningful event.

In 1972, the respected market analyst Yale Hirsch first detailed the now well-known January barometer. The theory behind this tool is simple. It simply infers that as January goes (for the stock market), so goes the year.

In other words, the theory is as follows:

- If the stock market is up in January, then it will also be up for the year.
- If the stock market is down in January, it will be down for the year.

Can it really be that simple? Can we simply go on vacation during the month of January and then, on our return, make a quick review of the month's action and place ourselves in a position to profit during the rest of the year? Well, after reviewing the data in this chapter, you will ultimately have to judge for yourself. But, as it turns out, there does appear to be a number of ways to analyze the action of the stock market during January that can prove useful for an investor as the rest of the year unfolds. Let's take these measures one at a time and then put them together into a comprehensive model. For the purposes of testing the January indicators, we will use a starting date of December 31, 1937.

THE FIRST FIVE DAYS OF JANUARY

As I have just stated, the January barometer states that as January goes, so goes the year. One even more dramatic assertion than the January barometer itself—which at least considers the action of an entire month before pronouncing judgment—is the assertion that the first five trading days of the year have some sort of predictive power for stock market performance during the rest of the year. In other words, the contention is that as the first five days of January go, so goes the year. Now on the face of it, that simply sounds a bit far fetched. Could it possibly be as simple as waiting for the first five trading days of the year to go by and then getting all the way in or all the way out of the stock market on the basis of the action of those five trading days? Most rational people would adopt a degree of skepticism regarding such an assertion. Still, before pronouncing judgment on the usefulness of this particular measure, let's take a look at the actual data and try to make an informed decision.

Technically, we could begin measuring market performance on the sixth trading day of the year. However, to make the test of the first five days consistent with the other tests in this section, we will use market performance from January 31 through December 31 to measure performance results.

For now, we will simply skip the month of January altogether, regardless of whether the first five days of the year show a gain or a loss. Then starting on February 1 we will either be

Long the Dow (if the first five days of January showed a net gain), or

Out of the stock market completely (if the first five days of January showed a net loss).

So if investors were to actually implement this approach, they would either

Sit out the month of January, then be in the market for 11 months, or

Sit out the entire year, depending on the action of the first five trading days of January.

Is this a viable strategy? Take a look at the numbers and decide for yourself.

Figure 2.1 depicts the growth of $1,000 since 1937 using this simple strategy. As you can see, in the long run, the market has tended to trend higher following a bullish first five days.

Before looking at a few interesting performance figures, let's define a few things.

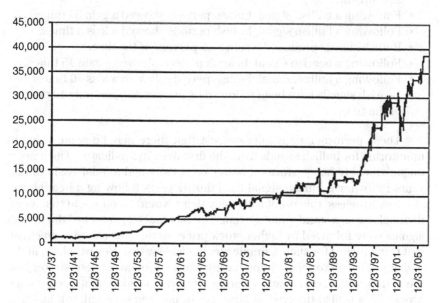

FIGURE 2.1   Growth of $1,000: Long Dow Feb. 1–Dec. 31, with net gains in first five trading days of January (since 1937)

- A bullish signal occurs when the first five trading days of January show a net gain.
- A bullish period extends from the close on January 31 following a bullish signal through December 31 of the same year.
- A bearish signal occurs when the first five trading days of January show a net loss.
- A bearish period extends from the close on January 31 following a bearish signal through December 31 of the same year.

Using these definitions, here are some of the important results to note:

- An investment of $1,000 only during bullish periods grew to $38,581 by December 31, 2007.
- The average daily gain between February 1 and December 31 following a bullish signal was 0.000381 percent.
- The average daily gain between February 1 and December 31 following a bearish signal was 0.000114 percent.
- The average daily gain during bullish periods was 3.33 greater than the average daily gain during bearish periods.
- The annualized rate of return during bullish periods since 1937 was 10.1 percent.
- The annualized rate of return during bearish periods since 1937 was 2.9 percent.
- Following a bullish signal, bullish periods showed a gain 37 times.
- Following a bullish signal, bullish periods showed a loss 8 times.
- Bullish signals produced a gain 82.2 percent of the time.
- Following a bearish signal, bearish periods showed a gain 15 times.
- Following a bullish signal, bullish periods showed a loss 10 times.
- Bearish signals have been followed by market declines only 40 percent of the time.

These performance results suggest that there may be some value in monitoring for bullish signals from the first-five-days indicator. The market unquestionably has performed better on a daily and annual basis during years following a bullish signal than during years following a bearish signal. Nevertheless, this is not a strategy that I would recommend that an individual use as a stand-alone system. The fact that 82 percent of the bullish signals were followed by higher stock prices in the year ahead is an excellent track record for such a simple mechanical system. Nevertheless, in the end, it is difficult to recommend basing one's entire investment strategy on the action of the stock market during a five-day window that occurs once a year. This is also the type of strategy—if one can even call it that—that most investors would not feel confident enough with to follow without wavering. So for now, we will categorize these results as interesting and come back to them when we have a few more pieces of the puzzle to incorporate.

THE LAST FIVE DAYS OF JANUARY

In following up on the January research done by Hirsch, and in search of another confirming indicator, I stumbled upon one that potentially serves as another useful piece of the puzzle and that has actually outperformed the first-five-days barometer over the past 70 years of data. The measure that I discovered involves doing the exact same analysis (i.e., considering just five trading days during the month of January) but looking at the last five trading days of January instead of the first five trading days.

Once again, for testing purposes, we will exclude the month of January and will use market performance between February 1 and December 31 to measure this indicator's performance results. So, for this measure, our strategy is as follows. Skip the month of January altogether. Then starting on February 1 we will be either

Long the Dow (if the last five days of January showed a net gain), or

Out of the stock market completely (if the last five days of January showed a net loss).

So, just as a person using the first-five-days strategy would do, a person using the last-five-days strategy would either

Sit out the month of January, then be in the market for 11 months, or

Sit out the entire year, depending on the action of the last five trading days of January.

Is using the last five days of January as an indicator really a viable strategy? Once again, let's take a look at the numbers and you can decide for yourself.

Figure 2.2 depicts the growth of $1,000 since 1937 using the last-five-days strategy. As you can see, in the long run, the market has tended to trend higher following a last-five-days bullish signal.

- A bullish signal occurs when the last five trading days of January show a net gain.
- A bullish period extends from the close on January 31 following a bullish signal through December 31 of the same year.
- A bearish signal occurs when the last five trading days of January show a net loss.
- A bearish period extends from the close on January 31 following a bearish signal through December 31 of the same year.

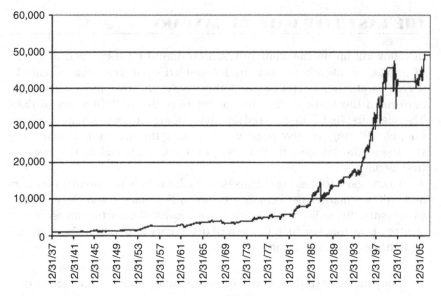

FIGURE 2.2 Growth of $1,000: Long Dow Feb. 1–Dec. 31, with net gains in last five trading days of January (since 1937)

Using these definitions, here are some of the important results to note:

- A $1,000 investment only during bullish periods grew to $49,138 by December 31, 2007.
- The average daily gain between February 1 and December 31 following a bullish signal was 0.000423 percent.
- The average daily gain between February 1 and December 31 following a bearish signal was 0.000069 percent.
- The average daily gain during bullish periods was 6.18 times greater than the average daily gain during bearish periods.
- The annualized rate of return during bullish periods since 1937 was 11.3 percent.
- The annualized rate of return during bearish periods since 1937 is 1.7 percent.
- Following a bullish signal, bullish periods showed a gain 35 times.
- Following a bullish signal, bullish periods showed a loss 7 times.
- Bullish signals produced a gain 83.3 percent of the time.
- Following a bearish signal, bearish periods showed a gain 17 times.
- Following a bullish signal, bullish periods showed a loss 11 times.
- Bearish signals have been followed by market declines only 39 percent of the time.

These results suggest that there may be some value in following bullish signals. Still, like the first-five-days strategy, this is not a strategy I would recommend that an individual use as a stand-alone system. The fact that 83 percent of the bullish signals were followed by higher stock prices in the year ahead is an excellent track record and strongly suggests that this is something that an alert investor should be aware of. Nevertheless, it is difficult to recommend basing one's entire investment strategy on the action of the stock market during a single five-day window that occurs once a year. So for now, we will catalog these results as interesting and come back to them when we have one more piece of the puzzle to incorporate.

THE JANUARY BAROMETER

As stated earlier, the implication of Yale Hirsch's January barometer is simple: If January is up, look for a gain between January 31 and December 31 of that year. The relevant questions to be answered, then, are, How reliable is this trend? and, Is this something that can actually be used to invest money with? As we did with the first-five-trading-days and the last-five-trading-days indicators, we will use market performance from February 1 through December 31 each year to measure performance results. So for this measure our strategy is as follows:

We will once again skip the month of January entirely. Then starting February 1 we will be either

Long the Dow (if the month of January shows a net gain), or
Out of the stock market completely (if the month of January shows a net loss).

So, a person using the January barometer strategy would either

Sit out the month of January, then be in the market for 11 months, or
Sit out the entire year, depending on whether the month of January showed a net gain or a net loss.

Figure 2.3 depicts the growth of $1,000 since 1937 using this strategy. As you can see, in the long run, the market has tended to trend higher following a bullish signal in the January barometer.

- A bullish signal occurs when the month of January as a whole shows a net gain.

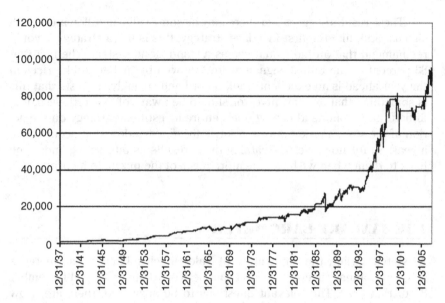

FIGURE 2.3 Growth of $1,000: Long Dow Feb. 1–Dec. 31, with net gains in January (since 1937)

- A bullish period extends from the close on January 31 following a bullish signal through December 31 of the same year.
- A bearish signal occurs when the month of January as a whole shows a net loss.
- A bearish period extends from the close on January 31 following a bearish signal through December 31 of the same year.

Having defined these terms, let's look at some relevant results:

- A $1,000 investment only during bullish periods grew to $89,570 by December 31, 2007.
- The average daily gain between February 1 and December 31 following a bullish signal was 0.000443 percent.
- The average daily gain between February 1 and December 31 following a bearish signal was 0.000074 percent.
- The average daily gain during bullish periods is 5.98 times greater than the average daily gain during bearish periods.
- The annualized rate of return during bullish periods since 1937 is 11.8 percent.
- The annualized rate of return during bearish periods since 1937 is 1.9 percent.

- Following a bullish signal, bullish periods showed a gain 43 times.
- Following a bullish signal, bullish periods showed a loss 4 times.
- Bullish signals produced a gain 91.4 percent of the time.
- Following a bearish signal, bearish periods showed a gain 9 times.
- Following a bullish signal, bullish periods showed a loss 14 times.
- Bearish signals have been followed by market declines 61 percent of the time.

As you can see, the January barometer sports a fairly impressive stand-alone track record. A market advance followed 91 percent of bullish signals, and a market decline followed 61 percent of bearish signals. In all, this method correctly called the direction of the stock market in 57 of 70 February-to-December periods. This works out to a very respectable 81 percent accuracy rate. Now let's see what happens if we turn this into a stand-alone trading system.

THE JANUARY BAROMETER AS A STAND-ALONE SYSTEM

First off, we will change the test just a little bit and assume that we will be in the stock market during the entire month of January while we wait for the January barometer to tell us what to do for the remainder of the year. As you can see in Figure 2.4, the Dow has shown a net gain—albeit a choppy one—during the month of January since 1937.

Here are the rules for the system we will test for trading using the January barometer:

- We will be long the Dow during the month of January every year.
- If January shows a net gain, we will continue to hold the Dow through the end of the year.
- If January shows a net loss, we will exit the market and hold cash through the end of the year.
- For this test, we will assume that, while we are out of the market, we will earn interest at a rate of 1 percent per year.

Now, let's get some idea as to whether there is any advantage to using this strategy. To do so, we will compare the results that we generate using this strategy to the results we might have generated using a simple buy-and-hold approach. Figure 2.5 displays the growth of $1,000 using this simple systematic approach versus a buy-and-hold approach since 1937.

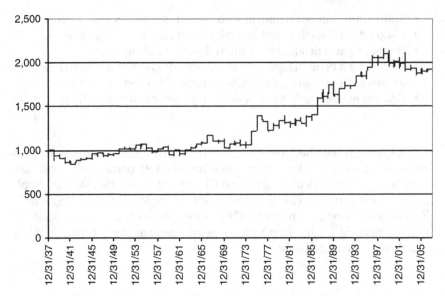

FIGURE 2.4 Growth of $1,000 invested in Dow only during January (since 1937)

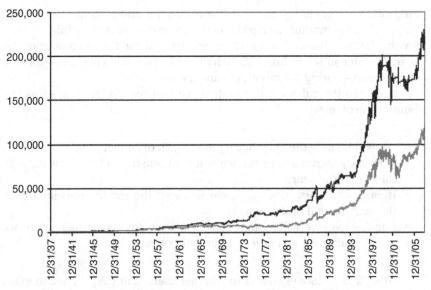

FIGURE 2.5 Growth of $1,000 invested in Dow using January barometer (black line) versus a buy-and-hold approach (gray line) (since 1937)

All told, $1,000 invested in the Dow using a buy-and-hold approach grew to $109,763 by December 31, 2007. At the same time, the same $1,000 invested in the Dow using the aforementioned January barometer strategy grew to $215,338 by December 31, 2007. The results generated from being in the stock market only when the January barometer signaled a bullish outlook are roughly double the returns generated from a buy-and-hold approach over the past 70 years.

Clearly, Yale Hirsch was on to something useful when he unveiled the January barometer back in 1972. Still, although this method enjoys not only a simple elegance but also a sterling track record, there appear to be ways to fine-tune it and increase its usefulness and moneymaking ability by combining all that we have covered so far in this chapter.

THE JAYNEWARY BAROMETER

Now let's take a look at a way to combine all of the information we have considered so far into one comprehensive January model. I have dubbed this model (slightly tongue-in-cheek) as the "JayNewary barometer." This model simply combines the first-five-days indicator, the last-five-days indicator, and the January barometer into one comprehensive model. The calculations are quite simple:

- If the first five trading days of January register a net gain, add one point to the model.
- If the last five trading days of January register a net gain, add one point to the model.
- If the month of January as a whole registers a net gain, add one point to the model.

That's all there is to it. As such, this model can range anywhere from a reading of 0 to a reading of 3. So do these various readings really have any implications for investors? In theory, one would expect higher readings for the JayNewary barometer to be followed by more bullish stock market price action, and likewise, lower readings to be followed by less favorable price action. Do the results bear this theory out? As is always the case in the stock market, the numbers will tell the tale.

Table 2.1 displays a number of the vital statistics highlighting stock market action following various readings from the JayNewary barometer. Figures 2.6 through 2.9 display the growth of $1,000 invested between February and December based on a given model reading from the

TABLE 2.1   Dow Performance versus JayNewary Barometer Readings

JayNewary Barometer Reading	No. of Times Up, Feb.–Dec.	No. of Times Down, Feb.–Dec.	Percentage Times Up, Feb.–Dec.	Average Percentage +(−)	$1,000 Becomes
0	1	5	16.7	(7.5)	521
1	9	9	50.0	(1.2)	1,281
2	20	2	90.9	10.5	4,896
3	22	2	91.7	13.3	17,408

JayNewary barometer. It is clear from this data that stock market investors can, in fact, use the month of January in a meaningful way.

To better understand the significance, or lack thereof, of a given reading, let's take a closer look at the action of the stock market following various readings from the JayNewary barometer.

JayNewary Barometer Readings of 0

On six occasions over the past 70 years, the JayNewary barometer has registered its most bearish reading of 0. Now, on the one hand,

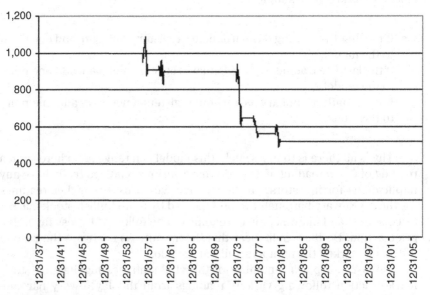

FIGURE 2.6   Growth of $1,000 Invested in the Dow Feb. 1–Dec. 31, with JayNewary Barometer Readings of 0 (since 1937)

statistics-minded investors might argue that there have simply not been enough years that have registered a JayNewary barometer reading of 0 from which to draw any meaningful conclusions. And, given that there have only been 6 such years among the 70 years tested that fit into this category, this could well be a valid argument. On the other hand, it might also make sense for investors to be thankful that there have not been more 0 readings from the JayNewary barometer over the years, given that the stock market has performed so poorly during these years.

As Table 2.1 shows, five of six times, the stock market registered a February-through-December decline following JayNewary barometer readings of 0, with an average decline of 7.5 percent. The best year, in fact the only year to show a profit, was 1977, with a gain of 7.7 percent. The worst performance between the end of January and the end of December during a 0-reading year was a 30.5 percent decline in 1974. As you can see in Table 2.1 and Figure 2.6, $1,000 invested only between February and December of those years in which the JayNewary barometer registered a reading of 0, would have been worth only $521 at the end of 2007. This represents a net loss of 47.9 percent, during a time when the Dow advanced 10.876 percent.

The primary thing to remember about a JayNewary barometer reading of 0 is this: If and when another such reading occurs, it does not necessarily mean that investors should stick their money into a mattress and their heads into the ground and then simply wait for December 31 to roll around before looking at the stock market again. These historical results do imply, however, that an alert investor should not fight the tape if the stock market shows signs of weakness during a year in which the JayNewary barometer registered a 0 reading. Sometimes, playing defense can go a long way toward helping investors maximize their profitability in the long run by keeping some powder dry with which to reinvest at lower prices. The bottom line: Give the bearish case the benefit of the doubt if the JayNewary barometer registers a reading of 0.

JayNewary Barometer Readings of 1

There have been 17 occasions when the JayNewary barometer registered a reading of 1. Following nine of those occasions, the Dow registered an advance during the February-through-December time frame. Another nine times witnessed a loss for the Dow. The average performance for all 17 years was a loss of 1.2 percent. Despite these fairly moderate averages, the year-to-year performances of 1-reading years have ranged all over the map. The best February-through-December performance following a 1 reading was 29.9 percent in 2003. The worst performance came the very year before that, in 2002, when the Dow registered a February-through-December decline of 22.2 percent. There have been five occasions—1941, 1946, 1969,

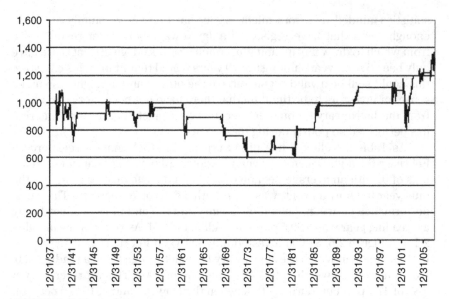

FIGURE 2.7 Growth of $1,000 invested in the Dow Feb. 1–Dec. 31, with JayNewary barometer readings of 1 (since 1937)

1973, and 2002—when the Dow registered a February-through-December loss in excess of 10 percent following a JayNewary barometer reading of 1.

Figure 2.7 displays the equity curve since 1937 for investing in the Dow following readings of 1. The equity curve depicted gives a clear indication of the random nature of market performance during 1-reading years.

Probably the main thing to keep in mind is that a JayNewary barometer reading of 1 has no apparent predictive value. In essence, when the JayNewary barometer registers a reading of 1 it is time to find a new indicator. In other words, do not expect a bias one way or the other on the basis of this reading. One possible exception—which has occurred only once, in 2007—is if the indicator that caused the JayNewary barometer to reach 1 is the original January barometer. In other words, if the month of January shows a net gain, but the first five days of January and the last five days of January are down, the JayNewary barometer will register a reading of 1. In this case, the original January barometer can serve as another indicator, as mentioned previously, and might still be considered in a bullish rather than a neutral light.

JayNewary Barometer Readings of 2

To put it as succinctly as possible, any JayNewary barometer reading greater than 1 should be considered a bullish sign for the 11 months ahead.

I will demonstrate why in a moment. At the same time, investors should not necessarily expect that everything will be sweetness and light following such readings. The stock market offers no sure things, and powerful countertrends are always a possibility. Investors must be prepared to deal with such events should they unfold. Nevertheless, the market performance following JayNewary barometer readings of 2 (and especially 3, as we will see shortly) is quite compelling. Let's see if I can back up that claim.

As Table 2.1 shows, a full 20 of 22 times—or an impressive 90.9 percent—the Dow registered a February-through-December advance following a JayNewary barometer reading of 2, with an average gain of 10.5 percent. The best year was 1958, when the Dow registered a February-through-December profit of 29.7 percent. In all, there were four years with 2 readings that witnessed returns of 20 percent or more by the Dow—1938, 1958, 1991, and 1998.

Figure 2.8 displays the growth of $1,000 invested only when the JayNewary barometer reads 2. In this case, that $1,000 would have grown to $4,896 by the end of 2007. The overall performance is quite positive; still, a close perusal of the equity curve depicted in Figure 2.8 reveals two important traits: (1) a long-term upward bias and (2) a fair amount of price volatility.

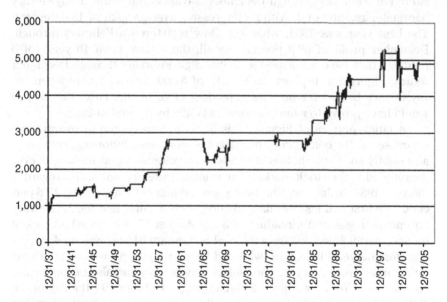

FIGURE 2.8 Growth of $1,000 invested in the Dow Feb. 1–Dec. 31 with a JayNewary barometer reading of 2 (since 1937)

Anyone contemplating the JayNewary barometer as part an investment process must consider the potential for downside price volatility. The one thing investors cannot afford to do is assume that a 2 reading "guarantees" higher stock prices and then stick their heads in the sand. To wit, in 1966, the Dow lost 20.1 percent between February and December, and in 2001, the loss during this time frame was a no less painful: 16 percent.

JayNewary Barometer Readings of 3

When examining any group of stock market indicators, one universal sign that indicators may be of value is when the performance of the stock market improves as the indicators become more bullish. With this in mind, it is worthy of note that the performance of the stock market does in fact improve the more bullish the JayNewary barometer becomes.

As we will see in a moment, no investor should ignore a JayNewary barometer reading of 3. Overall, the action of the stock market has been extremely bullish following 3 readings, and investors would be wise to make every effort to be aggressive and attempt to maximize their profitability in the 11 months following a 3 reading. As always, however, investors should remain aware of the potential for the stock market to surprise and whack them when they least expect it. We will talk more on this in a moment.

As Table 2.1 shows, 22 of 24 times—or 91.7 percent—the Dow registered a February-through-December advance following a JayNewary barometer reading of 3, with an impressive average gain of 13.3 percent. The best year was 1954, when the Dow registered a February-through-December profit of 38.3 percent. In all, there have been 16 years of 3 readings that have witnessed a double-digit February-through-December return. Figure 2.9 displays the growth of $1,000 invested only when the JayNewary barometer notches a reading of 3. In this case, that $1,000 would have grown to a fairly amazing $17,408 by the end of 2007.

A quick perusal of Figure 2.9 is likely to leave some investors quite impressed at the consistency of market performance following 3 readings, and rightly so. Nevertheless, it needs to be reiterated that nothing is ever guaranteed in the stock market. The primary case in point in this regard is the year 1987. In January, the Dow powered higher by a stunning 13.8 percent. The first and last five days also registered gains, and the JayNewary barometer registered a reading of 3. By August 25, the Dow had tacked on another 26.2 percent from its level of January 31 and was up 43.6 percent for the year. Investors, who had been enjoying a massive multiyear bull market, were ecstatic. And, unfortunately, they had also become quite complacent. From the August 25 high through October 19—the day of the 1987 market crash—the Dow lost a full 36.1 percent. Despite the fact that October 19 was actually low, and that the calendar year actually ended

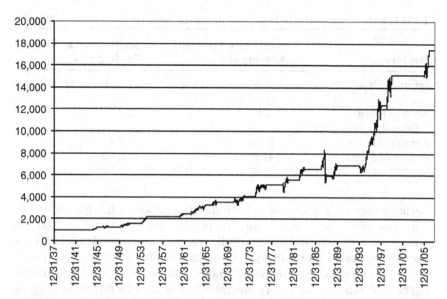

FIGURE 2.9 Growth of $1,000 invested in the Dow Feb. 1–Dec. 31, with JayNewary barometer readings of 3 (since 1937)

with a profit, the intervening decline was nevertheless devastating to many investors. There are two main things to remember here:

1. Do not rely on any one indicator to guide your investment strategy, no matter how good the overall long-term results look.
2. Do not let one adverse event dissuade you from using a method that has proved profitable in the long run.

In other words, the two biggest mistakes an investor could make given all of the information we have discussed regarding 3 readings, are

1. Investing solely on the basis of a JayNewary barometer reading of 3.
2. Ignoring a 3 reading solely because such a reading was in force during the sharp decline of August to October in 1987.

JayNewary Barometer Readings of 0 versus Readings of 3

Often, performance results of various methods are dismissed as random or not meaningful without a full weighing of the facts. It may make perfect sense to some people to say that they will ignore any January indicators

TABLE 2.2 Comparison of Market Performance during 0 Years versus 3 Years

Measure	JayNewary Barometer Reading of 0	JayNewary Barometer Reading of 3
February–December up	1 of 6, or 17% of the time	22 of 24, or 92% of the time
Average February–December performance	(7.5%)	13.3%
Annualized return	(12.3%)	14.7%
Growth of $1,000	($479)	$16,408

because they simply do not believe that the action in the month of January has any impact on the months of, say, June or October. And this makes sense to some individuals. Still, as a graduate of the School of Whatever Works, one thing I always encourage people to do is keep an open mind. This is especially true when a method shows negative results following bearish readings and more favorable market results following progressively more bullish readings. Such is the case with the JayNewary barometer. To drive this point home, let us once more consider the performance following 0 readings versus 3 readings since December 31, 1937.

Table 2.2 displays a variety of measures and the results generated following 0 readings versus 3 readings from the JayNewary barometer. In each case, the differences are quite stark.

What the future holds remains to be seen. But there can be little debate that the market has shown a strong tendency to perform much better when the JayNewary barometer is at its highest level rather than its lowest level.

THE ULTIMATE JANUARY BAROMETER SYSTEM

On the basis of the numbers that we have seen so far, it can be argued that 70 years of history suggest that there might be some value to tracking the performance of the stock market during the month of January and—given that action—gearing one's investments in a particular direction for the remainder of the year. So far, we have seen a couple of trends:

- The market tends to perform quite poorly when the JayNewary barometer registers a reading of 0.
- The market tends to perform exceptionally well when the JayNewary barometer registers a reading of 3.

- The market shows a tendency to rise when the JayNewary barometer registers a reading of 2 and/or if the original January barometer is bullish.
- A JayNewary barometer reading of 1 offers virtually no useful information whatsoever regarding the likely direction of the stock market over the impending 11 months.
- The market has registered a net gain during the month of January.

Now let's see if we can combine all of this information into an ultimate January barometer system (UJBS), Here are the trading rules that we will test:

- We will hold a long position in the Dow each year during the month of January.
- If the JayNewary barometer registers a reading of 3, we will go long the Dow using two-to-one leverage.
- If the JayNewary barometer registers a reading of 2 and/or if the month of January as a whole registers a gain, we will buy the Dow (without leverage).
- If the JayNewary barometer registers a reading of 1 and the month of January as a whole registers a loss, we will sit out the stock market and hold cash until the end of the year. For the purposes of this test, we will assume that we earn an annualized rate of interest of 1 percent.
- If the JayNewary barometer registers a reading of 0, we will sell short the Dow and hold that short position until the end of the year.

Table 2.3 summarizes the trading rules for our UJBS according to the time of year and the action of the stock market during the month of January.

First, a word of caution: The danger with an approach such as this one is that the rules typically lock us into a long, short, or cash position

TABLE 2.3 Trading Rules for the UJBS

Indication	Trade to Make
January	Hold Dow
February–December:	
JayNewary barometer = 3	Hold Dow*2
JayNewary barometer = 2 (or January up)	Hold Dow (no leverage)
JayNewary barometer = 1 (and January down)	Hold cash
JayNewary barometer = 0	Hold Dow short (no leverage)

for 11 months, regardless of the action of the stock market itself. So investors who decide to use this model should consider doing so with only a portion of their investment capital, on the chance that an unfavorable move eventually unfolds despite a bullish signal from our timing model. An alternative is to establish some sort of arbitrary stop-loss point at which investors move to cash after a loss of a given percentage amount. Despite this potential danger, however, the results are fairly compelling, as we will see in a moment.

Table 2.4 displays the cumulative results generated using these rules since December 31, 1937. The most compelling piece of information is the end result achieved using the system versus using a simple buy-and-hold approach. So, $1,000 invested in the Dow on December 31, 1937, would have grown to $109,763 by the end of 2007. During this same period, $1,000 invested using the rules detailed earlier on January market action each year would have grown to a fairly amazing total of $5,365,964. The year-by-year results appear in Table 2.4.

Here are some important performance numbers regarding the UJBS:

- The UJBS showed a gain during 50 of the past 70 years.
- A buy-and-hold approach showed a gain during 48 of the past 70 years.
- The UJBS showed a loss during 20 of the past 70 years.
- A buy-and-hold approach showed a loss during 22 of the past 70 years.
- The UJBS outperformed a buy-and-hold approach 34 times during the past 70 years.
- The UJBS underperformed a buy-and-hold approach 12 times during the past 70 years.
- The UJBS performed the same as a buy-and-hold approach 24 times during the past 70 years.
- During the 48 calendar years when the buy-and-hold approach showed a gain, the UJBS outperformed the buy-and-hold approach 20 times, performed the same 20 times, and underperformed just 8 times.
- During the 22 calendar years when the buy-and-hold approach showed a loss, the UJBS outperformed the buy-and-hold approach 14 times, performed the same 4 times, and underperformed just 4 times.
- All told, the UJBS performed as well as or better than the buy-and-hold approach 58 of 70 years, or 82.9 percent of the time.
- The average annual gain for the UJBS was 14.9, versus 8.1 percent for the buy-and-hold approach.

All in all, there can be little debate that the UJBS has handily beaten the Dow itself over the past 70 years on a buy-and-hold basis. Whether investors can actually bring themselves to use this method on a purely mechanical basis is a question that each investor must answer for him- or

TABLE 2.4 The UJBS: Year by Year

Year	Feb.–Dec. Position	UJBS	Buy/Hold	UJBS-BH	$1000 UJBS	$1000 BH
1938	Long	28.1	28.1	0.0	1,281	1,281
1939	Long	(2.9)	(2.9)	0.0	1,243	1,243
1940	Cash	(2.2)	(12.7)	10.5	1,216	1,085
1941	Cash	(4.3)	(15.4)	11.1	1,164	918
1942	Cash	(0.6)	7.6	(8.2)	1,157	988
1943	Long	13.8	13.8	0.0	1,317	1,124
1944	Long	12.1	12.1	0.0	1,476	1,260
1945	Long × 2	57.4	26.6	30.8	2,323	1,596
1946	Cash	7.2	(8.1)	15.3	2,490	1,466
1947	Long × 2	0.3	2.2	(2.0)	2,497	1,499
1948	Cash	(2.4)	(2.1)	(0.2)	2,438	1,467
1949	Long	12.9	12.9	0.0	2,752	1,656
1950	Long × 2	34.9	17.6	17.2	3,711	1,948
1951	Long × 2	14.4	14.4	0.0	4,244	2,228
1952	Long	8.4	8.4	0.0	4,602	2,415
1953	Cash	0.2	(3.8)	4.0	4,611	2,324
1954	Long × 2	97.6	44.0	53.6	9,111	3,346
1955	Long	20.8	20.8	0.0	11,003	4,041
1956	Cash	(2.7)	2.3	(5.0)	10,703	4,133
1957	Short	3.9	(12.8)	16.7	11,121	3,605
1958	Long	34.0	34.0	0.0	14,898	4,830
1959	Long	16.4	16.4	0.0	17,341	5,622
1960	Short	(8.4)	(9.3)	1.0	15,887	5,096
1961	Long × 2	32.9	18.7	14.2	21,118	6,050
1962	Cash	(3.4)	(10.8)	7.4	20,406	5,396
1963	Long × 2	29.7	17.0	12.7	26,465	6,313
1964	Long × 2	27.1	14.6	12.5	33,634	7,233
1965	Long × 2	18.4	10.9	7.5	39,813	8,020
1966	Long	(18.9)	(18.9)	0.0	32,273	6,501
1967	Long × 2	21.7	15.2	6.5	39,287	7,490
1968	Long	4.3	4.3	0.0	40,965	7,809
1969	Cash	1.2	(15.2)	16.4	41,441	6,623
1970	Long	4.8	4.8	0.0	43,437	6,942
1971	Long × 2	7.5	6.1	1.4	46,693	7,366
1972	Long × 2	28.6	14.6	14.0	60,024	8,440
1973	Cash	(1.1)	(16.6)	15.4	59,334	7,041
1974	Short	33.2	(27.6)	60.7	79,010	5,099
1975	Long × 2	63.6	38.3	25.2	129,225	7,053
1976	Long × 2	19.8	17.9	2.0	154,856	8,313
1977	Short	8.0	(17.3)	25.3	167,241	6,878
1978	Short	(13.1)	(3.1)	(9.9)	145,397	6,661
1979	Long	4.2	4.2	0.0	151,489	6,940

(Continued)

TABLE 2.4   (Continued)

Year	Feb.–Dec. Position	UJBS	Buy/Hold	UJBS-BH	$1000 UJBS	$1000 BH
1980	Long × 2	23.6	14.9	8.7	187,253	7,977
1981	Short	4.7	(9.2)	13.9	196,037	7,240
1982	Cash	0.5	19.6	(19.1)	196,991	8,660
1983	Long × 2	38.5	20.3	18.2	272,780	10,415
1984	Long	(3.7)	(3.7)	(0.0)	262,579	10,025
1985	Long	27.7	27.7	0.0	335,204	12,798
1986	Long	22.6	22.6	0.0	410,902	15,688
1987	Long × 2	(21.2)	2.3	(23.4)	323,850	16,043
1988	Long	11.8	11.8	0.0	362,224	17,944
1989	Long × 2	46.3	27.0	19.4	530,004	22,782
1990	Cash	(5.0)	(4.3)	(0.7)	503,320	21,793
1991	Long	20.3	20.3	0.0	605,591	26,221
1992	Cash	2.7	4.2	(1.5)	621,769	27,316
1993	Long	13.7	13.7	0.0	707,086	31,064
1994	Long × 2	(2.7)	2.1	(4.8)	688,182	31,729
1995	Long × 2	76.4	33.5	42.9	1,213,676	42,343
1996	Long × 2	48.7	26.0	22.7	1,804,392	53,358
1997	Long × 2	37.6	22.6	14.9	2,482,220	65,439
1998	Long	16.1	16.1	0.0	2,881,842	75,974
1999	Long × 2	50.4	25.2	25.2	4,333,936	95,135
2000	Cash	(4.0)	(6.2)	2.2	4,162,574	89,258
2001	Long	(7.1)	(7.1)	0.0	3,867,231	82,925
2002	Cash	(0.1)	(16.8)	16.7	3,863,597	69,025
2003	Cash	(2.6)	25.3	(27.9)	3,764,914	86,503
2004	Long	3.1	3.1	0.0	3,883,434	89,226
2005	Cash	(1.8)	(0.6)	(1.2)	3,813,108	88,684
2006	Long × 2	32.2	16.3	15.9	5,041,667	103,129
2007	Long	6.4	6.4	0.0	5,365,964	109,763
Average		**14.9**	**8.1**	**6.8**		

herself. One suggestion for using this system—and many of the other techniques detailed throughout this book—is to commit a portion of trading capital to this method and follow the rules exactly. Invest the rest of your investment capital any way you see fit.

THE EFFECT OF COMPOUNDING

As a side note, the results displayed in Table 2.4 illustrate the beneficial effect of compounding money at a higher rate of return. The huge discrepancy in the final dollar figures (roughly $5 million versus roughly $100,000) occurs because the UJBS earned an average annual return of 15 percent, whereas a buy-and-hold approach generated an average annual return of 8.9 percent. This 6.1 percent point advantage makes all the difference, especially the longer that the advantage continues to compound. The results in Table 2.4 also illustrate the point that many investment and financial advisers make when urging individuals to assume a certain degree of risk in their portfolios to generate a higher rate of return. Although investors who never do anything but earn interest on cash may never experience any losses, at the same time they have no chance of ever generating the kind of returns that can positively affect their way of life—and thus the importance of putting at least some money into investments that compound at a higher rate of return over time.

Table 2.5 displays a few comparative numbers. Keep in mind that the UJBS must be viewed as a long-term approach, as it can easily underperform a buy-and-hold approach during any given year or period of years. Still, note that looking at annual numbers, the UJBS outperformed a buy-and-hold approach 34 times, underperformed only 13 times, and generated the same annual return 23 times.

If an investor is able to adopt a longer-term mind-set, then the results simply look better and better. For example, if we look at five-year rolling rates of return, we find that the UJBS has outperformed a buy-and-hold approach 55 of 66 possible rolling five-year periods. If we look at ten-year rolling rates of return, we find that the UJBS has outperformed a buy-and-hold approach 55 of 61 possible rolling ten-year periods. Regardless

TABLE 2.5 More UJBS Statistics

Measurement	Results
No. of up years for UJBS	50
No. of up years for buy-and-hold	48
No. of down years for UJBS	20
No. of down years for buy-and-hold	22
UJBS return > buy-and-hold return (%)	34
UJBS return < buy-and-hold return (%)	12
UJBS return = buy-and-hold return (%)	24
Average annual % +(−) UJBS	14.9
Average annual % +(−) buy-and-hold	8.1
5-year rolling return: UJBS > buy-and-hold	55
5-year rolling return: UJBS < buy-and-hold	11
10-year rolling return: UJBS > buy-and-hold	55
10-year rolling return: UJBS < buy-and-hold	6

of which method you use, this is the type of long-term consistency that investors should be looking for. The consistency of any investment approach is what keeps investors on the straight and narrow. If doubt begins to creep into investors' heads about their investment approach, they are far more likely to change horses midstream and switch to a different investment approach just when the initial method is about to turn back toward a period of strong performance. So, long-term consistency is one of the keys elements of getting the most out of any given investment method.

To further illustrate the potential long-term usefulness of the UJBS, let's look at average annual returns by calendar decade. In other words, starting in 1940, we will look at the average annual return for the UJBS for each year in a given decade, and then we'll compare that average to the average annual return generated from a buy-and-hold approach throughout that entire decade.

Keeping with the theme of consistency, it is interesting to note in Table 2.6 that the UJBS has outperformed a buy-and-hold approach over each calendar decade since 1940, and in most cases by a significant margin. Remember from our discussion of Table 2.5 that it is the ability of any method to compound money at a higher rate of return that leads to maximum profitability in the long run.

Although there is no guarantee that the UJBS will continue to outperform a buy-and-hold approach during each and every decade ad infinitum, it is nevertheless a major point in its favor that it has displayed such a strong propensity to consistently outperform the stock market over a long period of time. It is also this type of consistency that can lead an investor to have enough confidence in the approach to stick with it through thick and thin to enjoy the long-term benefits.

TABLE 2.6   The UJBS: Decade by Decade

Decade	Average Annual Percentage UJBS	Average Annual Percentage Buy/Hold	UJBS Minus Buy/Hold
1940–1949	9.4	3.7	5.7
1950–1959	22.8	14.1	8.7
1960–1969	10.5	2.6	7.9
1970–1979	15.5	2.1	13.4
1980–1989	15.1	13.3	1.8
1990–1999	25.8	15.9	9.9
2000–2007*	3.3	2.6	0.7

*Through December 31, 2007.

To better view the long-term consistency of this model, I have broken the past 70 years of performance into two 35-year periods. Figure 2.10 displays the growth of $1,000 from 1937 through 1972 using the UJBS. Figure 2.11 displays the growth of $1,000 from 1972 through 2007 using the UJBS. In the long run, the results are simply outstanding. This performance is based on four key elements:

1. Maximizing gains when all the signs point in the right direction (i.e., by buying the Dow using two-to-one leverage when all three January measures are bullish).

2. Being long the Dow when a majority of January indicators are bullish.

3. Going short the Dow when no January indicators point in the right direction.

4. Sitting out completely when the January indicators are indeterminate.

By implementing these key elements into one objective system, it is possible to compound money at a much higher rate than would be possible using a buy-and-hold approach.

The results displayed in Figures 2.10 and 2.11 suggest that the UJBS can generate high rates of return over time. At the same time, like most

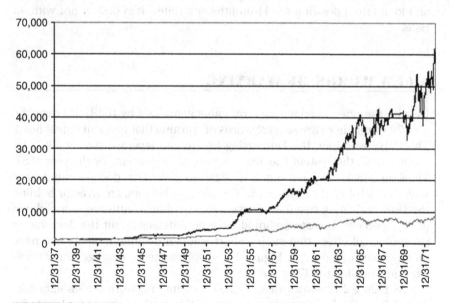

FIGURE 2.10 Growth of $1,000 invested with UJBS (black line) versus buy-and-hold (gray line), Dec. 31, 1937–Dec. 31, 1972

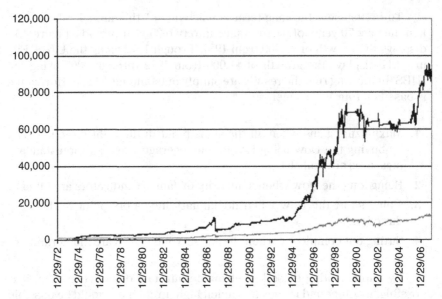

FIGURE 2.11 Growth of $1,000 invested with UJBS (black line) versus buy-and-hold (gray line), Dec. 31, 1972–Dec. 31, 2007

mechanical systems—particularly those that use leverage, can go short, and lock into a position for 11 months at a time—it is clearly not without risks.

A FEW WORDS OF WARNING

Despite the phenomenal long-term gains generated by the UJBS over the past 70 years, there are several words of warning that investors must heed. The UJBS was long the Dow using two-to-one leverage during 1987. By August 1987, the system was up in excess of 78 percent for the year 1987. Then the market topped out and began to sink. This decline culminated with the October 19, 1987, crash. From top to bottom, an investor holding the Dow and using two-to-one leverage would have suffered a drawdown of 63.1 percent. Investors should have no illusions about the devastating psychological effect that such a short, sudden decline in equity can have on any investor's psyche. Figure 2.12 displays the percentage drawdowns experienced since 1937 by the UJBS.

As Figure 2.12 shows, despite the excellent long-term profitability generated from the UJBS, an investor using this method would undoubtedly have experienced some crisis-of-confidence moments. The 1987 drawdown

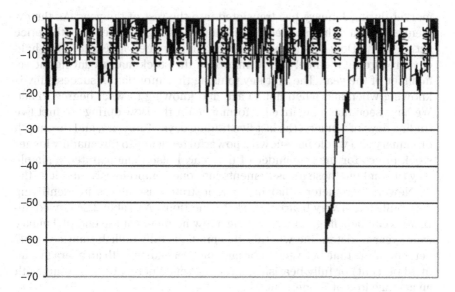

FIGURE 2.12 Percentage drawdown for UJBS since December 1937

is quite obvious: a downward spike dropping more than 60 percent. Even besides this extreme worst case, however, it should be noted that the UJBS experienced a number of drawdowns in excess of 20 percent along the way. So, the question that investors must ask before using any approach to trading—particularly a purely mechanical approach that, by design, locks them into a position for 11 months at a time—is, Will I be able to stick with it? Each investor must answer that question for him- or herself.

SUMMING UP

Theories come and theories go. Often, an idea will take hold and become accepted as fact even without a thorough vetting. The theory that the month of January might serve as a leading indicator for the remainder of the year has been a popular notion for more than three decades, ever since Yale Hirsch first popularized the January barometer in the early 1970s. Yet, most individuals either embrace or reject the notion of January as a predictor of stock market performance for the rest of the year on the basis of emotional or preconceived biases (e.g., "That's too easy") rather than a thoughtful inspection of the actual data.

In this chapter, we have taken a close look at the performance results generated during the month of January, and how the performance of the market during January has translated into the rest of the year. As the evidence presented has spelled out, it can be strongly argued that the price action of the Dow during the month of January does appear to often hold clues regarding the likely performance of the stock market during the remainder of the year. The first key to using this information successfully is knowing when and when not to act, and knowing to what degree to act. We have seen that a positive performance for the Dow during the first five trading days of January, the last five trading days of January, and the month of January as a whole has shown a powerful tendency to foreshadow higher stock prices for the remainder of the year. I also demonstrated a simple way to combine these measurements into one comprehensive model—the JayNewary barometer—that has demonstrated usefulness in identifying very bullish and very bearish market conditions. As Table 2.2 showed, investors can benefit greatly by taking a few moments at the end of January every year to determine whether this model is fully bullish (market up 92 percent of the time between February and December, with an average gain of 13 percent) or fully bearish (market down 83 percent of the time, with an average loss of 7.5 percent).

The other key to using January market performance to help you to profit is to recognize that the strategies discussed in this section must be followed consistently over time and that temporary losses must be endured to achieve the full benefit of the highlighted trends. For investors who are more comfortable following specific trading rules, I also detailed my UJBS, which considers the JayNewary barometer and the original January barometer, and can use leverage under extremely bullish conditions and go short under extremely bearish conditions. Whereas it is likely that the majority of investors would have trouble following this system on a purely mechanical basis (primarily because it locks into a position for 11 months regardless of subsequent market action), nevertheless, the long-term results that the model generates are fairly impressive.

Any simple, objective set of rules that generates returns far in excess of a simple buy-and-hold approach should never be dismissed out of hand. The January-based indicators and methods that we have discussed in this chapter deserve the attention of investors looking to maximize their long-term profitability.

CHAPTER 3

Holiday Seasonal Trends

L et's face it, who doesn't like a holiday? OK, certainly someone who has to work on a particular holiday—like police officers or firefighters or perhaps airline pilots—may not hold that particular holiday in such high regard. But, by and large, millions of people look forward to holidays, in some cases counting the days as they approach. And why not? A day off of work spent with family and close friends is a pleasurable experience, and most people look forward to the day's approach and enjoy it as it unfolds. Such days often involve a big meal with a special dessert and perhaps time spent watching a sporting event or a classic movie on television. Yes, there is definitely a lot of appeal to holidays of all different stripes. Often, the typical feeling around a holiday can be best described as general euphoria. It is interesting, then, to note that the stock market—the ultimate arbiter of human emotion regarding all things financial—seems to also have an affinity for stock market holidays. As we will see shortly, there has been a historical tendency for the stock market to share in some of the festivities by advancing around the holidays. To illustrate this phenomenon, let's take a closer look at the holidays and the trading days that surround them.

Many studies that I have seen have broken down the performance of the stock market by holiday and by the proximity of a given day to a particular holiday. In other words, a given study might report that the trading day two days before a particular holiday has outperformed the trading day directly following some other holiday. And although this information is interesting—and, in fact, we will cover this data later in this chapter—there nevertheless does not seem to be a valid argument as to why a particular

49

day of a particular proximity from a particular holiday should necessarily be any better or worse than any other particular day around any other given holiday. So, to account for this belief while still reporting all of the facts, we will look at the performance of the stock market during the trading days around various market holidays in several different ways:

- First, we will look at the trading day prior to each major U.S. stock market holiday.
- Second, we will look at the two trading days prior to each major U.S. stock market holiday.
- Third, we will look at the three days prior to and the three days following each such holiday as a whole.
- Last, we will cherry-pick the best holiday trading days and highlight the performance of the stock market during those dates.

From an examination of these data, we should be able to get a pretty good handle on what information is truly useful for stock market investors.

THE HOLIDAYS

For the purpose of our testing, we will start on December 31, 1933. From that date forward, we will examine the performance of the stock market during the trading days around the holidays listed in Table 3.1.

Regarding Presidents' Day, it should be noted that up until 1952 there were two market holidays in February, separately marking Lincoln's birthday and Washington's birthday. After 1952, these two holidays marking presidential birthdays were combined into one holiday, now Presidents' Day. In this study, Martin Luther King Day—which occurs on the third Monday of January—has been omitted only because it is a relatively new

TABLE 3.1 Major Stock Market Holidays

Major Stock Market Holidays

Lincoln's Birthday/Washington's Birthday/Presidents' Day
Good Friday
Memorial Day
Independence Day
Labor Day
Thanksgiving
Christmas
New Year's

holiday. Established in 1983, but observed by all 50 states for the first time only in 2000, this holiday simply has too little data available yet to analyze in any meaningful way.

THE TRADING DAY BEFORE EACH HOLIDAY

For much of the twentieth century on the day before a market holiday—and to a lesser extent, the day before that—the stock market showed a very strong propensity to advance. Whether the previously mentioned general euphoria explains this phenomenon can be debated; nevertheless, the long-term trend displayed in Figure 3.1 is unmistakable. Figure 3.1 displays the growth of $1,000 invested in the Dow only during the single trading day prior to each major stock market holiday between December 31, 1933, and December 31, 2007.

As you can see in Figure 3.1, from our start date of December 31, 1933, the upward trend continued unabated for more than 57 years. The equity curve then topped out prior to Memorial Day in 1991 and moved sideways to lower before finally breaking out to a new high just prior to Good Friday in 2007. Whether this breakout will be the start of a new long-term up leg is anyone's guess. Still, it seems fair to categorize the trading day before a holiday as a bullish time for the stock market overall.

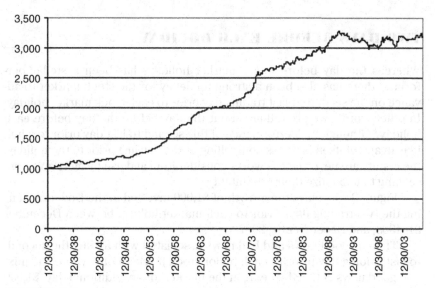

FIGURE 3.1 Growth of $1,000 invested in the Dow on day before market holidays, Dec. 31, 1933–Dec. 31, 2007

Here are some numbers to back up that assertion regarding the day before each major stock market holiday:

- A $1,000 investment would have grown to $3,147 between December 31, 1933, and December 31, 2007.
- The average daily return on the single trading day prior to any market holiday since December 31, 1933, was 0.001923 percent.
- The average daily return for all other trading days was 0.000227 percent.
- The average daily return on the trading day prior to market holidays was 8.4 times greater than the average daily return for all other trading days.
- The annualized return for the trading day prior to market holidays was 62.3 percent.
- The annualized return for all other trading days was 5.9 percent.
- Of the preholiday trading days, 62.2 percent showed a gain.
- All other trading days showed a gain just 51.9 percent of the time.

Clearly, the numbers suggest that over the past 70-plus years, the trading day before a major stock market holiday has been a good time to be in the stock market. Now, let's expand our horizons a bit and add the second trading day before each holiday to the mix to see what that does for our overall trading results.

TWO DAYS BEFORE EACH HOLIDAY

Whereas the day before major market holidays has been a stellar performer, there has also been a strong tendency for the stock market to advance on the second-to-last trading day prior to each stock market holiday. In other words, we are talking about the day before the day before each holiday. Although the performance of this second-to-last day prior to a holiday in and of itself is not as compelling as the day just prior to the holiday, the results are nevertheless worth consideration and use by alert investors seeking to maximize their profitability.

Figure 3.2 displays the growth of $1,000 invested in the Dow only during the two trading days prior to each market holiday between December 31, 1933, and December 31, 2007.

There is good news and bad news associated with adding the second-to-last trading day prior to each major stock market holiday into the mix. The good news is that, by being in the market for an additional day, $1,000 grew to $4,552 versus $3,147 if we had invested only on the day prior to

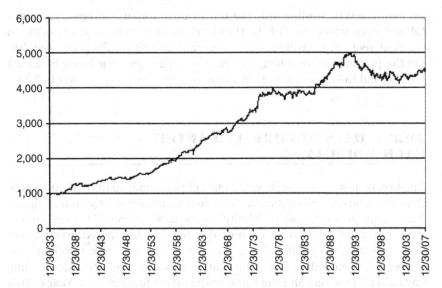

FIGURE 3.2 Growth of $1,000 invested in the Dow on the two trading days before market holidays (Dec. 31, 1933–Dec. 31, 2007)

each holiday. The cumulative results, however, are not quite as smooth as the results for just the single day prior to each holiday, as you can see from Figure 3.2. Also, the drawdown since the 1991 peak was a bit more pronounced and the cumulative return of the two-day preholiday period has yet to return to a new equity high.

Here are some numbers regarding stock market performance during the two trading days prior to each holiday:

- The average daily return for the two trading days prior to any market holiday since December 31, 1933, was 0.001263 percent
- The average daily return for all other trading days was 0.000230 percent.
- The average daily return on the two trading days prior to market holidays was 5.5 times greater than the average daily return for all other trading days.
- The annualized return for the two trading days prior to market holidays was 37.5 percent.
- The annualized return for all other trading days was 6 percent.

So, the bottom line is that adding the second-to-last trading day prior to market holidays into the mix does, in fact, increase the bottom line. Nevertheless, it does so in a slightly less efficient manner than what could be accomplished by trading only the day prior to major holidays. Now, let's take an even wider view of the trading days surrounding each holiday. In the next section, we will look at the overall trading results generated during the period encompassing the three trading days prior to each market holiday and the three trading days directly following each market holiday.

THREE DAYS BEFORE AND AFTER EACH HOLIDAY

The broadest way to look at stock market performance in relation to holidays is to consider all trading days in close proximity to any given holiday. For our purposes, "close proximity" is the three trading days before and the three trading days after each market holiday. In other words, we will assume a six-trading-day holding period around each market holiday. For the record, there will normally be some overlap between the three trading days after Christmas and the three trading days prior to New Year's. This overlap does not alter the results in any meaningful way.

Figure 3.3 displays the growth of $1,000 invested in the Dow only during the three trading days day prior to and following each market holiday between December 31, 1933, and December 31, 2007.

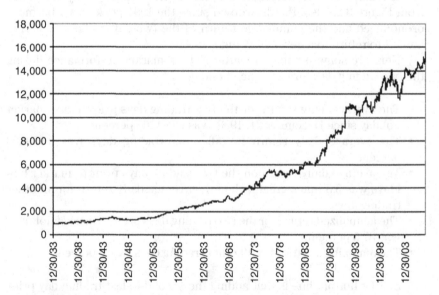

FIGURE 3.3 Growth of $1,000 invested in Dow on the three trading days before and after each market holiday (Dec. 31, 1933–Dec. 12, 2007)

Just as we saw in the earlier results, the results in Figure 3.3 clearly back up the assertion that the holidays are typically a good time to be in the stock market. Unlike the equity curves displayed in Figures 3.1 and 3.2, which topped out in 1991, the equity curve displayed in Figure 3.3 continued to drive to new highs well into the late 1990s. After a pullback during the bear market from 2000 to 2002, this equity curve has since powered to a series of new higher highs. In a nutshell, the general feeling of euphoria around the holidays continues to assert itself. The only difference is that, in recent years, the tendency toward favorable performance has been more spread out both before and after holidays rather than simply being concentrated in just the day or two before the holiday.

Here are some performance numbers generated by looking at the six-day trading period surrounding each stock market holiday from December 31, 1933, to December 31, 2007:

- A $1,000 investment would have grown to $15,247 between December 31, 1933, and December 31, 2007.
- The average daily return for the three days before and the three days after each stock market holiday since December 31, 1933, was 0.000810 percent.
- The average daily return for all other trading days was 0.000180 percent.
- The average daily return during the three days before and the three days after each market holiday was 4.5 times greater than the average daily return for all other trading days.
- The annualized return for the three days before and the three days after each market holiday was 22.6 percent.
- The annualized return for all other trading days was 4.7 percent.

The biggest problem with looking at holidays as they relate to the stock market is that there simply are not enough of them. Most people would be fairly content to earn 22.6 percent on an annual basis; however, the gross return for investors who decided to trade only the six-day period surrounding each stock market holiday would be quite a bit less than that amount because the investors would be in the market for only 48 trading days each year. Thus, our before-and-after holiday strategy simply does not provide enough total return to be viable as a stand-alone trading system. Nevertheless, this approach clearly could be added to some other set of rules to enhance overall investment performance. This will be done in the following chapter. For the sake of enlightenment, for now, let's zero in on the pre- and postholiday trading days that have generated the best market performance.

THE BEST HOLIDAY TRADING DAYS

All right, now it's time to go cherry-picking. As I mentioned earlier, I am not a big fan of highlighting that the first trading day before one holiday outperforms the second trading day after another holiday, and so forth while trying to make it sound as if there were some significance or rationale behind this. Nevertheless, while we are on the topic of stock market holidays, it is enlightening to at least examine which trading days perform the best and the worst around each given holiday. Table 3.2 displays the total percentage gain generated by investing an initial $1,000 only during the trading day listed every year since 1933. For example, look at the first trading day listed in Table 3.2—the third trading day prior to New Year's Day. If an investor started with $1,000 on December 31, 1933, and invested only on that one day every year since, he or she would have generated a total return of 18.1 percent (no interest is assumed while out of the market all the remaining days of the year). This method allows us to make apples-to-apples comparisons of the actual market performance for a given trading day over the years.

As Table 3.2 shows, there is no real rhyme or reason to the performance of the various pre- and postholiday trading days. The market performs best three days after certain holidays and best one day after other holidays—hence the reason that cherry-picking specific days is a potentially dangerous idea.

Still, let's look at a couple of noteworthy facts:

- The day before the holiday was the best performer for four holidays (Good Friday, Memorial Day, Independence Day, and Labor Day). Three days after the holiday was the best performer for two holidays (Presidents' Day and Christmas).
- Christmas and New Year's were the only holidays to show an average gain on all six trading days surrounding the holiday.
- Five holidays (New Year's, Presidents' Day, Good Friday, Independence Day, and Christmas) showed an average net gain over each of the three preholiday trading days.
- Four holidays (New Year's, Independence Day, Labor Day, and Christmas) showed an average gain over each of the three postholiday trading days.
- Probably the most significant statistic is that 39 of 48 of the trading days listed in Table 3.2 showed a net profit: a significant win of 81 percent.

Now, let's sort these data to identify the true winners and losers and to determine whether any truly useful trends ultimately emerge. Table 3.3

TABLE 3.2 A Chronological Listing of the Three Trading Days before and after Each Major Stock Market Holiday since 1933

Holiday	Trading Day	Percentage +(−)
New Year's	−3	18.1
New Year's	−2	25.6
New Year's	−1	6.8
New Year's	1	10.7
New Year's	2	45.0
New Year's	3	11.3
Presidents' Day	−3	2.3
Presidents' Day	−2	7.9
Presidents' Day	−1	3.6
Presidents' Day	1	3.5
Presidents' Day	2	(13.2)
Presidents' Day	3	12.7
Good Friday	−3	6.7
Good Friday	−2	9.5
Good Friday	−1	19.3
Good Friday	1	(7.8)
Good Friday	2	18.9
Good Friday	3	(0.2)
Memorial Day	−3	1.2
Memorial Day	−2	(10.4)
Memorial Day	−1	16.0
Memorial Day	1	(5.7)
Memorial Day	2	3.3
Memorial Day	3	3.8
Independence Day	−3	2.3
Independence Day	−2	21.6
Independence Day	−1	28.0
Independence Day	1	15.2
Independence Day	2	10.1
Independence Day	3	12.3
Labor Day	−3	4.0
Labor Day	−2	(4.8)
Labor Day	−1	36.2
Labor Day	1	2.2
Labor Day	2	1.1
Labor Day	3	1.0
Thanksgiving	−3	(17.2)
Thanksgiving	−2	8.8
Thanksgiving	−1	13.2
Thanksgiving	1	23.8
Thanksgiving	2	(3.4)

(Continued)

TABLE 3.2 *(Continued)*

Holiday	Trading Day	Percentage +(−)
Thanksgiving	3	(5.6)
Christmas	−3	4.0
Christmas	−2	5.3
Christmas	−1	22.3
Christmas	1	6.8
Christmas	2	4.9
Christmas	3	23.8

displays the same data as Table 3.2; however, in this table, the results are sorted from the best overall performance to the worst.

Once again, there is no real pattern that can be discerned from the data in Table 3.3. Nevertheless, as long as we are cherry-picking, let's take a look at the hypothetical results of investing during the better half of the trading days in Tables 3.2 and 3.3. In other words, assume that we are long the Dow only during the first 24 pre- and postholiday trading days listed at the top of Table 3.3. These top 24 trading days are listed in chronological order in Table 3.4.

Figure 3.4 displays the growth of $1,000 invested in the Dow only during the 24 trading days listed in Table 3.4 between December 31, 1933, and December 31, 2007.

As you can see, for most of the past 70-plus years, the most favorable holiday trading days generated a virtually endless string of gains.

Here are some performance numbers for the top 24 pre- and postholiday trading days:

- A $1,000 investment would have grown to $20,876 between December 31, 1933, and December 31, 2007.
- The average daily return for the top half of holiday trading days since December 31, 1933, was 0.00189 percent.
- The average daily return for all other trading days was 0.00015 percent.
- The average daily return for the top half of holiday trading days was 12.8 times greater than the average daily return for all other trading days.
- The annualized return for the top half of holiday trading days was 61 percent.
- The annualized return for all other trading days was 3.8 percent.

There is good news and bad news in these numbers. The good news is that the trading days highlighted in Table 3.4 have vastly outperformed

TABLE 3.3 Holiday Trading Days by Cumulative Performance

Holiday	Trading Day	Percentage +(−)
New Year's	2	45.0
Labor Day	−1	36.2
Independence Day	−1	28.0
New Year's	−2	25.6
Thanksgiving	1	23.8
Christmas	3	23.8
Christmas	−1	22.3
Independence Day	−2	21.6
Good Friday	−1	19.3
Good Friday	2	18.9
New Year's	−3	18.1
Memorial Day	−1	16.0
Independence Day	1	15.2
Thanksgiving	−1	13.2
Presidents' Day	3	12.7
Independence Day	3	12.3
New Year's	3	11.3
New Year's	1	10.7
Independence Day	2	10.1
Good Friday	−2	9.5
Thanksgiving	−2	8.8
Presidents' Day	−2	7.9
New Year's	−1	6.8
Christmas	1	6.8
Good Friday	−3	6.7
Christmas	−2	5.3
Christmas	2	4.9
Labor Day	−3	4.0
Christmas	−3	4.0
Memorial Day	3	3.8
Presidents' Day	−1	3.6
Presidents' Day	1	3.5
Memorial Day	2	3.3
Presidents' Day	−3	2.3
Independence Day	−3	2.3
Labor Day	1	2.2
Memorial Day	−3	1.2
Labor Day	2	1.1
Labor Day	3	1.0
Good Friday	3	(0.2)
Thanksgiving	2	(3.4)
Labor Day	−2	(4.8)

(*Continued*)

TABLE 3.3 *(Continued)*

Holiday	Trading Day	Percentage +(−)
Thanksgiving	3	(5.6)
Memorial Day	1	(5.7)
Good Friday	1	(7.8)
Memorial Day	−2	(10.4)
Presidents' Day	2	(13.2)
Thanksgiving	−3	(17.2)

the majority of all other trading days over the past 70-plus years. The bad news is that there is no real reason to believe that these specific trading days should continue to outperform going forward. Thus, the amazingly positive results must be viewed with a grain of salt.

TABLE 3.4 Top 24 Holiday Trading Days

No.	Holiday	Trading Day
1	New Year's	−3
2	New Year's	−2
3	New Year's	−1
4	New Year's	1
5	New Year's	2
6	New Year's	3
7	Presidents' Day	−2
8	Presidents' Day	3
9	Good Friday	−2
10	Good Friday	−1
11	Good Friday	2
12	Memorial Day	−1
13	Independence Day	−2
14	Independence Day	−1
15	Independence Day	1
16	Independence Day	2
17	Independence Day	3
18	Labor Day	−1
19	Thanksgiving	−2
20	Thanksgiving	−1
21	Thanksgiving	1
22	Christmas	−1
23	Christmas	1
24	Christmas	3

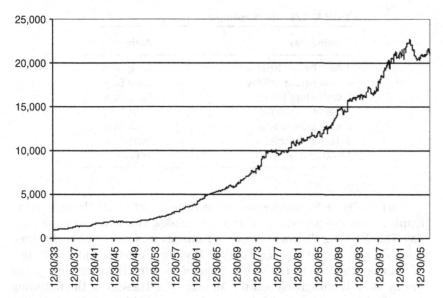

FIGURE 3.4 Growth of $1,000 invested in the Dow only during top 24 holiday trading days (Dec. 31, 1933–Dec. 31, 2007)

THE ULTIMATE HOLIDAY SYSTEM

There is a natural desire to want to incorporate the best holiday trading days that we just detailed into some form of systematic approach. However, I am going to refrain from acting on this desire and, instead, simply focus on a slightly broader approach to trading holiday markets. So, here are the trading rules that we will use for our ultimate holiday trading system (UHTS):

- On the single trading day just prior to each of the eight major stock market holidays listed at the outset of this chapter, we will hold the Dow using two-to-one leverage.
- On the two previous trading days (i.e., the second and third trading days prior to the holiday), we will hold the Dow using no leverage.
- Likewise, on the three trading days after each holiday, we will hold the Dow using no leverage.
- Finally, on all other trading days, we will assume that we are in cash and earning interest at a rate of 1 percent per year.

These rules are summed up in Table 3.5.

TABLE 3.5 UHTS Positions

Trading Day	Action
3 days before holiday	Long Dow
2 days before holiday	Long Dow
1 day before holiday	Long Dow × 2
1 day after holiday	Long Dow
2 days after holiday	Long Dow
3 days after holiday	Long Dow
All other days	In cash

Before displaying the results of this strategy, let's walk through an example of how this would work. Let's use Thanksgiving as our example holiday. Thanksgiving always occurs on a Thursday in November. So, the three trading days prior to Thanksgiving are Monday, Tuesday, and Wednesday of Thanksgiving week. The three trading days after Thanksgiving are the Friday after Thanksgiving and the Monday and Tuesday of the following week. So, our positions for the trading days around Thanksgiving look like those depicted in Table 3.6.

Figure 3.5 displays the growth of $1,000 invested in the Dow as detailed in Table 3.6 from December 31, 1933, through December 31, 2007.

A $1,000 investment in this manner since December 31, 1933, would have grown to $100,708 by December 31, 2007. By way of comparison, $1,000 invested in the Dow on a buy-and-hold basis during the same time would have grown to $132,781. Although the UHTS underperformed a buy-and-hold approach, please remember that this system was only in the market about 18 percent of the time. The key thing to note, then, is not so much that the system should be used as a stand-alone method, but simply that investing near the major market holidays can afford investors the potential to maximize their longer-term profitability.

TABLE 3.6 Example UHTS Positions around Thanksgiving

Trading Day	Trading Day	Action
3 days before holiday	Monday before Thanksgiving	Long Dow
2 days before holiday	Tuesday before Thanksgiving	Long Dow
1 day before holiday	Wednesday before Thanksgiving	Long Dow × 2
1 day after holiday	Friday after Thanksgiving	Long Dow
2 days after holiday	Monday after Thanksgiving	Long Dow
3 days after holiday	Tuesday after Thanksgiving	Long Dow

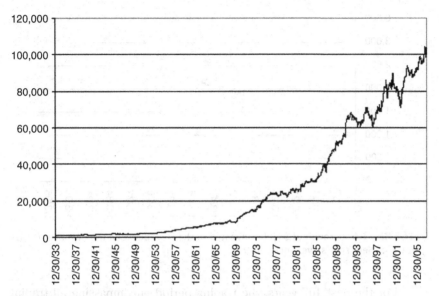

FIGURE 3.5 Growth of $1,000 invested with UHTS since 1933

THE MOST WONDERFUL WEEK OF THE YEAR (USUALLY)

One last holiday-related trend to highlight is typically already encompassed within the three days before and three days after each holiday period that we have already discussed. Specifically, I want to highlight the performance of the Dow between the first trading day after Christmas through—and including—New Year's Eve. The length of this trading period can vary from year to year, but it typically encompasses between three and five trading days, depending on the day of the week that Christmas falls on. For example, in 2007, this period lasted four days—Wednesday, December 26; Thursday, December 27; Friday, December 28; and Monday, December 31. How has the stock market performed during this particular time frame over the years? Figure 3.6 displays the growth of $1,000 invested in the Dow only during the trading days between Christmas and New Year's Day every year since 1900. As you can see, there has been an upward long-term trend.

The numbers are just as compelling as the graph shown in Figure 3.6. Consider the following performance figures (using the Dow as a proxy for the market):

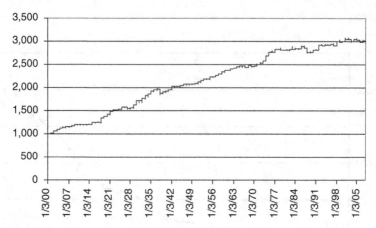

FIGURE 3.6 Growth of $1,000 invested in the Dow between the day after Christmas and New Year's Eve since 1900

For the past 107 years, the trading period encompassing all trading days after Christmas and through New Year's Eve:

- Advanced 85 times, or 78.7 percent of the time.
- Declined 23 times, or 21.3 percent of the time.
- The average return has been 1.02 percent.
- The 85 winners experienced an average gain of 1.6 percent.
- The 22 losers experienced an average loss of 1 percent.
- The average daily percentage gain for trading days that fall into this time frame has been 0.002259 percent. This works out to a stunning 76.6 percent on an annualized basis.
- The average daily percentage gain for all other trading days (i.e., those that do not fall into this time frame) has been 0.000210 percent. This works out to just 5.4 percent on an annualized basis.
- The average daily percentage gain for the trading days between Christmas and New Year's has been 10.8 times greater than the average daily gain for all other trading days (0.002259 divided by 0.000210 percent)
- The maximum gain was 7.3 percent, and the worst loss was 5.1 percent.

From here, there is some bad news and some potentially good news. The bad news is that, over the past 19 years, the Dow has shown an advance only 11 times, or 58 percent of the time. And the average gain over the past 19 years has been 0.36 percent, versus 1.05 percent measured over the past 108 years. So it could be argued that the strength of this trend is abating.

The good news is that the trend has continued to work quite well with small-cap stocks during the same time.

Over the past 20 years, the Russell 2000 has shown a gain 17 times during the period from post-Christmas through New Year's Eve, with an average gain of 1.59 percent. The maximum gain was 5.8 percent, and the biggest loss was 3.6 percent. Another figure of note looking at the performance of the Russell 2000 during this period over the past 20 years: The average daily percentage gain for trading days that fall into this time frame has been 0.003927 percent. This works out to 168.5 percent on an annualized basis.

Talk about a season of good cheer.

SUMMING UP

Most individuals would likely agree that they look forward to and enjoy holidays. As we have seen in this chapter, investors have had much to look forward to around the holidays as well. There is no way to know for sure whether the heightened euphoria that accompanies most holidays is the reason that the stock market—once again, the ultimate barometer of human emotion when it comes to investing—tends to show strength around these dates. But the bottom line is that there can be little debate that the average daily gain for the stock market around holidays has historically been far in excess of those registered by all other non-holiday-related trading days.

The one caveat that should be noted from the data we have analyzed is that the strength of the one- and two-day trading periods prior to each holiday have shown less strength and consistency in the past 10 to 15 years than they did in the roughly 60 years prior to that time. Is it possible that the holiday effect is wearing off? Or that because so many people are now aware of these historical trends that they are now becoming muted? Yes, it is possible. Unfortunately, that determination can only be made in the fullness of time. For now, the good news is that the near-holiday trading days continue to show results better than those of the average trading day. So, for now, investors may be able to gain an edge by being in the stock market during trading days around each major stock market holiday.

As we saw in this chapter, the single trading day prior to each major stock market holiday appears to be the strongest. However, to generate the most meaningful returns, investors need to expand their horizons a bit and consider investing during the three trading days before and the three trading days after each holiday. Investors who are willing to roll the dice a bit might consider cherry-picking some of the better-performing pre- and postholiday trading days, as listed in Table 3.4. Probably the best way to use holiday trading days to maximize investment results is to consider implementing the UHTS, as laid out in Table 3.5. Active traders might also wish to remember to take advantage of the typical rally between Christmas and New Year's.

CHAPTER 4

Monthly Seasonal Trends

M any people who have analyzed and participated in the stock market over the years have come to the conclusion that the fluctuations of stock prices are purely random in nature. In essence, such people conclude that there is no real rhyme or reason to price movements, and, that therefore, it is impossible to predict with any degree of accuracy when or if the stock market is more likely than not to rise or fall. Yet, upon close analysis, there is one underlying theory that seems to make sense regarding the movement of stock prices. This theory relates to the impact of supply and demand. Because stocks are bought and sold just like any other good, they are susceptible to the impact of prevailing supply and demand. If a large number of investors decide to buy the same stock at the same time, this will result in a great deal of demand for shares of that stock. Because there are only so many shares of a given stock available at any given point in time, this spike in demand should result in upward pressure on the price of the stock as sellers take advantage of the increased demand to unload shares at a more favorable price. Likewise, if a large number of investors decide to sell a particular stock at the same time, this will result in a great deal of supply of that stock in the marketplace. This increased supply will result in selling pressure that most likely leads to lower prices.

To sum up the interplay between supply and demand as succinctly as possible, we can simply state, "Money moves the market." In other words, if money is moving aggressively into the stock market to buy stocks, we can expect that this demand for stocks causes prices to rise as buyers raise their bids to accumulate the desired shares of stock. Likewise, if there is a great deal of selling going on as the majority of traders attempt to exit stock positions, we should expect that prices will fall as would-be buyers pull their bids and wait for the decline to run its course before stepping up to buy. Finally, if neither buyers nor sellers are dominating the market at a particular point in time, it would make sense that the market drifts, or fluctuates within a given range, until such time that buyers again start escalating demand or that sellers start ramping up supply.

Does this theory of money moves the market hold up in the real world of the marketplace? In this chapter, we will attempt to answer that question by looking at the performance of the stock market during particular days of the month when we would anticipate that buyers were moving cash into the market, thus generating an increased demand that should, in theory, propel stock prices higher. We will also compare the market's performance during these days to the performance during all other trading days to determine whether there is, in fact, any real significant difference. We will then zero in on the very best trading days of the month, factor in something most commonly referred to as the "Santa Claus rally," and, finally, detail a comprehensive model that builds all of the preceding into one systematic approach. The results may surprise you.

THE BEST DAY OF THE MONTH

Before revealing the best trading day of the month for the stock market, let's first analyze a bit more closely the theory that money moves the market. In today's world, people who rarely ever think about investing in general, or the stock market specifically, invest a great deal of money in the stock market. Thanks to the advent of individual retirement accounts (IRAs) in the early 1980s and 401(k) programs and several other retirement savings programs, a great many individuals have set things up so that a certain amount of money is deducted from each paycheck and put directly into some designated investment vehicle. In many cases, the investment vehicle of choice is some form of mutual fund, most typically a stock fund. Because these deductions occur automatically, and always go into the same investment vehicles, it can be argued that there is automatic demand for the affected investment vehicles, most notably stocks and bonds. If, in fact, money does move the market, then as a corollary, if we can determine when money moves into the market, we can surmise that stock prices would be more likely to rise during that time. In fact, this theory seems to hold water. To illustrate this idea, consider the following theoretical scenario.

A great many individuals are paid at the end of each month (many also are paid in the middle of the month, but we will get to that a little later). So, let's assume that many individuals are paid on the last working day of the month. Now let's say that a portion of their paychecks are sent directly to a stock mutual fund for investment. So, by the end of the next working day (i.e., the first trading day of the next month), the fund manager has a pretty good idea of how much new cash has become available for him or her to invest. Because the majority of mutual funds have a charter that compels them to put any new cash invested to work in the stock market as quickly as possible, in most cases, the fund manager will put that new cash to work in the stock market as soon as possible. To do so, he or she must go into the marketplace and buy stocks. This influx of cash creates buying demand for stocks. If the manager waits until the majority of incoming investment capital is accumulated, then the most likely time he or she would put that money to work is the second trading day of the month. Further, if a great many individuals are automatically investing a great deal of money into a great number of mutual funds at the same time, it makes sense that there would typically be strong demand for stocks on the second trading day of every month. Intuitively, this sounds like a reasonable theory, but how does it actually work in practice? As it turns out, it works out as one would figure.

An analysis of monthly trading days reveals that the best trading day of the month since January 1, 1901, has been the second trading day of the month. Is this a coincidence? One can make an argument either way. But if the theory that I presented a moment ago makes any sense at all, then there is a strong case that the fact that the second trading day of the month has been shown to be the most consistently bullish trading day over the past 100-plus years is no coincidence at all. Figure 4.1 displays the growth of $1,000 invested in the Dow only on the second trading day of each month since the start of the year 1901.

A close look at Figure 4.1 reveals that this second-day trend has been a bit choppy in recent years. Still, we can also see that there were previous such periods in the past. The early 1900s, the middle of the 1930s, and the 1970s all saw little or no new net gains accumulated during the second trading day of the month. Still, the decades of the 1940s, 1950s, 1960s, 1980s, and 1990s saw consistent gains accumulated on the second trading day of the month. In essence, it can be argued that the second day of the month tends to perform best when the overall trend of the stock market is bullish. This makes intuitive sense as buyers tend to be more aggressive during a bull market.

To fully appreciate the strength of the second-day trend, consider the following numbers:

- The one-year rate of change for the stock market as a whole has shown a gain 63.9 percent of the time since January 1, 1901.

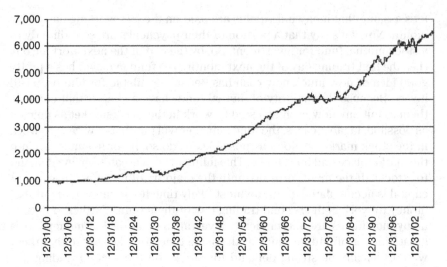

FIGURE 4.1   Growth of $1,000: Long Dow only on the second trading day of each month since Jan. 1, 1901

- The one-year rate of change for the second-day-of-the-month method has shown a gain 72.9 percent of the time since January 1, 1901.
- The average daily gain for the Dow since January 1, 1901, has been 0.00024 percent.
- The average daily gain for the second trading day of each month since January 1, 1901, has been 0.001512 percent.
- The average daily gain for the second trading day of each month was 6.3 times the average daily return for all trading days.
- The average annualized gain for all trading days other than the second trading day of the month has been 4.8 percent.
- The average annualized gain for the second trading day of the month has been a stunning 46.3 percent! In other words, if every trading day gained as much as the average second trading day of the month, the stock market would gain 46.3 percent per year.

Clearly, the only real problem with our second-day strategy is that there is only one second day per month. As a result, although the average daily returns are spectacular, the cumulative returns are not great enough to justify using this trend as a stand-alone method. Active short-term traders should remain aware of this trend and may be able to use it to initiate short-term bullish trades (again, this method seems to generate the most gains when the trend of the overall market is clearly up). But average investors will have to broaden their horizons just a bit to make any real use of this undeniably strong trend.

THE TRADING DAYS OF THE MONTH

Now instead of focusing on just the one best day of the month, let's broaden our search to try to identify days of the month that have demonstrated a tendency to be strong performers. One of the easiest ways to find the best-performing days is to first isolate and, if possible, eliminate the worst-performing days. An in-depth look at the typical daily results for each month over the past 100-plus years reveals some extremely interesting and potentially useful patterns. To preface this analysis of monthly trading days, let me first say that the money-moves-the-market mantra that I invoked earlier—based on the idea that money typically flows into the market at the end, the beginning, and the middle of the month—seems to hold up quite nicely with this new focus. Now, let's take a closer look at the actual performance numbers.

Our theory for now, which we will either prove or disprove, is that each month unfolds in five basic waves:

1. Money moves into the market at the beginning of the month.
2. There is a lull until about the middle of the month.
3. More money moves into the market in the middle of the month.
4. There is another lull prior to the end of the month.
5. More money moves into the market at the end of the month.

In essence, we are talking about three buying waves at the beginning, middle, and end of the month and two selling waves in between. In testing the daily data, I started on January 1, 1901. I then looked at each trading day for each month. In other words, I considered separately trading day 1, trading day 2, trading day 3, and so on. One complicating factor in this analysis is that not every month has the same number of trading days. At present, most months contain somewhere between 20 and 22 trading days. However, at times in the past, there have been as many as 25 trading days in a month. This is because (if you can imagine this) for certain periods during the twentieth century (basically from the 1930s to the 1950s), the stock market was open on Saturday. So to account for this, I also measured the performance of certain trading days starting at the end of the month, designating the last trading day of each month as trading day −1, the next-to-last trading day of each month as trading day −2, and so forth. This allows for better analysis and identification of end-of-the-month trends. The results are instructive and appear in the tables that follow.

TABLE 4.1 Cumulative Percentage Gain for Trading
Days 1–5

Day of Month	Cumulative Percentage Gain
Trading day 1	223
Trading day 2	524
Trading day 3	303
Trading day 4	65
Trading day 5	31

Monthly Wave 1: Trading Days 1 to 5

For each trading day of the month, I have calculated the cumulative gain
on $1,000 invested in the Dow only during that particular trading day every
month since December 31, 1900. For example, in Table 4.1, the value 223
percent is next to trading day 1. This means that $1,000 invested in the
Dow only on the first trading day of every month since December 31, 1900,
would have grown to $3,232, or a total gain of 223 percent.

As Table 4.1 shows, each of the first five trading days registered a net
gain over the past 100-plus years. Also, trading days 1, 2, and 3 garnered
significantly higher profits, and trading day 2 was by far the top performer.
Figure 4.2 displays the growth of $1,000 invested only during the first five
trading days of each trading month since December 31, 1900.

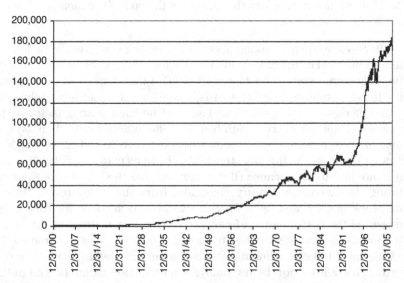

FIGURE 4.2 Growth of $1,000 invested during Trading Days 1–5 each month
since Dec. 31, 1900

As you can see in Figure 4.2, the first five trading days of the month have tended to be a very good time to be in the stock market. Although there have certainly been some losing periods along the way, over the long run, the stock market has consistently trended higher during the first five trading days of the month.

Monthly Wave 2: Trading Days 6 to 8

Following the typical early month strength during trading days 1 through 5, there tends to be something of a lull in the stock market as buying pressure abates. Table 4.2 displays the cumulative results for trading days 6, 7, and 8.

As Figure 4.3 shows, there is a world of difference between the performance of the market during the first five days (see Figure 4.2) and that of trading days 6, 7, and 8.

It seems clear that buying pressure typically abates after the first several trading days of the month. During the first thirty years of the 1900s, this period was almost universally bearish. Since that time, there have been several multiyear periods of uptrends. Still, little or no money has been made on the whole over the past 70-plus years, and the past 107 years as a whole have witnessed a loss of slightly more than 70 percent during trading days 6, 7, and 8 of each month.

Monthly Wave 3: Trading Days 9 to 12

Monthly wave 3 confirms the idea that money moves the market. This wave encompasses trading days 9 through 12 each month. As you can see in Figure 4.4, for most of the past century, there was no trend whatsoever during this midmonth period. Then suddenly in the early 1980s—at about the time that IRAs came into existence—this period began to show consistently strong gains. My preferred explanation for this change in character during the midmonth period is that many people are paid not only at the end of the month but also at midmonth. Thus, at midmonth, there is a regular flow of money from employers to employees, and automatically

TABLE 4.2 Cumulative Percentage Gain for Trading Days 6–8

Day of Month	Cumulative Percentage Gain +(−)
Trading day 6	(42)
Trading day 7	(11)
Trading day 8	(45)

FIGURE 4.3   Growth of $1,000 invested during trading days 6-8 each month since Dec. 31, 1900

from employees to some form of investment account. This automatic flow of cash to the market is a constant source of demand for stocks during midmonth. There can be no debate that the stock market has performed exceptionally well during midmonth over the past several decades—after not performing consistently during the same period previously.

As Figure 4.4 shows, the stock market has trended sharply higher during this midmonth bulge over the past several decades. Also, there is an unmistakable difference in the performance of the stock market during this period from the performance for trading days 6, 7, and 8 (see Figure 4.3).

Another point that should be made is that midmonth and end-of-month paychecks provide a constant source of demand for stocks. Remember that

TABLE 4.3   Cumulative Percentage Gain for Trading Days 9-12

Day of Month	Cumulative Percentage Gain +(−)
Trading day 9	99
Trading day 10	(8)
Trading day 11	23
Trading day 12	22

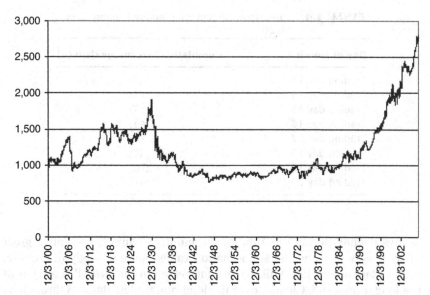

FIGURE 4.4 Growth of $1,000 invested during trading days 9–12 each month since Dec. 31, 1900

none of this means that the stock market will advance during these periods each and every month. During any given month, other outside influences may cause enough selling pressure to push down stock prices despite the regular inflow of cash. The only implication is that it does seem useful to remember that there is consistently a potentially positive influence for the stock market during these time frames because of the automatic inflow of investment capital.

Monthly Wave 4: Trading Days 13 to 20

Once the midmonth bulge of trading days 9 through 12 plays out, a lack of buying pressure is typically commonplace. This is illustrated in Table 4.4 by the fact that between trading days 13 and 20, only trading day 17 has shown an average daily profit over the past 100-plus years. All the other days have shown a net loss. Given that since December 31, 1900, the Dow has advanced from 71 points to more than 14,000—a gain of about 20,000 percent—it can be considered statistically significant that such an extended string of days in the month would consistently fail to produce gains.

As Figure 4.5 shows, it is important to remember that the numbers in Table 4.4 should not be interpreted to mean that the stock market will

TABLE 4.4   Cumulative Percentage Gain for Trading Days
13–20

Day of Month	Cumulative Percentage Gain (–)
Trading day 13	(8)
Trading day 14	(1)
Trading day 15	(27)
Trading day 16	(43)
Trading day 17	29
Trading day 18	(8)
Trading day 19	(12)
Trading day 20	(1)

always decline during this time of the month. Figure 4.5 reveals a great
many instances when the stock market rallied quite strongly during this
mid- to late-month lull. Still, we are interested in the overall direction of
the long-term trend. Clearly, over the long run, trading days 13 through 20
have not been a great time to be in the stock market.

Now let's look at another subset of this late-month lull. To do this, we
begin by counting backward starting at the end of each month.

FIGURE 4.5   Growth of $1,000 invested during trading days 13–20 each month
since Dec. 31, 1990

Monthly Wave 4a: Trading Days −7, −6, and −5

As I mentioned earlier, a complicating factor in analyzing daily intramonth trends is that not every month has the same number of trading days. So, to get a clearer picture of month-end trends, we will count backward from the last trading day of the month to determine whether any trends become apparent. For our purposes, the last trading day of the month is trading day −1, the next-to-last trading day is trading day −2, the day before that is trading day −3, and so on. In analyzing the last seven trading days of each month, two trends become apparent.

The first trend involves trading days −7, −6, and −5 of each month. For example, October 31, 2007 would be trading day −1. From there we can simply count backward as follows:

> October 31, 2007 = Trading day −1
>
> October 30, 2007 = Trading day −2
>
> October 29, 2007 = Trading day −3
>
> October 26, 2007 = Trading day −4
>
> October 25, 2007 = Trading day −5
>
> October 24, 2007 = Trading day −6
>
> October 23, 2007 = Trading day −7

So, for October 2007 we would look at the performance of the Dow on October 23, 24, and 25, because these dates represent trading days −7, −6, and −5 for that month. As you can see in Table 4.5, trading days −7, −6, and −5 each showed an average loss over the past 100-plus years.

Figure 4.6 displays the growth of $1,000 invested in the Dow only during the seventh-, sixth-, and fifth-to-last trading days of every month since December 31, 1900. As you can see, following a period of extremely strong performance between about 1919 and 1931, this time of month was Death Valley for stock prices for more than fifty years. Since the start of the great bull market in 1982, this time period has shown a slight net gain.

TABLE 4.5 Cumulative Percentage Gain for Trading Days −7, −6, and −5

Day of Month	Cumulative Percentage Gain (−)
Trading day −7	(21)
Trading day −6	(18)
Trading day −5	(55)

FIGURE 4.6 Growth of $1,000 invested during trading days −7, −6, and −5 each month since Dec. 31, 1900

It should be reiterated that these trading days are not destined to lose money every month. And, as I just illustrated with the rally of 1919 to 1931, if trading days −7, −6, and −5 show a large net gain over the next twelve years, it would not necessarily be an aberration or an unprecedented achievement. Nevertheless, our primary interest remains in the long-term trend. There can be little debate that the long-term trend during this period near the end of the month has been quite unfavorable for the stock market and, by extension, for stock market investors.

Monthly Wave 5: The Last Two Trading Days of the Month

In stock market circles, much is made of the alleged phenomenon of window dressing. "Window dressing" is when investment management professionals dress up their portfolios at the end of a month or quarter to impress current and would-be investors with their ability to pick high-quality securities. Although this sounds like a bit of a foolhardy endeavor and not necessarily like something that such a professional should be spending time on, the fact is that there is probably something to this. Whatever the cause, there is clearly something of note going on in the stock market at the end of the month.

TABLE 4.6 Cumulative Percentage Gain for Trading Days
−1 and −2

Day of Month	Cumulative Percentage Gain
Trading day −2	128
Trading day −1	279

This trend is clearly illustrated by the results shown in Table 4.6. As you can see, the last trading day of the month and the next-to-last trading day of the month have generated extremely positive results over the past 100-plus years.

Over the past 100-plus years, the last trading day of the month has been the third most profitable trading day of the month, behind only trading days 2 and 3. Figure 4.7 displays the growth of $1,000 invested in the Dow only during the last two trading days of each month since December 31, 1900.

As you can see in Figure 4.7, the growth in equity accumulated during the last two trading days of the month is not a straight line. There have been several sharp drawdowns of note along the way. In fact, the equity curve for this two-day period topped out in early 1996 and has not reached a new high since. Nevertheless, it seems reasonable to expect this period to resume its bullish tendency at some point in the future.

FIGURE 4.7 Growth of $1,000 invested during trading days −1 and −2 each month since Dec. 31, 1900

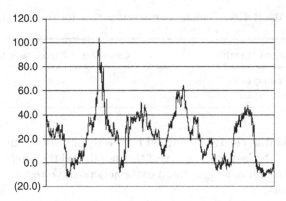

FIGURE 4.8 Ten-year rolling percentage rate of return for the last two trading days of the month since 1901

Figure 4.8 displays the rolling ten-year percentage gain or loss for this two-day period since 1901. As you can see, previous instances when the ten-year rate of return was negative were invariably followed by periods of very strong performance in the same time frame. Therefore—with the caveat that nothing in the stock market is guaranteed—it should not surprise investors if the last two trading days of the month generate some strong positive returns in the years ahead.

THE WORST TRADING DAYS OF THE MONTH

As we have just seen, there seem to be several intramonth trends or patterns at work on a regular basis in the stock market. The beginning, middle, and end of the month have shown a strong tendency to exhibit bullish behavior, whereas the intervening mid-early and mid-late periods have generated a net loss over the past 100-plus years of stock market movement. To fully illustrate a time to be in the market and a time to be out of the market, let's consider the results of an investor who invested only during the weakest periods of the month as measured over the past 100 years.

For the purposes of this test, assume that an investor bought and held the Dow only during the following periods each month:

- Trading days 6, 7, and 8.
- Trading days 13, 14, 15, 16, 17, 18, 19, and 20.
- Trading days −7, −6, and −5 (with the last trading day of each month being designated as trading day −1).

FIGURE 4.9 Growth of $1,000 invested only during the 14 worst days of the month

Figure 4.9 displays the dismal results for such an investor who had bought and held the Dow only during these worst trading days.

This performance is truly dismal. Between December 31, 1900, and December 31, 2007, the Dow itself advanced from 70.71 to 13,264.82, for a gain of 18,659 percent. During that same time, an initial $1,000 invested each month only during the worst days would have shrunk to just $92, a staggering loss of 90.8 percent. It takes a moment for the horrid nature of this performance to fully sink in—and note that this performance was based on an objective, repetitive set of rules. In other words, we are simply highlighting the performance of the same trading days month in and month out every year for more than 108 years. Although this performance is awful, it opens up some interesting possibilities for alert investors.

THE BEST TRADING DAYS OF THE MONTH (PART 1)

Because we have now been able to identify a series of days during which the stock market has exhibited poor performance, the next obvious question is, What if we simply avoided those days and invested in the stock

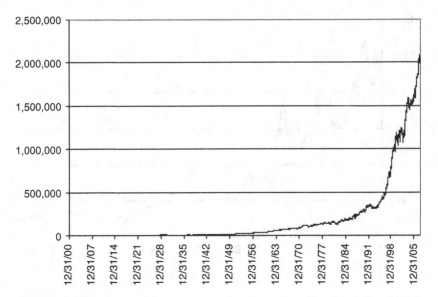

FIGURE 4.10 Growth of $1,000 invested only on all trading days other than the 14 worst days of the month

market only on all other trading days? To analyze this possibility, we will test the following strategy:

- We will hold a long position in the Dow on all trading days each month except for trading days 6 through 8, 13 through 20, and −7, −6, and −5. In other words, we will simply exclude all of the worst trading days that we just highlighted.

Figure 4.10 illustrates the growth of $1,000 invested using the rules just detailed since December 31, 1900. You will note a slight difference between the performance in this figure and that depicted in Figure 4.9.

The stark difference in the equity curves displayed in Figures 4.9 and 4.10 is hard to mistake. In all, $1,000 invested only on the non-worst days of each month grew to $2,029,812 by December 31, 2007. This figure does not include any interest that might have been earned while out of the market and in cash.

To further illustrate the differences in performance between the worst days of the month and the non-worst days, consider Table 4.7, which highlights decade-by-decade performance during both the worst and the non-worst periods of each month.

TABLE 4.7 Decade-by-Decade Performance; Non-Worst Days versus Worst Days

Decade	Total Non-Worst Days (%) +(−)	Total Worst Days (%) +(−)	Non-Worst Minus Worst Days
1901–1909	80.3	(22.3)	102.7
1910–1919	10.0	(1.6)	11.6
1920–1929	185.1	(18.7)	203.8
1930–1939	30.5	(53.7)	84.2
1940–1949	80.2	(26.1)	106.2
1950–1959	175.0	23.4	151.6
1960–1969	118.6	(46.1)	164.7
1970–1979	73.6	(39.6)	113.2
1980–1989	94.5	68.8	25.5
1990–1999	281.3	9.5	271.8
2000–2007	97.2	(41.5)	138.7

As I have mentioned throughout, there are no guarantees that seasonal trends that have prevailed in the past for the stock market will continue to prevail in the future. Still, the fact that the non-worst monthly days have outperformed the worst monthly days by such a wide margin every single decade over the past 100 years is about as much of a favorable historical test as any investor could ask for. As I also mentioned earlier, this is the type of consistent performance that breeds confidence in investors, which in turn allows them to follow a given approach long enough to enjoy its benefits.

Now let's put the days of the month under a slightly stronger microscope and see whether there is a way to wring more out of these trends.

THE BEST TRADING DAYS OF THE MONTH (PART 2): THE MONTH-END/NEW-MONTH PATTERN

As we have already seen, there is a definite propensity for the stock market to rally at the beginning and end of the month. Once again, this does not mean that the stock market will rally at the end and the beginning of every month. Nor does it mean that this period cannot go months at a time without generating any meaningful new profits. Nevertheless, with these caveats firmly in mind, it appears beneficial to take a closer look at these trends and the impact they may have for investors who are prepared to act and take advantage of them.

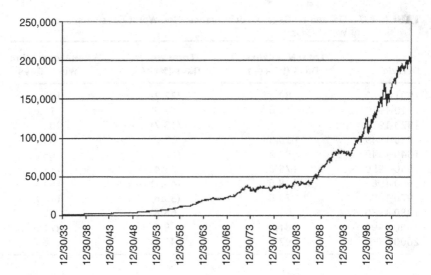

FIGURE 4.11 Growth of $1,000 invested only during the last two trading days of each month and the first four trading days of each month since Dec. 31, 1933

We will consider first the six contiguous days of the last two days of the month and the first four days of the following month. For the purposes of this test, we will assume that an investor is long the Dow only during these six days each month and is out of the market completely during all other trading days. We will start at the close on December 31, 1933. To highlight only the effect of stock market performance, we will assume that no interest was earned during those days that we were out of the stock market. Figure 4.11 displays the growth of $1,000 since December 31, 1933, that could have been generated by being long the Dow only during these six trading days every month.

The results depicted in Figure 4.11 are compelling. There are a few interesting facts to note about the overall performance of the stock market during these six days a month:

- Average daily gain during the six-day favorable period was 0.001037 percent.
- The average daily gain during all other trading days of the month was 0.000014 percent.
- The average daily gain during the six-day favorable period has been 72.0 times greater than the average daily return on all other trading days of the month.
- The annualized rate of return during the six-day favorable period was 29.9 percent.

- The annualized rate of return during all other trading days was 0.4 percent.
- A $1,000 investment in the Dow only during the favorable six-day period each month grew to $202,335 between December 31, 1933, and December 31, 2007.
- A $1,000 investment in the Dow during only all other nonfavorable days shrank to $656 during the same time frame.

To put it another way, the Dow gained 20,136 percent during the favorable days and managed to lose 34 percent during the unfavorable days. To put this into proper perspective, you must recognize that all of the money and more that has been made in the stock market during the past 70-plus years has occurred on just six trading days per month! Being in the stock market during all of the rest of the trading days during this time would actually have cost you money. This is almost impossible for many individuals to believe. And it certainly calls into question the theory of random stock market price action. Still, the numbers are what they are and there appears to be some wisdom in taking action to maximize profitability during those days when the market is most likely to generate profits. Investors, of course, are entitled to draw their own conclusions.

The Midmonth Pattern

Earlier, I talked about the idea that money moves the market. More specifically, I detailed that when money moves aggressively into the market to buy stocks, stock prices are more likely to rise than they are during other times when there is no pressing demand for stocks. In this section, I try to prove this theory. We have seen in this chapter how month-end window dressing and new money moving automatically into the stock market at the beginning of each month creates automatic and repetitive demand for stocks, which typically serves to push stock prices higher. For the bulk of the past century, there was no similar phenomenon during the middle of the month. Then, in the very early 1980s, IRAs came into existence. As a result, over time, millions of individual investors began automatically investing money from their midmonth paycheck into the stock market. Has this development had any effect on the stock market as a whole since that time? Let's take a look at some numbers, and then you can judge for yourself.

Figure 4.12 displays the growth of $1,000 invested in the Dow only during trading days 9, 10, 11, and 12 each month between December 31, 1933, and December 31, 1979.

As you can see in Figure 4.12, there is little rhyme or reason to the performance of the stock market during the middle-four-day period

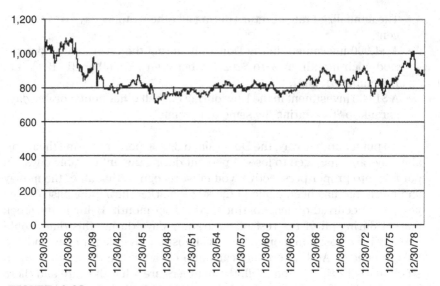

FIGURE 4.12 Growth of $1,000 invested in the Dow during trading days 9–12 each month from 1933 through the end of 1979

between the end of 1933 and the end of 1979. It can be argued that a lack of capital flowing into the market resulted in other factors influencing the stock market. Sometimes these factors might be favorable and other times unfavorable. Because the factors are random and change over time, the results are without a clear trend. In fact, the stock market actually lost money during these trading days between 1933 and 1979, with $1,000 shrinking slightly to $874. But, beginning in the 1980s, and following the introduction of IRAs, this automatic, built-in midmonth demand began to exert a steadily favorable influence on stock prices. Figure 4.13 displays the growth of $1,000 invested in the Dow only during trading days 9, 10, 11, and 12 each month between December 31, 1979, and December 31, 2007.

As you can see in Figure 4.13, unlike the 47-year period prior to 1980, which was essentially flat, there has been a definite tendency for the stock market to advance during the favorable four days at midmonth since 1980. The difference in performance prior to 1980 and after 1980 is made quite obvious by the vertical line at December 31, 1979, in Figure 4.14.

The data to the left of the vertical line in Figure 4.14 represent the era of no built-in demand for stocks during the midmonth period, and the data to the right of the vertical line represent the era of built-in demand for stocks during the midmonth period. Do you notice a difference?

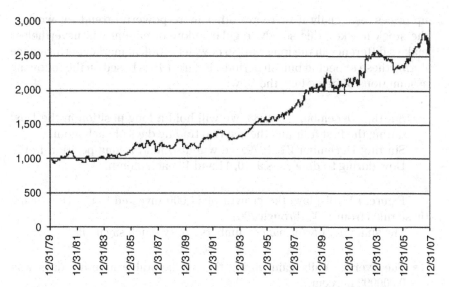

FIGURE 4.13 Growth of $1,000 invested in the Dow during trading days 9-12 each month from 1980 through the end of 2007

The Monthly 10

At this point, given the evidence that we have seen so far, we are operating on the theory that money indeed moves the market. We have identified two periods of the month—(1) the contiguous period containing the last two trading days and the first four trading days of each month and (2) trading days 9 through 12—as typically bullish periods. That bullishness apparently results from an automatic flow of capital into the stock market at these times each month. Although this inflow will not always be enough to push

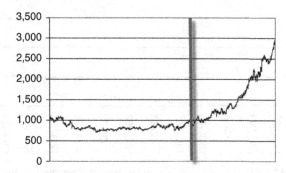

FIGURE 4.14 Growth of $1,000 invested in the Dow during trading days 9-12, each month from 1933 through the end of 2007

up prices, especially if there are other more powerful trends at work in the stock market, this steady, regular inflow of capital will nevertheless make a difference in the long run. So now, let's look at market performance during these expected bullish periods. Figure 4.15 is based on the following assumptions of being long the Dow:

- Starting December 31, 1933, we will hold a long position in the Dow during the first four and the last two trading days of each month.
- Starting December 31, 1979, we will also hold a long position in the Dow during trading days 9, 10, 11 and 12 each month.

Figure 4.15 displays the growth of $1,000 invested in the Dow using these rules from 1933 through 2007.

The summary performance numbers pretty much say it all:

- The average daily gain during the ten favorable monthly days was 0.000993 percent.
- The average daily gain during all other trading days of the month was −0.000070 percent.
- The annualized rate of return during the six-day favorable period was 28.4 percent.

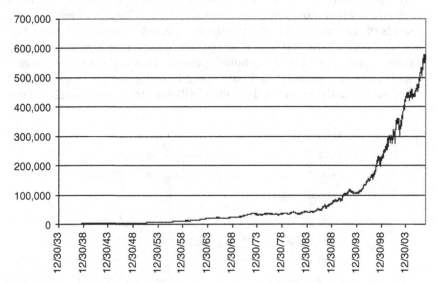

FIGURE 4.15 Growth of $1,000 invested only during the last two trading days and first four trading days of each month since Dec. 31, 1933, in addition to trading days 9–12 since Dec. 31, 1979

- The annualized rate of return during all other trading days was −1.8 percent.
- A $1,000 investment in the Dow only during the ten favorable days each month grew to $562,500 between December 31, 1933, and December 31, 2007.
- A $1,000 investment in the Dow during only all other nonfavorable days shrank 76.4 percent to just $236 during the same time frame.

Random-walk theorists will argue that all trading days are created equal. The results we have just seen suggest that, at the very least, some days are apparently more equal than others.

THE MOST WONDERFUL TIME OF THE YEAR

Now, let's look at a period of time that overlaps part of three different months and that has proved quite favorable for stock investors over the years. Much has been made over the years of the so-called Santa Claus rally in the stock market. Whereas most analysts focus on the days surrounding Christmas itself, there may be a much more powerful force at work.

For the purposes of this test, during the Santa Claus rally period, we will be long the Dow for the two days before Thanksgiving through the fifth trading day of the following January.

Figure 4.16 displays the growth of $1,000 invested in the Dow only during this approximate time frame of 1.3 months every year since December 31, 1933.

As you can see in Figure 4.16, Santa Claus does seem to have a tendency to visit Broad and Wall during the holidays. Of course, as with any other seasonal trend, it is important to note that the market does not advance during this time frame every single year. Whereas this trend has been highly reliable for many decades, the fact remains that there will be times when this period will witness a market decline with possible losses. Still, the long-term upward trend depicted in Figure 4.16 is fairly unmistakable.

Here are some performance numbers for the Santa Claus rally:

- The average daily gain during the Santa Claus rally was 0.000898 percent.
- The average daily gain during all other trading days of the year was 0.000210 percent.
- The average daily gain during the Santa Claus rally was 4.3 times greater than the average daily gain during all other trading days.

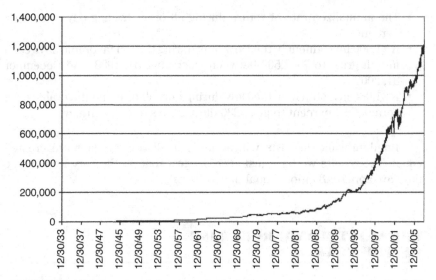

FIGURE 4.16 Growth of $1,000 invested during the Santa Claus rally from Jan. 3, 1900–Dec. 31, 2007

- The annualized rate of return during the Santa Claus rally was 25.4 percent.
- The annualized rate of return during all other trading days was 5.4 percent.
- The Santa Claus rally has shown a gain in 59 of the past 75 years, or 78.7 percent of the time.
- The average performance for the Santa Claus rally has been a gain of 2.92 percent.
- The biggest gain was 13.3 percent during 1971–1972.
- The worst loss was 6.2 percent during 1977–1978.
- The average gain during the 59 up periods was 4.1 percent.
- The average loss during the 15 down periods was 2.0 percent.

As I remind throughout this book, the stock market is the ultimate arbiter of human emotion for all things financial. And, because human emotion is such a strong factor in determining the trend of the stock market at any given point in time, it should not be surprising that during the glad tidings and good cheer of the Thanksgiving, Christmas, and New Year's holidays that the stock market shows a tendency to rally. Some people will dismiss this notion out of hand, but let's stop and think about it for a moment.

For a great many people, the holidays are the one time of year when they step back from their day-to-day lives and actually take stock of themselves and what is going on around them. Thanksgiving is just that—a time to reflect on all the blessings that encompass one's life. The Christmas season—and other religious holidays in December—is a time of great hope and joy. And many people view New Year's as the dawn of something new and, in the hopes and dreams of many people, something better. All of this good feeling, joy, and hopefulness can manifest in many ways. The desire to better one's lot in life certainly falls into that category. So, it is not a coincidence that the stock market tends to rally between Thanksgiving and the New Year. It is simply a perennial period of good feeling exerting its influence.

MONTHLY 10 COMBINED WITH THE SANTA CLAUS RALLY

We have identified ten trading days of the month that have historically witnessed well-above-average returns for the stock market. In addition, we have identified a season of the year—the Santa Claus rally—when the stock market typically exhibits strength. The obvious next step is to add the Santa Claus rally to our ten favorable monthly days and see what kind of results we can generate. For this test, we will buy and hold the Dow each and every year only during the following days:

- The first four trading days of every month.
- The last two trading days of every month.
- Trading days 9, 10, 11, and 12 of every month.
- All days between and including the two trading days prior to Thanksgiving through the fifth trading day of the next year.

So, during all months except November, December, and January, we will be in the market only for ten trading days. During November, we will be in the market during the first four trading days, trading days 9 through 12, and all days between the close of the third trading day prior to Thanksgiving (i.e., entering the market at the close on the Monday of Thanksgiving week) and the end of the month. During December, we will be in the market for all trading days. During January, we will be in the market for 11 trading days—the first 5 days (as part of the Santa Claus rally), trading days 9 through 12, and the last 2 trading days of the month.

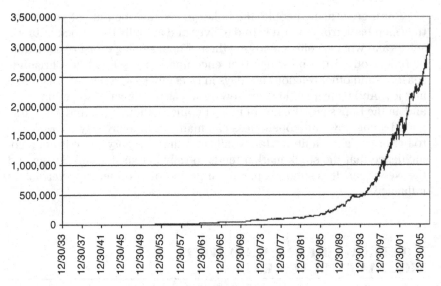

FIGURE 4.17 Growth of $1,000 invested in the Dow using rules of monthly 10 plus Santa Claus rally, from Dec. 31, 1933–Dec. 31, 2007

Now, let's look at the results that these rules would have generated. Figure 4.17 displays the growth of $1,000 invested in the Dow using these rules from December 31, 1933, through December 31, 2007.

The equity curve depicted in Figure 4.17 is inarguably impressive. So are the performance numbers that go along with it:

- The average daily gain during favorable periods was 0.00092 percent.
- Average daily gain during all other trading days of the month was −0.00015 percent.
- The annualized rate of return during the six-day favorable period was 26.1 percent.
- The annualized rate of return during all other trading days was −3.7 percent.
- A $1,000 investment in the Dow only during the ten favorable monthly days each month grew to $1,200,209 between December 31, 1933, and December 31, 2007.
- A $1,000 investment in the Dow only during all other nonfavorable days shrank 88.9 percent to just $111 during the same time frame.

As with a number of the seasonal trends detailed in this book, it is at first hard to believe how compelling the results are. The performance of the monthly 10 plus Santa Claus rally certainly falls into that category. To think that a person who had insisted on being invested in the Dow during only the nonfavorable days would have suffered a relentless 88.9 percent loss is almost too much to comprehend. The first reaction of many individuals will be that there is no way to guarantee that these kinds of results will continue ad infinitum. And they would be correct. Nevertheless, it is not a stretch to believe that the stock market is strongest in the following situations:

- When money is moving into the market with the express purpose of buying stocks.
- When people are feeling most optimistic.

On this basis, the results generated using this method make sense. As we have established, money moves systematically into the stock market at the beginning, end, and middle of each month. Likewise, the most predictable season of optimism regarding all things in general occurs during the winter holidays. There is no reason that astute investors should not attempt to take advantage of these trends.

THE ULTIMATE MONTHLY DAYS SYSTEM

As a near-final tweak of our analysis of trends among days of the month, we will now take a page from the previous chapter and add in the holiday factor to create what I unabashedly call the "ultimate monthly days system" (UMDS). This system will follow the same trading rules as the Monthly 10 plus Santa Claus rally but will also be in the market during the trading days prior to each major stock market holiday. The rules for this system are to hold the Dow as follows:

- The last two trading days of each month.
- The first four trading days of each month.
- Trading days 9, 10, 11, and 12 of each month.
- The period starting two days prior to Thanksgiving and extending through the fifth trading day of the following January.
- The trading day prior to each major stock market holiday.
- On all other trading days, be in cash and earn interest at a rate of 1 percent per year.

Figure 4.18 displays the results that might have been generated using these rules since December 31, 1933.

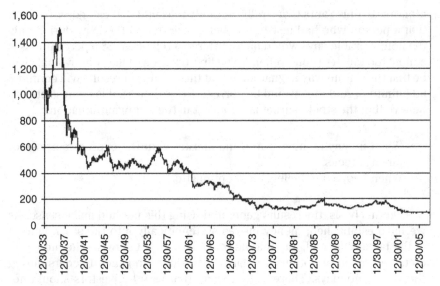

FIGURE 4.18 Growth of $1,000 invested in the Dow with UMDS between Dec. 31, 1933, and Dec. 31, 2007

The addition of the pre- and postholiday trading days—even including, for the sake of consistency, those that we already know are unprofitable—into the mix and the factoring in of a modest amount of interest while out of the stock market, results in a meaningful improvement in overall profitability. As you can see in Figure 4.18, $1,000 invested since December 31, 1933, using these rules would have grown steadily through December 31, 2007.

Here are the performance numbers for the UMDS:

- The average daily gain during favorable periods was 0.000925 percent.
- The average daily gain during all other trading days of the month was −0.000168 percent.
- The annualized rate of return during the six-day favorable period was 26.2 percent.
- The annualized rate of return during all other trading days was −4.2 percent.
- A $1,000 investment in the Dow only during the ten favorable monthly days plus interest earned in cash grew to $3,027,390 between December 31, 1933, and October 17, 2007.
- A $1,000 investment in the Dow only during all other nonfavorable days fell a staggeringly 90.7 percent to just $93 during the same time frame.

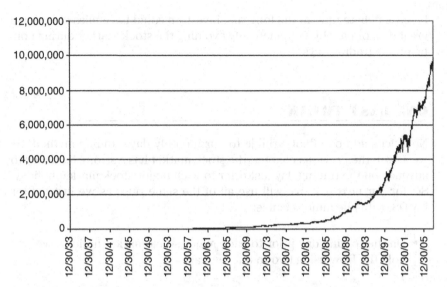

FIGURE 4.19 Growth of $1,000 invested in the Dow only during UMDS nonfavorable days between Dec. 31, 1933, and Dec. 31, 2007

To fully appreciate the potential benefit of avoiding the stock market during those periods that are deemed unfavorable by UMDS, consider the results that appear in Figure 4.19. This equity curve displays the sad state of affairs that typically grips the market during trading days that are deemed unfavorable according to UMDS and drives home the notion that there is a time to be in the stock market and a time to be out. In this vein, our UMDS appears to do a pretty good job of separating the good days from the bad.

It is worth pointing out that the performance of the stock market during nonfavorable days is by no means a straight-line decline. In fact, a close examination of the equity curve displayed in Figure 4.19 reveals a number of times when the stock market rallied strongly even though, according to our trading rules, it should not have done so. One of the hardest things for any investor to accept is that he or she will never be correct 100 percent of the time. As you see in Figure 4.19, there would have been any number of times in the past 100-plus years when investors following UMDS trading rules would have been sitting on the sideline while the stock market rallied strongly. The longer these rallies last and the more pronounced they become, the more tempted investors are to stray from their trading rules and to wing it on the basis of extrapolating current, temporary trends. Consistency and discipline are two keys to trading and investment success for all individual investors. Thus, although Figure 4.19 does reveal a number of periods of rising equity (i.e., periods when UMDS was wrong), there can be little debate that, in the long run, investors could have missed out on a great deal of pain by systematically avoiding the stock market during non-favorable trading days.

ONE LAST TWEAK

Now, let's add one final wrinkle to our monthly days trading method. As we saw in the previous chapter, the stock market has a strong tendency to advance on the trading day just prior to each major stock market holiday. So, for our next test, we will use all of the same rules as we just did for UMDS, with one minor change:

- On the trading day prior to each major stock market holiday, we will hold the Dow using two-to-one leverage.

Adding this minor tweak generates a tremendous increase in the overall returns. In this case, $1,000 grows to more than $9,000,000 between December 31, 1933, and December 31, 2007. So, let's refer to this method as our "ultimate, ultimate monthly days system" (UUMDS). This increase in overall returns illustrates the potential usefulness of applying leverage to any trading method that has an expectation of a positive return. This final dollar amount basically displays the net effect of compounding money at a rate of 13 percent per year over the course of 70-plus years.

Figure 4.20 displays the growth of equity over the years using the rules laid out earlier.

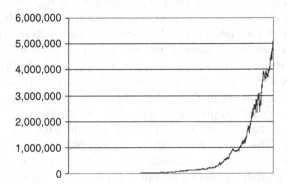

FIGURE 4.20 Growth of $1,000 invested in the Dow using the UUMDS including the use of two-to-one leverage on the trading day before each stock market holiday (Dec. 31, 1933–Dec. 31, 2007)

Table 4.8 displays the year-to-year results versus a buy-and-hold approach.

A few important notes regarding the performance depicted in Figure 4.20 and Table 4.8. This system by no means beats the market every year. In fact, the UUMDS has outperformed a buy-and-hold approach only 49 times and has underperformed a buy-and-hold approach 25 times on a calendar-year basis. Thus, investors who are focused on beating the market year in and year out, and who view a year that underperforms the market averages as a failure—even if they make a lot of money—may have a great deal of difficulty following this particular system.

If you are wondering how the overall performance can be so much better when the system outperforms the market only about 66 percent of the time, the answer is risk control. The primary difference between the system itself and the stock market as a whole comes down to the fact that the system almost invariably performs better than the overall market when the overall market is weak. Preservation of capital is a topic that gets a lot of lip service from market professionals and amateurs alike. But not everyone really knows how to achieve capital preservation. The UUMDS achieves it almost systematically. To illustrate, consider that since 1933 there have been 23 calendar years that have witnessed a decline by the Dow. Then note that during all 23 of these down years for the Dow, the UUMDS has outperformed the Dow. In other words, while the Dow is losing money, the UUMDS is either making money or losing a lot less than the Dow itself. This is an example of capital preservation in action.

It should also be noted that the UUMDS is not a cash machine in that it does not make money every year. The UUMDS has shown a calendar-year gain 67 of 74 times. This is a marked improvement over a buy-and-hold approach that showed a gain during only 51 of 74 years. So, the good news is that the system has experienced 16 more profitable years than has the Dow itself. Still, the bad news is that investors using this system would still have experienced nine losing calendar years. Here are a few more facts and figures of interest regarding the UUMDS:

- The best-performing calendar year was 1938, with a gain of 59.4 percent.
- The worst-performing calendar year was 1966, with a loss of 8.9 percent.
- The largest drawdown in equity was 20.5 percent, which started on August 17, 1987, and bottomed out on December 4, 1987. A new equity high was reached on September 2, 1988. The biggest drawdown using a buy-and-hold approach was 52.2 percent, which started on March 10, 1937, and bottomed out on April 28, 1942. Since that time, declines

TABLE 4.8   UUMDS Year-by-Year

Year	UUMDS	Buy and Hold	Difference (%)	UUMDS $1,000 ($)	Buy/Hold $1,000 ($)
1934	2.1	4.1	(2.1)	1,021	1,041
1935	13.3	38.5	(25.2)	1,157	1,443
1936	17.0	24.8	(7.8)	1,353	1,801
1937	12.4	(32.8)	45.2	1,521	1,210
1938	59.4	28.1	31.3	2,425	1,549
1939	2.2	(2.9)	5.1	2,478	1,504
1940	4.6	(12.7)	17.3	2,592	1,313
1941	(4.8)	(15.4)	10.6	2,468	1,111
1942	29.6	7.6	22.0	3,197	1,195
1943	8.9	13.8	(5.0)	3,480	1,360
1944	9.3	12.1	(2.8)	3,804	1,525
1945	18.3	26.6	(8.3)	4,501	1,931
1946	9.3	(8.1)	17.5	4,921	1,774
1947	11.9	2.2	9.7	5,508	1,813
1948	(1.7)	(2.1)	0.4	5,413	1,775
1949	11.9	12.9	(1.0)	6,058	2,003
1950	15.4	17.6	(2.2)	6,994	2,356
1951	28.3	14.4	13.9	8,974	2,695
1952	12.9	8.4	4.5	10,130	2,922
1953	2.1	(3.8)	5.9	10,342	2,812
1954	27.1	44.0	(16.8)	13,146	4,048
1955	11.3	20.8	(9.4)	14,635	4,889
1956	27.0	2.3	24.8	18,590	5,000
1957	11.8	(12.8)	24.6	20,782	4,361
1958	28.6	34.0	(5.3)	26,735	5,842
1959	16.4	16.4	0.0	31,130	6,800
1960	9.4	(9.3)	18.8	34,069	6,165
1961	23.3	18.7	4.6	42,015	7,319
1962	33.6	(10.8)	44.4	56,117	6,528
1963	20.2	17.0	3.2	67,466	7,637
1964	6.7	14.6	(7.9)	71,973	8,750
1965	15.5	10.9	4.7	83,158	9,702
1966	(8.9)	(18.9)	10.1	75,769	7,865
1967	10.7	15.2	(4.5)	83,849	9,060
1968	9.3	4.3	5.0	91,647	9,447
1969	6.1	(15.2)	21.3	97,260	8,012
1970	25.9	4.8	21.1	122,470	8,398
1971	23.9	6.1	17.8	151,760	8,911
1972	20.3	14.6	5.7	182,527	10,210
1973	(4.7)	(16.6)	11.9	173,903	8,517
1974	13.2	(27.6)	40.8	196,900	6,169
1975	23.1	38.3	(15.2)	242,376	8,533

TABLE 4.8 (Continued)

Year	UUMDS	Buy and Hold	Difference (%)	UUMDS $1,000 ($)	Buy/Hold $1,000 ($)
1976	11.1	17.9	(6.8)	269,245	10,057
1977	0.7	(17.3)	17.9	271,055	8,320
1978	5.0	(3.1)	8.1	284,524	8,058
1979	3.5	4.2	(0.7)	294,424	8,396
1980	13.4	14.9	(1.5)	333,841	9,650
1981	(3.9)	(9.2)	5.3	320,760	8,759
1982	15.5	19.6	(4.1)	370,434	10,476
1983	11.9	20.3	(8.3)	414,643	12,599
1984	7.9	(3.7)	11.6	447,376	12,128
1985	11.7	27.7	(16.0)	499,514	15,482
1986	2.3	22.6	(20.3)	511,090	18,978
1987	21.2	2.3	18.9	619,456	19,408
1988	22.2	11.8	10.4	757,051	21,707
1989	28.8	27.0	1.9	975,238	27,560
1990	7.8	(4.3)	12.1	1,051,021	26,363
1991	32.6	20.3	12.3	1,394,028	31,720
1992	7.7	4.2	3.5	1,501,516	33,044
1993	(1.3)	13.7	(15.0)	1,482,166	37,578
1994	8.7	2.1	6.6	1,611,336	38,383
1995	24.8	33.5	(8.7)	2,010,247	51,222
1996	13.2	26.0	(12.8)	2,275,301	64,547
1997	23.0	22.6	0.3	2,797,664	79,162
1998	10.9	16.1	(5.2)	3,103,594	91,906
1999	36.0	25.2	10.8	4,221,105	115,086
2000	13.3	(6.2)	19.5	4,783,510	107,976
2001	10.3	(7.1)	17.4	5,276,102	100,315
2002	(7.6)	(16.8)	9.2	4,876,920	83,500
2003	37.6	25.3	12.3	6,709,832	104,644
2004	5.7	3.1	2.5	7,091,446	107,938
2005	1.1	(0.6)	1.7	7,166,807	107,282
2006	17.7	16.3	1.4	8,436,862	124,756
2007	12.7	6.4	6.3	9,506,979	132,781
Average	**13.8**	**8.1**	**5.7**		

of 30 percent or more occurred in 1970–1971, 1973–1974, 1987, and 2000–2002.

• The average annual rate of return for the UUMDS was 13.8 percent, compared to an average annual return of 8.1 percent for a buy-and-hold approach.

SUMMING UP

Many individuals who follow and deal in the stock market claim that the price movements of the market are random and that there is no way to predict from day to day, month to month, or year to year which way prices are headed. And, certainly, there are many investors who have tried unsuccessfully to time the market who would likely agree with this assessment. Yet, the information detailed in this chapter provides a strong refutation of this random-walk theory. This information suggests that, in the long run, there is a genuine rhythm or ebb and flow to the stock market. I have also suggested a reason why this ebb and flow takes place—simply summarized as money moves the market. In a nutshell, as investment dollars flow into the stock market, the prices of stocks rise naturally as a result of the increased demand for stocks. I also suggested that, as of this point in time, there is a constant and consistent flow of investment dollars into the stock market at particular times of the month (i.e., the very end into the beginning of the month and the middle of the month). This is a simple reflection of the fact that millions and millions of dollars are automatically transferred at these times from employees' paychecks directly into some type of stock market investment vehicle, whether a mutual fund or some type of private investment account. As long as this trend continues, the stock market should retain a constant inflow of dollars at these specific times each month. And, as you saw in this chapter, this inflow makes a huge difference in terms of stock market performance.

In addition to demonstrating what happens to stock prices when money is theoretically flowing into the stock market, we also saw what tends to happen to stock prices during the lulls in between the periods of high demand for stocks. When there is not a strong demand for stocks, stock prices have a tendency to fall under their own weight. By tracking this theoretical flow of money each month, we are able to separate the days of the month into favorable and nonfavorable days. And, as I showed, the favorable days have outperformed the nonfavorable days by a staggering margin over the past 100-plus years. The consistency of this trend was highlighted in Table 4.7, where we looked at the performance of the stock market on a decade-by-decade basis and compared the performance of the market during the favorable days and the nonfavorable days. To date, the favorable days have outperformed the unfavorable days each and every decade over the past century, in most cases by a wide margin. I will leave it to random-walk theorists to explain how this could be possible, other than the explanation that money moves the market.

Also in this chapter, I tightened things up a bit and identified several periods in each month when performance has typically been best in the long run. These ten trading days a month have witnessed the stock market advance at an annualized rate of 28 percent since 1933. All other trading days witnessed the stock market decline at an annualized rate of 2 percent per year since 1933. From there we examined the so-called Santa Claus rally and combined that with our days-of-the-month methods to create the ultimate monthly days system. Last, we added in the effect of holiday trading days, as discussed in Chapter 3, to create one last model that I dubbed the ultimate, ultimate monthly days system.

It appears, from the data presented in this chapter, that investors could adopt some of the methods described herein and use them on a purely systematic basis to beat the market. Nevertheless, despite the seemingly overwhelming evidence presented that certain times of the month outperform others quite consistently, a certain leap of faith is involved in adopting such a trading method on a purely mechanical basis. Most investors would be best served by either considering investing a portion of their investment capital using some of the monthly day methods detailed in this chapter or using some of the monthly days information discussed in this chapter as a filter for their own trading methods, to put the odds on their side as much as possible.

CHAPTER 5

Yearly Seasonal Trends

T he stock market fluctuates on the basis of a vast array of economic and emotional factors. But, whatever the causes may be, in the end the results can all be measured with numbers. Because there is so much hard numerical data available regarding the stock market, the market lends itself to a great deal of analysis and number crunching. Oftentimes when people start crunching numbers to analyze the stock market, the more numbers they crunch, the more they feel compelled to crunch more numbers, and so on and so forth. And, eventually, people can get so bogged down in numbers that they can no longer tell the forest from the trees. The same thing can happen to those who attempt to analyze macroeconomic trends that they believe will ultimately affect stock prices. Whether it is gross domestic product or inflation, interest rates or currency fluctuations, deficits or corporate profits, the amount of data to be analyzed is virtually limitless. Ultimately, all of this can lead to an affliction commonly known as "analysis paralysis." When one looks at a great deal of different forms of data, almost never will all of the data point to the same conclusion. As a result, investors may find that some of the data suggest that a bullish trend for stock prices is about to unfold, whereas the rest of the data point to the opposite conclusion. So, what's an investor to do?

As you will see in this chapter, it can be quite useful to step back once in a while from some of the day-to-day fluctuations of the stock market, and all the myriad factors that are purported to influence stock prices, to simply consider the market's movements in the context of a much broader, long-term time frame. So, in this chapter, we will look at the market on a year-to-year basis and, even more broadly, on a decade-by-decade basis to see whether there are any longer-term trends that prevail in the marketplace that we can use as a road map to point us in the right direction toward the most likely trend for the stock market.

DECENNIAL PATTERNS (PART 1: RANKING THE YEARS)

Each decade consists of ten calendar years. For our purposes we will consider a year ending in the number 0 to be the first year of a new decade. So, for example, 1900, 1910, 1920, and so on, are the first years of new decades. As such, we can then refer to the years in the decade simply as year 0, year 1, year 2, and so on to year 9. The first thing we want to do is consider the average performance of each year across decades to see whether any trends stand out. Before performing this analysis, however, I should point out that in the end we will find that some particular year performed the best, another performed the worst, and everything else fell somewhere in between. So the goal is not to find the best year or two across decades and to say, "Aha!" as though we have uncovered some unknown nugget of information. What we are really looking for are any anomalies or trends that jump out and perhaps take us by surprise by virtue of their persistent strength (or weakness) and consistency.

Table 5.1 displays the average annual return for each decade year starting in 1900.

TABLE 5.1 Average Annual Return by Year Number across Decades

Year No.	Average Annual Percentage +(−)	Overall Rank
0	(6.7)	10
1	(1.9)	8
2	3.0	7
3	9.0	4
4	7.8	5
5	31.4	1
6	7.0	6
7	(4.1)	9
8	19.7	2
9	10.2	3

A few items of note do pop out from a cursory glance at Table 5.1:

- The early part of the decade tends to be weak. In fact, years 0 and 1 averaged an annual loss (6.7 percent and 1.9 percent, respectively), and year 2 averaged only a small annual gain of 3.0 percent. These three years ranked as Nos. 10, 8, and 7, respectively.
- The stock market has shown a tendency to advance during the middle portion of the decade on average, with years 2, 3, 4, 5, and 6 all showing average gains.
- Year 5 was the obvious leader, sporting a fairly amazing 31.4 percent average annual gain.
- Over the decades, the stock market has demonstrated a tendency to top out in year 6 or 7, followed by a short, steep decline (year 7 averaged a loss of 4.1 percent), followed by a strong advance into the end of the decade.
- Year 8 was the second-best performer with an average annual gain of 19.7 percent.

Just from this simple analysis, investors can glean some very useful information that can help them plan their investment strategy. The fact that the stock market has shown a marked tendency to be weak in the early years of a decade illustrates the need for investors to show patience at times. The fact of the matter is that it is not always possible to maximize profitability at all times. During the early portions of a new decade, investors may do well to give the bearish case the benefit of the doubt and to place a premium on capital preservation more than on maximization of profitability.

Once we get into year 2 of a new decade, the potential for generating gains increases significantly. It is typically after several years of weakness or substandard gains that many individuals become disenchanted with the stock market and turn away in disgust or despair. Of course, that is exactly the time and conditions under which a new bull market is typically born. So, investors must take care not to become psychologically bogged down in a bearish mind-set if the stock market does show weakness during the first several years of a new decade.

As I mentioned earlier, it was a foregone conclusion before we looked at any numbers that one particular year would emerge as the top performer. As it turns out, that year is year 5. What is striking, however, is that the average annual return during this year is far in excess of anything typically experienced in any other calendar year. The average annual return for year 5 of each decade was more than 31 percent. The next closest year in terms of performance was year 8, with an average gain slightly more than 19 percent. After that, performance drops down to 10 percent for year 9. So, clearly investors should be prepared to attempt to maximize their profitability during year 5 of each decade.

Another trend that becomes apparent is the tendency for the stock market to pause sometime during year 6, or more often during year 7, and to stage a short but oftentimes very sharp decline. Typically this decline serves as something of a pause that refreshes. Following the typical mid-decade rally, the market seems to digest those gains a bit and pull back sometime during years 6 or 7. This pullback then typically serves to set the stage for a late-decade rally during years 8 and 9.

Now let's zero in on and compare a couple of strategies that use nothing but calendar years.

DECENNIAL PATTERNS (PART 2: THE BEST AND WORST YEARS)

For the sake of argument, and with the benefit of perfect hindsight, let's examine the kind of results that investors might have achieved had they simply avoided the stock market completely during a handful of years each and every decade over the past century. For the purposes of this test, we will examine the performance of three different investment strategies over the past 100-plus years. These different strategies are detailed separately in Table 5.2.

The strategies listed in Table 5.2 are all fairly simple and straightforward. Strategy A simply buys and holds the Dow. Strategy B is fully invested in the Dow during seven of the ten years in each decade. Strategy C is fully invested only during the other three years of each decade—years 0, 1, and 7. So, how does the performance of these different strategies compare? The results may surprise you.

We will start this test on January 3, 1900. As a frame of reference, let's look first at the results generated using strategy A, the buy-and-hold

TABLE 5.2 Yearly Trading Strategies

Strategy	Details
Strategy A	Hold the Dow using a buy-and-hold approach.
Strategy B	Hold the Dow only during years 2, 3, 4, 5, 6, 8, and 9 of every decade.
Strategy C	Hold the Dow only during years 0, 1, and 7 of every decade.

TABLE 5.3 Three Strategies (1900–2007)

Strategy	$1,000 Becomes ...
Strategy A	$ 199,142
Strategy B	1,764,664
Strategy C	113

approach. A $1,000 investment in the Dow at the close on January 3, 1900, would have grown to $199,142 by December 31, 2007. Trading strategy B, which would have been out of the Dow during all years ending in 0, 1, or 7, would have grown to $1,764,664 during the same time frame, for a return that is about 8.9 times greater than that of the buy-and-hold approach. To round things out, $1,000 invested using strategy C—holding the Dow only during years ending in 0, 1, or 7, shrank an alarming 89 percent and would have been worth only $113 by the end of 2007! These results are summarized in Table 5.3.

Figure 5.1 displays the growth of $1,000 using strategies A and B. The magnitude of the outperformance simply from skipping the same three years each decade is striking and unmistakable.

On the much more depressing side, Figure 5.2 displays the growth of $1,000 invested in the Dow only during years ending in 0, 1, or 7.

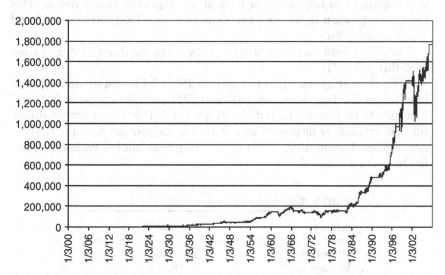

FIGURE 5.1 Growth of $1,000 investing in Dow since 1900 (dark line skips years 0, 1, and 7 each decade; light line represents a buy-and-hold approach)

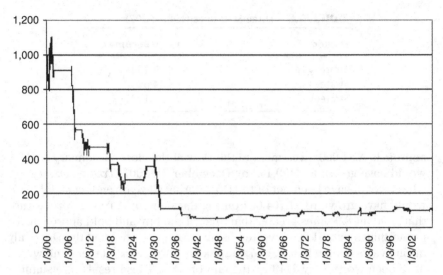

FIGURE 5.2   Growth of $1,000 investing in the Dow only during years 0, 1, and 7 since 1900

Now, it might seem to some that, given the results in Figures 5.1 and 5.2, the obvious conclusion is that investors should simply sit out the stock market during years 0, 1, and 7 every decade. However, before anyone comes to the conclusion that these years should be completely avoided, it is important to take a closer look at the historical yearly trends. This time, let's break it down into two time periods—1900 through 1941 and 1942 through 2007.

Table 5.4 displays the growth of $1,000 using our three strategies from 1900 through 1941.

The most staggering fact revealed in Table 5.4 is that an initial $1,000 invested in the Dow between 1900 and 1941 only during years 0, 1, and 7 would have lost an incredible 94 percent! This unbelievably dreadful performance is displayed in Figure 5.3. As you can see, these years encompassed some of the most devastating bear market action the market has ever witnessed.

TABLE 5.4   Three Strategies (1900–1941)

Strategy	$1,000 Becomes . . .
Strategy A	$ 1,666
Strategy B	28,225
Strategy C	59

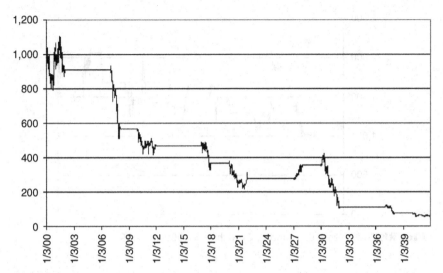

FIGURE 5.3 Growth of $1,000 invested in Dow only during years 0, 1, and 7 (1900–1941)

This horrible performance during years 0, 1, and 7 of each decade through 1941 could easily convince someone to simply skip these years completely. However, before reaching this conclusion, investors should consider the ramifications of adopting such an all-or-nothing strategy since 1941. Table 5.5 displays the growth of $1,000 using our three strategies starting in 1942 and extending through 2007.

It is important to note that strategy C actually made money between 1942 and 2007. In fact, it just about doubled in value from $1,000 to slightly less than $2,000. This performance is displayed in Figure 5.4.

The return generated during years 0, 1, and 7 as depicted in Table 5.5 and Figure 5.4 is still substandard compared to that of strategy B, with which $1,000 grew to more than $62,000 over the same time. Nevertheless, the key point to consider here is that, had investors followed strategy B and simply been out of the stock market during all years 0, 1, and

TABLE 5.5 Three Strategies (1942–Present)

Strategy	$1,000 Becomes . . .
Strategy A	$119,546
Strategy B	62,521
Strategy C	1,912

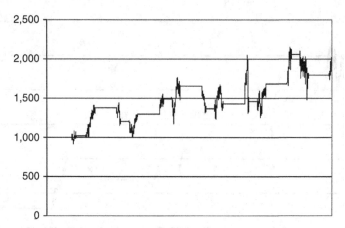

FIGURE 5.4   Years 0, 1, and 7, Growth of $1,000 since 1942

7 since 1942, they would have underperformed a buy-and-hold strategy by almost two to one. Even though the net gain during years 0, 1, and 7 since 1942 has not been great, and despite the choppy nature of the gains, as shown in Figure 5.4, a profit is a profit, and there is no point in pursuing a strategy that may underperform a buy-and-hold approach by almost 50 percent.

So, the bottom line is that investors should not necessarily avoid or participate in the stock market solely on the basis of the last digit in a particular year. The real key to using this type of information is to allow it to serve more as a frame of reference than as a trading rule. Despite this, there are several patterns that serve as useful guidelines throughout a given decade. We'll look at these next.

DECENNIAL PATTERNS (PART 3: THE DECENNIAL ROAD MAP)

If we put all of the annual performance figures by decade together, we find that there are a number of strong tendencies that may exert an influence on the stock market over the course of any particular decade. Figure 5.5 displays what we will hereafter refer to as the "decennial road map." The average performance, based on where we are in a given decade, is shown in Figure 5.5, with the month numbers listed along the bottom. A few tendencies become obvious from a perusal of Figure 5.5. We will look at these tendencies next.

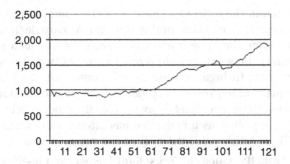

FIGURE 5.5 Decennial road map: the average decade performance month by month

DECENNIAL TENDENCIES

There are four common trends that have played out strongly across the course of each decade over the past century. Being aware of these potential trends can give alert investors a significant edge over other investors by allowing them to understand whether a given movement in the stock market is likely to continue or reverse. Let's discuss these trends individually, and then look at how they have played out in the past century.

1. **The early lull:** As you can see in Figure 5.5, the average market performance during the first part of the decade is typically not too exciting. For whatever reason, the stock market tends to have trouble making much headway during the first two or two and a half years of each decade. Often this extended period of sideways action or decline causes many investors to lose interest in and exit the stock market. It is often this capitulation that sets the stage for what follows next.

2. **The mid-decade rally:** In the middle of Figure 5.5, note a sharp move to the upper right, smack dab in the middle of the decade. We will talk more about the year 5 phenomenon in a bit, but suffice it to say that the most consistent trend across the decades is a meaningful rally in the middle of the decade. The bottom line is that investors typically do well to give the bullish case the benefit of the doubt during the middle of the decade rather than worry too much about whether the market is about to top out. That typically does not happen until a little later in the decade. Even then, in many cases that top is only a temporary one.

3. **The 7/8 sell-off:** Following strong mid-decade performance, the stock market has a tendency to consolidate and put in a significant

low—often in the form of a sharp sell-off—somewhere in year 7 or 8, which is then followed by another uptrend. A sharp decline in the stock market during this time frame has typically served as a useful buying opportunity. Investors should remain aware of two things. First, if the market starts to break during year 7, some sort of defensive action may be prudent to preserve capital. Second, investors should avoid the temptation to turn completely away from the stock market if it sells off in year 7 or year 8, as this decline has often set the stage for a significant rally to follow once the decline has run its course.

4. **The late rally**: Once the 7/8 sell-off has worked itself out, the stock market has often staged a strong rally into the end of the decade. In fact, years 8 and 9 have ranked as the third- and second-best years of the decade, respectively, on average over the past century. Once again, as during the middle of the decade, if the stock market gets rolling in year 8 or 9—particularly if preceded by a meaningful sell-off—investors would do well to invest aggressively to maximize profitability while the stock market is trending higher.

Now, we know how a decade should generally unfold. But, there are obvious questions to be answered when we move from average performance as measured over a number of decades to actual performance on a decade-by-decade basis. The primary question we want to answer is, How closely does the stock market's performance each decade correlate to what we expect given the average performance of all decades? To answer this question, let's review the performance of the stock market during each decade since 1900 to see just how consistently these trends play out.

DECADE-BY-DECADE PERFORMANCE

No one should get the idea that every decade will follow the road map that appears in Figure 5.5. Remember that the performance shown there represents average performance across decades since 1900. As with any type of data under analysis, the actual data points can vary quite a bit from the average. So, let's look at performance decade by decade and assess whether our decennial road map can actually help investors make money or whether it is just a nice theory. We will first look at 1900 through 1909 compared to the average, then 1910 through 1919, and so on. We'll sum things up at the end and measure how closely the actual decade-to-decade performance compares to the average.

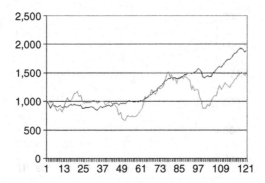

FIGURE 5.6 Growth of $1,000 invested in the Dow from 1900–1909 (versus decennial road map)

1900–1909

Figure 5.6 shows the growth of $1000 invested in the Dow versus the decennial road map from 1900 through 1909.

Whereas the magnitude of the movements of the Dow from 1900 to 1909 did not match the road map, on closer analysis, we still find that all the key tendencies did play out. The first portion of the decade saw no real gains. Between January 1900 and March 1903, the Dow was unchanged. It then proceeded to lose 37 percent in just eight months. From that point, the Dow rallied 143 percent into late January 1906. Thus, the expectations of both the early lull and the mid-decade rally were fulfilled. Between January 1906 and November 1907, the Dow lost 48 percent, thus fulfilling the expectation of the 7/8 sell-off. By late 1909, the Dow had rallied 89 percent from its 1907 low, fulfilling the expectation of the late rally. In summary, all four of the major decennial tendencies occurred from 1900 to 1909.

1910–1919

Figure 5.7 displays the growth of $1,000 invested in the Dow versus the decennial road map from 1910 through 1919.

Again, the actual performance of the Dow between 1910 and 1919 does not match the average performance, yet, all of the key tendencies are present and accounted for. The market was down fairly substantially until the middle of the decade. In fact, as of Christmas Eve 1914, the Dow was down 46 percent since December 31, 1909. Over the next 23 months, the Dow staged a mid-decade rally of 107 percent. After that came the 7/8 sell-off, which saw the Dow plunge 40 percent in just over a year, finally bottoming out in December 1917. From that low, the market then rallied 81 percent before reaching a temporary peak in November 1919.

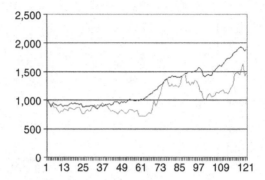

FIGURE 5.7 Growth of $1,000 invested in the Dow from 1910–1919 (versus decennial road map)

1920–1929

Figure 5.8 displays the growth of $1,000 invested in the Dow versus the decennial road map from 1920 through 1929.

The 1920s are remembered as the Go, Go Years and the Roaring Twenties, and for the vaunted and reviled stock market crash of 1929. Still, during this decade, the stock market generally followed our decennial road map, with one notable exception. Between the end of 1919 and August 1921, the Dow dropped 40 percent. From there the market rallied 64 percent by October 1922, and then drifted sideways for two years. Then came the real roaring part—the one intradecade trend that did not occur during the 1920s was the 7/8 sell-off. From May 1924 to the ultimate top in September 1929, the Dow rallied a stunning 332 percent. As anyone who knows anything about the stock market or U.S. history knows, this

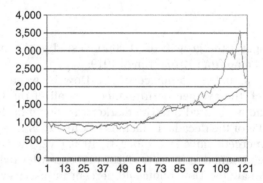

FIGURE 5.8 Growth of $1,000 invested in the Dow from 1920–1929 (versus decennial road map)

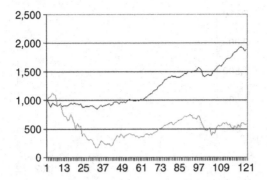

FIGURE 5.9 Growth of $1,000 invested in the Dow from 1930–1939 (versus decennial road map)

late rally was destined not to last. From the closing high on September 3, 1929, through December 31 of that same year, the Dow lost a staggering 35 percent. This decline continued into the 1930s and heralded the onset of the Great Depression.

1930–1939

Figure 5.9 displays the growth of $1,000 invested in the Dow versus the decennial road map from 1930 through 1939.

The 1930s are remembered primarily as the era of the Great Depression. As you can see in Figure 5.9, the 1930s were simply not a good time. For the decade as a whole, the Dow lost about 41 percent. Nevertheless, Figure 5.9 reveals that, at least to some extent, the four major tendencies played out during the 1930s. The market was obviously extremely weak in the early years (losing a staggering 83 percent from December 31, 1929, to the 1932 low). From there a substantial mid-decade rally ensued, with the Dow rallying 337 percent between 1933 and 1937. That top was followed by the 7/8 sell-off and a market decline of about 48 percent into March 1938. Over the next eight months, the Dow gained a robust 60 percent; thus, it can be argued that the market did fulfill the expected late rally. Following that November 1938 peak, however, the market meandered sideways through the end of the decade.

1940–1949

Figure 5.10 displays the growth of $1,000 invested in the Dow versus the decennial road map from 1940 through 1949.

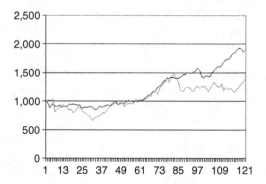

FIGURE 5.10 Growth of $1,000 invested in the Dow from 1940–1949 (versus decennial road map)

The 1940s are remembered for World War II and the growth of industry as the United States ramped up industries to produce materials needed for the war effort. By and large, the 1940s did witness the four primary decennial tendencies we have discussed. The market was weak in the early years, which is not surprising given that most of the world was involved in a war and the future of civilization was hanging in the balance. Between the end of 1939 and April 1942, the Dow lost 38 percent. By the end of 1944, the Dow was essentially unchanged for the decade. From its April 1944 interim low into February 1947, the Dow staged a mid-decade rally of 37 percent. This was followed by a swift three-month decline of 12 percent. This 7/8 sell-off bottomed in May 1947. The late rally took the Dow 22 percent higher into the close of the decade.

1950–1959

Figure 5.11 displays the growth of $1,000 invested in the Dow versus the decennial road map from 1950 through 1959.

With World War II out of the way and U.S. industry hitting on all cylinders, the 1950s were a great time to be in the stock market. Except for the stock market's strength during the early part of the decade, the equity curve for the 1950s closely resembles that of our decennial road map. The market was down about 1 percent into July 1950. It then staged a rare early decade rally, leaping 48 percent by January 1953. From there, the market experienced another lull, falling 13 percent by September 1953. Then followed a fairly standard mid-decade rally, rallying 43 percent by August 1956. The 7/8 sell-off bottomed out in October 1957, with the Dow 19 percent off of its August 1956 high. The Dow then staged the perfect late rally, closing the decade at a new all-time high, a full 62 percent off of the 7/8 sell-off low.

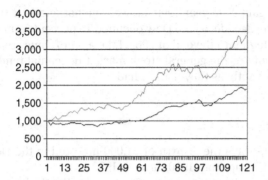

FIGURE 5.11 Growth of $1,000 invested in the Dow from 1950–1959 (versus decennial road map)

1960–1969

Figure 5.12 displays the growth of $1,000 invested in the Dow versus the decennial road map from 1960 through 1969.

Amid the wars, protests, assassinations, and social upheaval, the 1960s were a time of great turmoil in the United States. This fact was not lost on the stock market, which turned in profitable but spotty performance during the turbulent decade. After a moderate advance of 8 percent between the end of 1959 and November 1961, the Dow then fulfilled the early lull by plummeting 27 percent over the next seven months, finally bottoming out in June 1962. From there came an extended mid-decade rally of 86 percent, which lasted until February 1966. The 7/8 sell-off came early as the Dow then fell 25 percent in eight months, bottoming out at 744 in October 1966. The late rally lasted until the end of November 1968 and the Dow witnessed

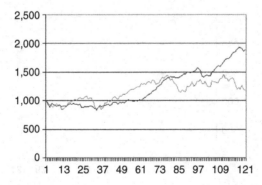

FIGURE 5.12 Growth of $1,000 invested in the Dow from 1960–1969 (versus decennial road map)

a 32 percent gain. The year 1969 showed uncharacteristic weakness for a last year of the decade, as the Dow declined 19 percent from the November 1968 closing high into the end of 1969. Like a lot of things that happened in the 1960s, many of the general stock market decennial tendencies played out, just not exactly as they usually had.

1970–1979

Figure 5.13 displays the growth of $1,000 invested in the Dow versus the decennial road map from 1970 through 1979.

The 1970s witnessed more upheaval in the United States as the Vietnam War and the Watergate scandal, which ultimately led to the resignation of President Richard Nixon, dominated U.S. events in the first half of the decade. The second half of the decade was affected by soaring inflation, high interest rates, and a struggling economy under President Jimmy Carter. As a result, the 1970s stock market saw little gain. On the whole, the Dow gained just less than 5 percent for the entire decade. In terms of our decennial road map, the market followed some of the usual trends but not all of them.

Rather than a traditional early lull, the stock market rallied during the first three years of the decade and topped out in January 1973, a full 31 percent above its 1969 closing level. The Dow then plummeted 45 percent by December 1974. Calling this an early lull might be a bit of stretch, but by the end of 1974, the Dow was down 23 percent to date in the decade. The market then followed the script, staging a strong mid-decade rally with a 74 percent gain between December 1974 and April 1976. The market experienced a 7/8 sell-off that culminated in a plunge during October 1978.

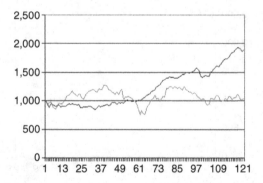

FIGURE 5.13 Growth of $1,000 invested in the Dow from 1970–1979 (versus decennial road map)

An attempt at a late rally was, for the most part, aborted by a backdrop of soaring inflation and a prime interest rate of 20 percent.

It should be noted that although the Dow was mostly flat during the last few years of the decade, the majority of stocks—particularly smaller-cap stocks—advanced fairly strongly. Between the end of 1977 and the end of 1979, the Dow was virtually unchanged. During this same time, the OTC Composite Index gained almost 50 percent. So, it could be argued that there was in fact a late rally, but it occurred among smaller-cap stocks and not large-cap stocks.

1980–1989

Figure 5.14 displays the growth of $1,000 invested in the Dow versus the decennial road map from 1980 through 1989.

The 1980s marked the beginning of a major new bull market, as well as a return to the classic decennial road map performance. The stock market first experienced a classic early lull, which eventually bottomed in August 1982, following an early 22 percent rally and a subsequent 24 percent decline into August 1982. As of August 12, 1982, the Dow was down 7 percent for the decade. The market then staged an exceptionally strong mid-decade rally that lasted until mid-1987 and carried the Dow 250 percent above its 1982 low by August 1987. The 7/8 sell-off unfolded quickly after that, with the Dow losing 36 percent in a matter of months and culminating with the crash of October 1987. The market then staged a strong late rally in 1988 and 1989, ultimately overcoming the loss incurred during the crash and reaching new highs by the end of the decade, with a 58 percent advance off the October 1987 low.

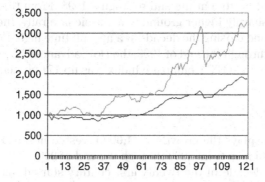

FIGURE 5.14 Growth of $1,000 invested in the Dow from 1980–1989 (versus decennial road map)

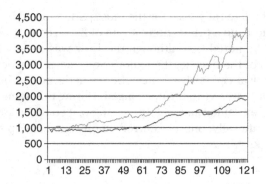

FIGURE 5.15 Growth of $1,000 invested in the Dow from 1990–1999 (versus decennial road map)

1990–1999

Figure 5.15 displays the growth of $1,000 invested in the Dow versus the decennial road map from 1990 through 1999.

The 1990s witnessed the greatest single-decade performance of any decade in the past 100-plus years. From start to finish, the Dow registered a stunning gain of 350 percent. Once again, although the magnitudes of the price movements were different from the decennial road map averages, the market did witness most of the four tendencies. The market experienced a slight early lull in 1990, losing 14 percent between December 31, 1989, and October 1990. From there, the Dow advanced steadily, if unspectacularly through 1994. The mid-decade rally witnessed the Dow advance 130 percent between April 1994 and August 1997. The 7/8 sell-off then followed, with the Dow dropping 13 percent over the next two and a half months. Following another rally, the market experienced a sharp sell-off and significant bottom at the end of August 1998. From there, the market exploded to sharply higher ground in a classic late rally, fueled by the Internet boom and closing the decade at a new all-time high. From the end of August 1998 through the end of 1999, the Dow advanced 53 percent. During the same time, the OTC Composite Index was up 171 percent.

2000–2007

Figure 5.16 displays the growth of $1,000 invested in the Dow versus the decennial road map from 2000 through the end of 2007.

The first decade of the twenty-first century started out following the decennial road map almost perfectly. The market was weak during almost all of the first three years: 2000, 2001, and 2002. From there the market

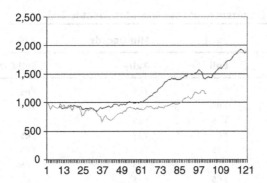

FIGURE 5.16 Growth of $1,000 invested in the Dow from 2000-2007 (versus decennial road map)

advanced slowly but steadily into late 2007. Between December 31, 1999, and the eventual low on October 9, 2002, the Dow lost a little more than 36 percent. The Dow then rallied 94 percent to a new all-time high in October 2007. After peaking there, the Dow dropped 10 percent in a little more than a month. Following a brief bounce, the market plunged again in late 2007 and the first week of 2008. On this basis, it can be argued that the market has so far experienced an early lull, a mid-decade rally, and quite possibly a 7/8 sell-off. If this is the case, then investors should watch the market for signs of the late rally to position themselves to take advantage of the next leg of a bull market. As we will see later in this Chapter, that rally—if it comes—will most likely unfold between February 28, 2008, and September 30, 2009.

Summary of Decade Tendencies

Table 5.6 summarizes the occurrences of the four common tendencies for the stock market during any given decade. Specifically, I have totaled the number of times that each of the four intradecade trends has occurred, to get an idea of the kind of consistency we might anticipate from each.

The results in Table 5.6 arguably confirm that there is some validity to the idea of intradecade trends. Since 1900, eight decades witnessed what would fulfill our idea of an early lull. This may encompass a quiet market that makes little or no headway during the early years of a decade, such as the 1980s, or it may be a situation where the stock market declines in a more meaningful way, such as during the early 2000s.

The most reliable intradecade trend has been the mid-decade rally. Every decade since the turn of the 1900s has witnessed a powerful stock market advance sometime between years 5 and 6. In most cases, the bulk of

TABLE 5.6   Occurrences of Four Major Intradecade Trends

Decade	Early Lull	Mid-Decade Rally	7/8 Sell-Off	Late Rally
1900–1909	Yes	Yes	Yes	Yes
1910–1919	Yes	Yes	Yes	Yes
1920–1929	Yes	Yes		Yes
1930–1939	Yes	Yes	Yes	Yes
1940–1949	Yes	Yes	Yes	Yes
1950–1959		Yes	Yes	Yes
1960–1969	Yes	Yes		
1970–1979		Yes	Yes	
1980–1989	Yes	Yes	Yes	Yes
1990–1999		Yes	Yes	Yes
2000–2009	Yes	Yes	Yes	?
Total Yes	**8**	**11**	**9**	**8**
Total No	**3**	**0**	**2**	**2**

that advance occurred during year 5. But even during those decades when year 5 did not witness a powerful advance, the market still managed to crank out a strong mid-decade rally. For example, for the 2005 calendar year, the Dow posted a loss, albeit a meager one, of less than 1 percent. Still, between October 25, 2004, and May 10, 2006, the Dow posted a net gain of just less than 23 percent. So remember this: Regardless of what the headlines may say or how the stock market may be acting heading into the second half of year 4 of each decade, if the stock market starts to rally, make sure that you are on board. And, remember not to be anxious to take a profit too quickly, as the mid-decade rally tends to last many months.

The 7/8 sell-off occurred during 9 of the past 11 decades. In some cases, the decline was quite large (e.g., the 36 percent peak-to-trough decline in 1987), whereas at other times the decline was more along the lines of a typical correction. In any event, if at some point you find yourself in a year 7, the market has rallied sharply over several years, and all the news seems to be cheery and bright, remember the market's tendency to correct during this time frame and be prepared to take action to preserve your capital.

The last intradecade trend to watch for is the late rally, which has occurred in some form or another in eight of the past ten decades. Only time will tell if such a rally will unfold during the 2000s. In any event, as no one is advocating that investors use these trends systematically, this argument is an academic one.

According to this analysis, investors who keep an eye out for these trends as each decade progresses may be able to give themselves an advantage over the majority of investors, who typically just drift with the current market tide. After the market is flat to lower over a multiyear period—as it often is during the first several years of a decade—many investors lose hope or interest and are ill prepared to profit from any ensuing advance. On the other hand, investors who are aware of the market's propensity to advance during the middle of each decade will be poised and ready to jump in aggressively as the latter stage of year 4 approaches. Likewise, after a sharp 7/8 sell-off, many investors mistakenly assume that the party is over and that it is time to exit the stock market. Here again, alert investors who know that a sharp market decline during this time frame is fairly typical will be far more likely to keep their wits about them and profit, should the late rally ultimately occur.

Now that we have examined the typical stock market movements across decades in view of several generalities, let's narrow the focus to a handful of specific intradecade time frames that have demonstrated a tendency to be very fortuitous for stock market investors.

INTRADECADE TRENDS OF NOTE

As we have seen so far, our decennial road map can be useful in terms of suggesting a logical course of action at different points of each decade. On the basis of the four tendencies that I have highlighted so far, alert investors may have a pretty good idea of when to follow a trend and when to fade a trend. Ultimately, the goal is to identify the most persistent trends and to take advantage of those. So, let's dig a little deeper and take a look at a handful of intradecade trends that have been amazingly consistent over the years in their highlighting of extremely favorable conditions for stock market investors. We'll take these trends one at a time and then combine them into one comprehensive model.

Intradecade Trend 1: October of Year 4 through March of Year 6

In the previous section, we highlighted the propensity of the stock market to stage a mid-decade rally. Backing up this theory, Table 5.7 displays an interesting data set from the past century. As you can see in Table 5.7, until 2005, every year ending in 5 (e.g., 1905, 1915, 1925) showed a gain, and in most cases a very substantial gain. Even with the small loss suffered by the Dow in 2005, the average performance for year 5 since 1905 has been a

TABLE 5.7 Dow Performance during Year 5

Year	Dow Percentage +(−)
1905	38.2
1915	81.7
1925	30.0
1935	38.5
1945	26.6
1955	20.8
1965	10.9
1975	38.3
1985	27.7
1995	33.5
2005	(0.6)
Average Percentage +(−)	**31.4**

fairly astounding 31.4 percent. It should be noted that the Dow was virtually the only major market average to show a loss for the year 2005. The S&P 500 was up 3.0 percent, the Nasdaq 100 was up 1.5 percent, and the Russell 2000 small-cap index was up 3.3 percent. So, even though the Dow was down for the year, thus ending its string of winners, it can be argued that overall the year was up for stocks in general.

This performance is noteworthy. However, as it turns out, simply looking at year 5 in a decade proves a bit too narrow of a test. What really gets interesting is when we broaden the horizons to include just a little bit more of the mid-decade period. Now, let's expand this period to include October through December of year 4 and January, February, and March of year 6. In other words, instead of just focusing on the 12 months that comprise year 5, we will consider the 18 months from the close on September 30 of year 4 through March 31 of year 6. The results appear in Table 5.8.

As you can see in Table 5.8, the average gain achieved by the Dow during this 18-month period was 41.7 percent. As impressive as the results in Table 5.8 may be, the display of these results in Figure 5.17 is even more compelling. Figure 5.17 displays the growth of $1,000 invested in the Dow only during this 18-month mid-decade period for each decade since 1900.

For anyone looking for a low-risk time to be invested in the stock market, it would be hard to beat the mid-decade bullish period identified here. In fact, it is stunning to consider that the bulk of all gains in the stock market have come during this 18-month period each decade. To wit, consider that $1,000 invested in the Dow during this 18-month period each decade would have grown to $40,948. However, $1,000 invested in the Dow during all other days since December 31, 1900, would have grown to just $4,581.

TABLE 5.8 Dow Performance from September 30, Year 4–March 31, Year 6

Mid-Decade	Dow Percentage +(−)
Sept. 30, 1904–Mar. 31,1906	68.3
Sept. 30, 1914–Mar. 31,1916	30.6
Sept. 30, 1924–Mar. 31,1926	36.2
Sept. 30, 1934–Mar. 31,1936	68.8
Sept. 30, 1944–Mar. 31,1946	36.1
Sept. 30, 1954–Mar. 31,1956	42.0
Sept. 30, 1964–Mar. 31,1966	5.6
Sept. 30, 1974–Mar. 31,1976	64.4
Sept. 30, 1984–Mar. 31,1986	50.7
Sept. 30, 1994–Mar. 31,1996	45.4
Sept. 30, 2004–Mar. 31, 2006	10.2
Average Percentage +(−)	**41.7**

Figure 5.18 displays the 18-month mid-decade rally as in Figure 5.17, but it overlays the growth achieved by investing only during all other trading days not included in this favorable 18-month period.

As you can see in Figure 5.18, taking advantage of the mid-decade rally is essential to any investors who want to maximize their long-term

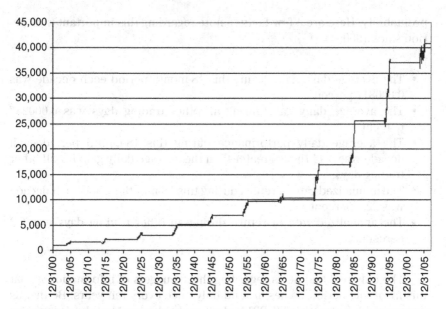

FIGURE 5.17 Growth of $1,000 invested in the Dow only during the 18-month mid-decade bullish period since 1900

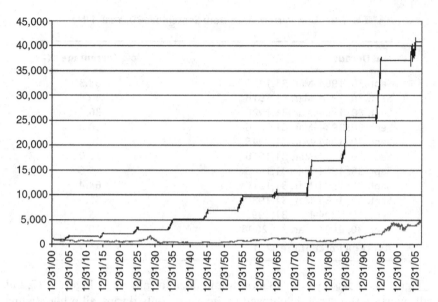

FIGURE 5.18 Growth of $1,000 invested in the Dow only during the 18-month mid-decade bullish period since 1900 (black line) versus $1,000 invested in Dow during all other 102 months within each decade (gray line)

profitability. Here are a few facts to note regarding this important time period since 1900:

- The average daily gain during this 18-month period each decade was 0.000817 percent.
- The average daily gain during all other trading days was 0.000237 percent.
- The average daily performance during this 18-month period each decade was 3.44 times greater than the average daily gain for all other trading days.
- The annualized rate of return during this 18-month period each decade was 22.8 percent.
- The annualized rate of return during all other trading days was 6.2 percent.

The only real bad news regarding these nuggets of information is that this favorable period comes around only once every ten years. Be that as it may, come September 30, 2014, alert investors should look to maximize their profits in the stock market regardless of the news of the day.

Intradecade Trend 2: March of Year 8 through September of Year 9

Two other trends highlighted in the previous section were the 7/8 sell-off and the late rally. As it turns out, there is a particular time frame in each decade that has typically allowed investors to profit from these two trends. The next favorable intradecade trend that I want to highlight extends from the close on the last trading day of February of year 8 through the end of September of year 9. The returns posted during this 19-month period each decade since 1900 appear in Table 5.9.

As you can see in Table 5.9, the average gain achieved by the Dow during this 19-month period of each decade has been 31.6 percent. Figure 5.19 displays the growth of $1,000 invested in the Dow only during this 19-month period each decade since December 31, 1900. Here, $1,000 invested only during this time frame grew to $13,338. Although the results are not quite as impressive as the results for the mid-decade rally, the late rally has typically offered investors another profit-maximizing opportunity.

Here are a few facts to note regarding this important 19-month late rally since 1900:

- The average daily gain during this 19-month period each decade was 0.000517 percent.
- The average daily gain during all other trading days was 0.000297 percent.
- The average daily performance during this 19-month period each decade was 1.74 times greater than the average daily gain for all other trading days.

TABLE 5.9 Dow Performance from February 28 of Year 8 through September 30 of Year 9

March of Year 8-September of Year 9	Dow Percentage +(−)
Feb. 28,1908–Sept. 30, 1909	64.4
Feb. 28,1918–Sept. 30, 1919	38.6
Feb. 28,1928–Sept. 30, 1929	76.3
Feb. 28,1938–Sept. 30, 1939	17.7
Feb. 28,1948–Sept. 30, 1949	9.1
Feb. 28,1958–Sept. 30, 1959	43.6
Feb. 28,1968–Sept. 30, 1969	(3.3)
Feb. 28,1978–Sept. 30, 1979	18.4
Feb. 28,1988–Sept. 30, 1989	30.0
Feb. 28,1998–Sept. 30, 1999	21.0
Average Percentage +(−)	**31.6**

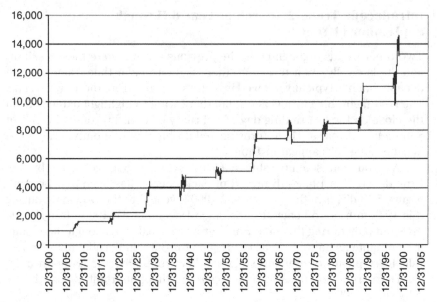

FIGURE 5.19 Growth of $1,000 invested in the Dow only during the 19-month late rally period since 1900

- The annualized rate of return during this 19-month period each decade was 13.9 percent.
- The annualized rate of return during all other trading days was 7.8 percent.

Clearly, investors should give the bullish case for the stock market the benefit of the doubt during this late rally time frame. Likewise, investors should remember that any sharp market declines heading into this time frame may be outstanding buying opportunities, and they should be prepared to take advantage of such a decline to position themselves to profit from the late rally, should it unfold as it has more often than not.

Intradecade Trend 3: October of Year 2 through December of Year 5 of Even-Numbered Decades

The last intradecade seasonal trend that I want to mention is near and dear to my heart, only because, as I mentioned in the preface, it is based on the first seasonal trend I ever remember hearing about. Interestingly, as I pointed out in the preface, when I first heard about this particular seasonal trend, I remember thinking, "That's the dumbest thing I've ever heard in my life." This trend actually occurs once every twenty years, so many number

TABLE 5.10 Dow Performance between October 1 of Year 2 and December 31 of Year 5 (Every 20 Years)

October of Year 2 through December of Year 5	Dow Percentage +(−)
Sept. 30, 1902–Dec. 31, 1905	45.4
Sept. 30, 1922–Dec. 31, 1925	62.7
Sept. 30, 1942–Dec. 31, 1945	76.8
Sept. 30, 1962–Dec. 31, 1965	67.4
Sept. 30, 1982–Dec. 31, 1985	72.6
Sept. 30, 2002–Dec. 31, 2005	41.2
Average Percentage +(−)	**61.0**

crunchers may argue that the sample size is too small to be meaningful. And, statistically speaking, they may have a valid argument. Nevertheless, the performance results are quite compelling, so let's take a closer look.

The period that we'll examine now begins on the first trading day of October during year 2 of every other decade starting in 1902 (i.e., 1902, 1922, 1942). The favorable period then extends through the next 27 months until the end of December of year 5. I first heard of this trend sometime early in 1982, and I remember distinctly raising an eyebrow and asking how in the world what happened in the stock market 20 or 40 or 60 or 80 years ago could make the least bit of difference today. But my tune changed a bit after the Dow advanced 72.6 percent between September 30, 1982, and December 31, 1985.

The performance results for the Dow during this 27-month period every 20 years since 1900 are shown in Table 5.10.

Figure 5.20 displays the growth of $1,000 invested in the Dow only during this 27-month period every 20 years starting in 1900, and $1,000 invested only during this time frame grew to $17,063.

A close look at Figure 5.20 reveals that the market has experienced some volatile action within this overall favorable time frame. Nevertheless, there is little doubt that the overall trend of the stock market has been quite bullish during these 27 months. The only bad news regarding this particular cycle is that investors will have to wait until September 30, 2022, before they can take advantage of this trend again. Here are a few facts to note regarding this important period since December 31, 1900:

- The average daily gain during this 27-month period each decade was 0.000604 percent.
- The average daily gain during all other trading days was 0.000271 percent.

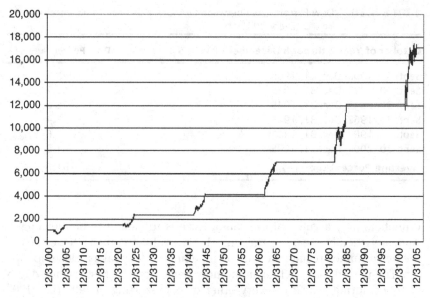

FIGURE 5.20 Growth of $1,000 invested in the Dow only during this 27-month Year 2–Year 5 rally every 20 years

- The average daily performance during this 27-month period each decade was 2.23 times greater than the average daily gain for all other trading days.
- The annualized rate of return during this 27-month period each decade was 16.4 percent.
- The annualized rate of return during all other trading days was 7.1 percent.

Clearly, it can be argued that, in each decade, some time frames have been more favorable to the stock market than others. Here, we have objectively identified three such time frames that can give alert investors a tremendous advantage in knowing when to act to maximize their profitability. Now, let's take a look at the kind of results that could have been generated by combining these three favorable time frames into one comprehensive strategy.

INTRADECADE CYCLES COMBINED

We have talked about the mid-decade rally, the late decade rally, and for lack of a better term, the early- to mid-decade rally that occurs once every

20 years. In reality, the decennial road map serves as more of a guide than a road map. The three intradecade cycles that we just discussed, however, are objective and can be used at specific times again and again, decade after decade. Let's take a look at the actual road map that we can follow using these three cyclical patterns.

For the purposes of this test, we will refer to the cycles as follows:

Mid-Decade Cycle: Starting at the close of trading on September 30 of year 4 through the close of trading on March 31 of year 6, of every decade, starting in 1902.

Late-Decade Cycle: Starting at the close of trading on February 28 of year 8 through the close of trading on September 30 of year 9 of every decade.

20-Year Cycle (every other decade): Starting at the close of trading on September 30, 1902 (and 1922, 1942, 1962, 1982, 2002) through the close of trading on December 31 of the next year 5.

Table 5.11 displays the dates for each cycle since 1900 along with the performance of the Dow during each cycle. Note that every 20 years there will be some overlap between the 20-year cycle—which extends through the end of year 5—and the mid-decade cycle, which encompasses all of year 5.

The numbers in the far-right-hand column of Table 5.11 strongly suggest that the time periods identified in the two left-hand columns are outstanding times for investors to make money in the stock market. Riding the big waves up is the best way to make money in stocks in the long run. Too many investors sit on the sidelines after an advance begins, waiting—or, more accurately, hoping—for a second-chance pullback in the market, which may or may not come. And, if the pullback doesn't come, they have to decide when to jump on the bandwagon. Likewise, after the market has staged a decent advance, many investors are tempted to essentially cash in their chips and exit the market, rather than risk giving back their hard-earned profits. Yet, selling too soon is another way that many investors cost themselves a great deal of profit potential.

Sometimes one of the hardest things for an investor to do is nothing. In other words, just sitting idle and allowing profits to accumulate can be very difficult. The cycles that I have detailed offer investors some objective guidelines for determining when to jump into the market and, just as important, when to take some money off the table. No one should expect to buy at the bottom and sell at the top simply by using these particular time cycles. The goal is simply to be in the market and to stay there when

TABLE 5.11 Intradecade Cycles

Buy Date	Sell Date	Cycle	Percentage +(−)
Sept. 30, 1902	Mar. 31, 1906	20-yr. + mid-decade	46.0
Feb. 28, 1908	Sept. 30, 1909	Late decade	64.4
Sept. 30, 1914	Mar. 31, 1916	Mid-decade	78.2
Feb. 28, 1918	Sept. 30, 1919	Late decade	31.6
Sept. 30, 1922	Mar. 31, 1926	20-yr. + mid-decade	45.9
Feb. 28, 1928	Sept. 30, 1929	Late decade	76.3
Sept. 30, 1934	Mar. 31, 1936	Mid-decade	68.8
Feb. 28, 1938	Sept. 30, 1939	Late decade	17.7
Sept. 30, 1942	Mar. 31, 1946	20-yr. + mid-decade	83.1
Feb. 28, 1948	Sept. 30, 1949	Late decade	9.1
Sept. 30, 1954	Mar. 31, 1956	Mid-decade	42.0
Feb. 28, 1958	Sept. 30, 1959	Late decade	43.6
Sept. 30, 1962	Mar. 31, 1966	20-yr. + mid-decade	59.7
Feb. 28, 1968	Sept. 30, 1969	Late decade	(3.3)
Sept. 30, 1974	Mar. 31, 1976	Mid-decade	64.4
Feb. 28, 1978	Sept. 30, 1979	Late decade	18.4
Sept. 30, 1982	Mar. 31, 1986	20-yr. + mid-decade	102.9
Feb. 28, 1988	Sept. 30, 1989	Late decade	30.0
Sept. 30, 1994	Mar. 31, 1996	Mid-decade	45.4
Feb. 28, 1998	Sept. 30, 1999	Late decade	21.0
Sept. 30, 2002	Mar. 31, 2006	20-yr. + mid-decade	46.3
Feb. 28, 2008	Sept. 30, 2009	Late decade	?
Sept. 30, 2014	Mar. 31, 2016	Mid-decade	?
Feb. 28, 2018	Sept. 30, 2019	Late decade	?

the environment is friendly. These cycles seem to do a pretty good job of accomplishing that task.

There are two things to note from Table 5.11. The first is simply to remember that these cycles are objective. In other words, there is no guesswork or analysis involved. An investor could have simply bought on the dates in the left-hand column and sold on the dates in the column to the right. Second, had investors done just that, they would have generated the returns displayed in the far-right-hand column. The objective simplicity involved in this analysis can make using seasonal and cyclical trends easy to use. Of course, the numbers in the far-right-hand column point out the potential usefulness.

Buying and holding for years or months at a time given a particular cycle can be psychologically difficult. While any particular cycle is in force, there is no end of news and information coming out that can affect one's outlook. However, at a minimum, investors can use these cycles as a filter that causes investors to give the bullish case the benefit of the doubt. Of the 21 periods listed in Table 5.11, the Dow registered a gain 20 times. The only loss was of a modest 3.3 percent between February 1968 and September 1969. Also, 19 of the 20 profitable periods have registered gains in excess of 17 percent. Clearly, if you are looking for an environment in which the stock market may register large gains, you should be aware of these key intradecade cycles.

To further analyze the performance of the Dow during these key periods, we will break market history into two periods. The first is 1900 through 1949, and the second extends from 1950 through 2007. Figure 5.21 displays the growth of $1,000 invested during the three intradecade cycles we have discussed, from December 31, 1900, through December 31, 1949.

As you can see, there are periods of volatility, and investors who had relied solely on these trends to decide whether to be in or out of the stock market would have to sit through some not-insignificant drawdowns along the way. Still, a little perspective goes a long way. Figure 5.22 shows the performance of the Dow during all trading days that did not fall into one of the three intradecade cycles.

As you can see in Figure 5.22, the results for any investor who had been unfortunate enough to invest only in all of the nonfavorable days, as

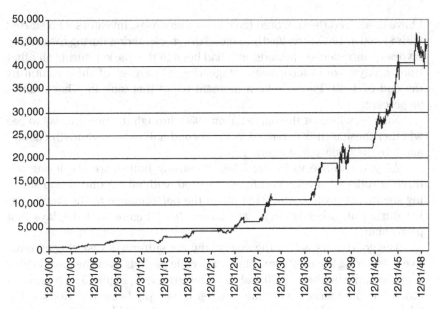

FIGURE 5.21 Growth of $1,000 invested in the Dow during three intradecade trends from 1900–1949

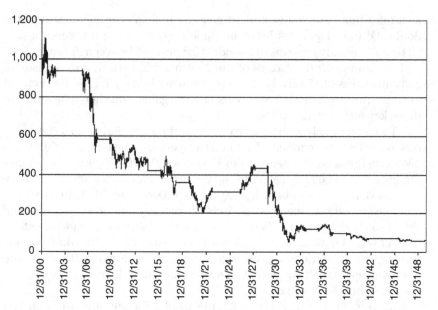

FIGURE 5.22 Growth of $1,000 invested in the Dow during all trading days that do not fit into three intradecade trends from 1900–1949

I have described them, would have been disastrous. Investors who started with $1,000 in 1900, steadfastly avoided the stock market during these three favorable intradecade periods, and had been in the market during all other trading days would have lost a staggering 93 percent of their capital by the end of 1949. Please take a moment to let that sink in. That's minus 93 percent.

Now let's look at the period from 1950 through the present day to see whether these trends persisted in the second half of the twentieth century and into the twenty-first century.

As you can see in Figure 5.23, the strong bullish trends during our three intradecade cycles continue unabated, with all but one period showing significant profits. And what about the performance of the stock market during all other trading days since 1950? Figure 5.24 displays that performance.

The good news is that the market did not suffer a devastating cumulative loss during the nonfavorable intradecade periods over the past 50-plus years, as it did between 1900 and 1949. Nevertheless, Figure 5.24 reveals an indeterminate market and a fair number of sharply bearish periods. All in all, investors would have enjoyed more peace of mind by missing some of the nonfavorable periods.

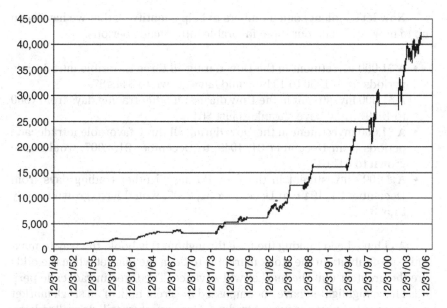

FIGURE 5.23 Growth of $1,000 invested in the Dow during three intradecade trends from Dec. 31, 1949–Dec. 31, 2007

FIGURE 5.24 Growth of $1,000 invested in the Dow during all trading days that do not fit into three intradecade trends from 1949–Dec. 31, 2007

Now let's look at some numbers to help quantify all that we have seen up to now regarding our three favorable intradecade periods:

- A $1,000 investment in the Dow during all three favorable intradecade periods from 1900 to 1949 would have grown to $44,487.
- A $1,000 investment in the Dow during all other trading days from 1900 to 1949 would have shrunk to just $64.
- A $1,000 investment in the Dow during all three favorable intradecade periods from December 31, 1949, to December 31, 2007, would have grown to $41,617.
- A $1,000 investment in the Dow during all other trading days from December 31, 1949, to December 31, 2007, would have grown to only $1,593.

As I have been making the case throughout this book, the way to maximize profitability in the stock market is to be in the market when the odds are the greatest that the market will advance. The three intradecade periods I have highlighted have encompassed the great bulk of all stock market advances in the past century of trading. Alert investors will do well to keep these time frames in mind as the years go by.

SUMMING UP

So far in this book, I have been presenting evidence that makes the argument that, over time, the fluctuations of the stock market are not based on a series of random events. Quite to the contrary, the evidence presented makes the case that the stock market—like many other things in life—fluctuates on a cyclical and repetitive (i.e., seasonal) basis. In this chapter, we first highlighted the tendency of the stock market to perform better during the second half of the decade (years ending in 5, 8, and 9 were the top three performers, gaining 31.4 percent, 19.7 percent, and 10.2 percent, respectively) than during the first half of the decade (years 2, 1, and 0, were the seventh, eighth, and tenth or worst-performing years of the decade, respectively).

We next examined the tendency for the market to follow—albeit to varying degrees—a fairly standard pattern from decade to decade over the past century. Although not every decade is a picture-perfect copy of our decennial road map (see Figure 5.5), the high degree to which each decade experiences four common trends—the early lull, the mid-decade rally, the 7/8 sell-off, and the late rally—is at best a highly unlikely coincidence. As we saw in Table 5.6, the market experienced a flat-to-down period during the early part of the decade during 8 of the past 11 decades. The mid-decade rally was the most consistent intradecade trend, as each of the past 11 decades has witnessed a meaningful mid-decade rally. The market has experienced a meaningful decline during year 7 or year 8 in 9 of the past 11 decades and, likewise, has subsequently experienced a late rally during 8 of the last 10 decades (with the end of the 2000–2009 decade yet to be written).

As if these general tendencies in the context of each decade were not enough, I also highlighted three key intradecade time frames that have, time and again, encompassed some of the most favorable stock market action recorded in the past century. Before anyone completely dismisses the notion of seasonality in the stock market, a quick review of Table 5.11 may be in order. For example, $1,000 invested in the Dow on a buy-and-hold basis since December 31, 1901, would have grown 18,659 percent to $187,595 by the end of 2007. And $1,000 invested only during the 21 periods listed in Table 5.11—which are simply the same time frames repeated over and over across the decades—would have grown 185,039 percent to a fairly staggering $1,851,398 during the same time frame. This represents about 9.9 times more profit than what would have been achieved using a buy-and-hold approach.

That sounds like something that might be worth remembering.

CHAPTER 6

Repetitive Time Cycles of Note

I f you listen to enough market commentary, it is almost inevitable that at some point you will hear someone refer to a particular cycle in the stock market. For example, you might hear an analyst say that the ten-week cycle is due to bottom on such and such a date or within a given time frame. Or, it could be the 10-day cycle or the 46-day cycle, or—there is no end to the possibilities. A detailed study of various such cycles typically leads to inferior results. In a nutshell, the problem with cycle analysis is that too often what analysts refer to is not exactly what they claim that it is. For example, a stock market pundit may say, "The 50-day cycle is due to bottom sometime in the next week." And this begs the question, If it is a 50-day cycle, shouldn't we know on exactly which day the cycle will bottom? In other words, if there truly is a 50-day cycle in the stock market, then it should repeat every 50 days—otherwise, it is not a 50-day cycle. Basically, anytime a purported cycle is due to bottom on or about a particular date, you can assume that you are talking about something that is very subjective in practice.

In my research, I have come across only a small handful of repetitive cycles that can be followed on such an objective basis. In other words, each cycle lasts the exact same amount of time, and the next cycle's exact start or end dates can be identified in advance. For example, if we purported to examine a 43-day cycle, then that cycle would begin anew every 43 days without exception. And although the cycles that I detail in this chapter are few in number, they have shown to be quite powerful in practice. Using exact cycles over and over allows us to make an objective assessment regarding the relative usefulness of a cycle that is supposedly at work in the market.

In the lexicon of cycle analysis, the start of a new cycle is the "cycle bottom." The use of this term is based on the somewhat-optimistic assumption that the stock market will make a meaningful low concurrent with the start of each new cycle. Whereas this notion is typically based in pure fantasy, as we will see in this chapter, it is possible in a handful of cases to use cycles to identify low-risk buying opportunities and favorable market trends that will typically last for at least a certain period of time. This knowledge can give alert investors a tremendous edge in knowing when to act aggressively to maximize their profitability.

In this chapter, we will look at three specific cycles that have objectively identifiable start and end dates and that can be tested back over a long period of time. These three cycles vary quite a bit in duration, which means that they are unrelated to one another. This offers greater utility than looking at, say, two cycles that routinely overlap. Also, as we will see at the end of this chapter, when one or more of these cycles do overlap, we can gain some useful information about the prospects for the stock market. The cycles that we will discuss in this chapter are the following:

- The 212-week cycle.
- The 40-week cycle.
- The 53-day cycle.

Many individuals have a great aversion to considering cycles when it comes to investing. The primary drawback for many people is that, in most cases, there is no logical explanation as to why a given cycle has worked in the past; thus, it can be quite difficult for some individuals to develop any confidence that a given cycle will continue to work in the future. Thus, they will tend to dismiss things that they cannot explain. This is entirely understandable. For investors who typically focus on both hard fundamental data, such as earnings, sales, and profit margins, and on the perceived value of the operations of each company under analysis, it is quite a leap of faith to go from buying when sales and earnings are rising to buying because a given cycle is about to bottom. Nevertheless, I encourage individuals to read this chapter with an open mind. I have been following these three key cycles for more than 15 years in real time and the results have been nothing short of remarkable.

THE 212-WEEK CYCLE

I first read about this cycle back in 1982 in some works from Peter Eliades, the editor of a stock market advisory newsletter and a leading proponent of market cycles at the time. As I mentioned in Chapter 1, Eliades was and is one of the leading pioneers in the area of research regarding cyclicity and seasonality in the stock market. The cycle that he mentioned in 1982 was something that he referred to as "the 212-week cycle." That cycle is exactly four years and four weeks (52 weeks times four is 208 weeks, plus 4 more weeks is 212 weeks). Much has been written and said about the supposed four-year cycle in the stock market. In fact, one can make a strong argument that an important stock market low has been made about once in every four-year cycle, dating back to the late 1800s. However, the purpose of this book is to try to quantify things rather than just make vague suggestions, such as "a new four-year cycle should begin sometime in the next year." The 212-week cycle answers this question with an objective answer.

For our test of the 212-week cycle, we will start on December 31, 1937. Our first cycle will begin at the close of trading on May 16, 1938. From this point, we will count forward exactly 1,484 calendar days (212 weeks times 7 days a week equals 1,484 days) to find the next new cycle start date of June 8, 1942, then July 1, 1946, and so on. Each new cycle start date appears in Table 6.1. We will then look at the action of the stock market following the start date for each new cycle to see whether there are any useful trends that we can take advantage of.

As I will explain as we go, a detailed analysis of stock market action on and around this series of dates leads to two important conclusions:

1. No one should assume in any way that a major stock market bottom— preceded by a plunge to the low and followed by a robust upside reversal—will occur exactly every 1,484 calendar days.

2. Despite that conclusion, the beginning of each new 212-week cycle appears to offer investors an excellent buying opportunity over the ensuing six months.

To back up these assertions, consider the data that appears in Table 6.1. First, Table 6.1 displays the start dates for each new 212-week cycle since 1938. It also displays the performance of the Dow during the first six months directly following each new cycle start date. Last, it displays the worst decline by the Dow as measured from the price on the start date of the new cycle during the first six months of each new cycle. In other words, it shows you the worst loss you would have had to sit through if you had bought the Dow at the close on the date that the new cycle began and had sold six months later.

It is clear from the numbers displayed in Table 6.1 that the first six months of a new 212-week cycle can be a very good time to be invested

TABLE 6.1 Market Performance in First 6 Months after New 212-week Cycle Start

New 212-Week Cycle Date	Dow Percentage +(−) 6 Months Later	Worst Decline within 6 Months of New Cycle Start Date
5/16/1938	31.3	(6.6)
6/8/1942	9.7	(2.7)
7/1/1946	(14.2)	(21.0)
7/24/1950	18.1	(1.5)
8/16/1954	29.6	(4.0)
9/8/1958	18.6	0.0
10/1/1962	19.9	0.0
10/24/1966	12.7	(0.3)
11/16/1970	21.2	(0.8)
12/9/1974	34.7	0.0
1/1/1979	3.6	0.0
1/24/1983	19.7	0.0
2/16/1987	23.0	0.0
3/11/1991	1.6	(2.9)
4/3/1995	13.9	0.0
4/26/1999	(−3.9)	(5.6)
5/19/2003	14.1	(0.0)
6/11/2007	0.1	(5.1)
Average	**14.5**	**(2.8)**
Median	**16.1**	**(0.6)**

in the stock market. Of the 18 new cycles that have started since 1938, 16 were followed by a higher price for the Dow six months later. This works out to an 89 percent accuracy rate. And the gains on average were quite impressive and well beyond the typical six-month average gain of 4 percent or 5 percent. In fact, the average gain registered was 14.5 percent, and the median gain was even higher at 16.1 percent. Equally important is the data contained in the third column of Table 6.1. This data essentially shows how much pain investors would have had to tolerate had they taken the plunge and bought on the day the new cycle started. This is important because, as most investors know, if the market goes down too much after you get in, there comes a point when it is prudent to simply cut your losses and move on.

To illustrate this point consider the following scenario:

1. Based on the start of a new cycle, an investor buys a Dow index fund on a specific date with the idea of holding it for six months.

2. The Dow index fund then drops 15 percent, and the investor feels compelled to cut his losses. Thus, he sells and suffers a 15 percent loss.

3. The Dow index fund then reverses to the upside and ends the six months with a profit of 15 percent.

The history book will record that the latest six-month cycle was a winner because the market registered a 15 percent gain in the six months after the cycle's start date. Unfortunately, the individual in this example booked a 15 percent loss rather than a 15 percent gain because the market first went in the wrong direction and he felt compelled to preserve capital by cutting his losses. This is not necessarily a mistake on his part. Cutting losses and preserving capital are essential actions for most investors to ensure that the worst-case scenario never plays out. So, the point here is not that investors should not cut a loss simply because a historically reliable indicator has given a buy signal. The point is to note that the practical and actual usefulness of any indicator is diminished if buy signals are too often followed by periods of sharp declines before rallies to generate a profit.

This is why the numbers in the far-right-hand column of Table 6.1 are so important. If the losses in the interim are too great, then investors may not be able to stick around long enough to enjoy any benefits that accrue. Fortunately, the news on this front is good. Of the 18 new cycles listed in Table 6.1, only one experienced a drawdown from the original buy price in excess of 6.6 percent: 1946, when the Dow fell as much as 21 percent after the start of the new 212-week cycle that began at the close on July 1, 1946. Ultimately, the Dow rallied back slightly to end the first six months after the new cycle start date with a loss of 14.2 percent. No one would consider this to be a good signal. And many investors would likely have sold somewhere along the way during those first six months. Fortunately, this occurrence was the exception to the rule. In fact, following 8 of the 18 new cycle start dates in Table 6.1, the market advanced the next day and never looked back. In all, 15 of the 18 new cycles never witnessed a drawdown in excess of 5 percent. As I mentioned a moment ago, on only one occasion did the Dow register an interim decline in excess of 6.6 percent. Different investors have different pain thresholds, but the vast majority of investors are likely able to sit through a 6 percent to 7 percent drawdown. This makes the 212-week cycle quite an intriguing concept to a great many investors.

Even more compelling than the numbers in Table 6.1 is Figure 6.1, which displays the equity curve that would have been achieved by investing in the Dow only during the first six months after each 212-week cycle start date since 1938. Figure 6.1 shows the growth of equity during the first six months of a new 212-week cycle, followed by a long horizontal line until the start of the next new cycle. This flat line represents the roughly three

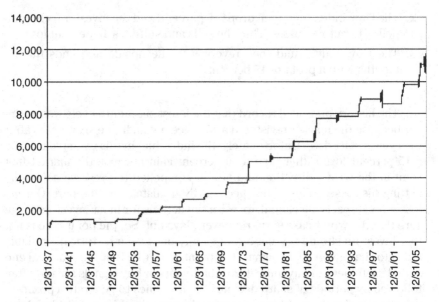

FIGURE 6.1 Growth of $1,000 invested in the Dow for 6 months after each 212-week cycle start date since Dec. 31, 1937

and half years that the cycle is not relevant and during which a systematic application of the six-month rule would result in a flat position.

The results displayed in Figure 6.1 highlight the amazing consistency of this cycle. Whereas it may not be true that the stock market hits a major bottom every four years, it can be argued that a major buying opportunity does occur every four years, regardless of whether that opportunity is preceded by a major sell-off.

Here are a few performance facts to note regarding this useful cycle since 1938:

- The average daily gain during this six-month period every 212 weeks was 0.001069 percent.
- The average daily gain during all other trading days was 0.000194 percent.
- The average daily gain during the bullish six-month period was 5.5 times greater than the average daily gain during all other trading days.
- The annualized rate of return during this bullish six-month period was 30.9 percent.
- The annualized rate of return during all other trading days was 5.0 percent.

- A $1,000 investment only during the six months after each new 212-week cycle start date grew to $11,104 by December 31, 2007.
- A $1,000 investment during all days except the six months after each new 212-week cycle start date grew to just $9,885 during the same time.

The most interesting fact to note here is that you would have made more money by investing only during these bullish six months that occur only once every four years than you would have by investing during all other trading days combined. This is a fairly stunning realization and points to the powerful nature of this cycle. To put it another way, you would have made more money being in the market just 12 percent of the time than you would have during the other 88 percent of trading days.

To better appreciate the power of this cyclical trend, take a look at Figure 6.2, which displays the growth of $1,000 invested in the Dow only during the six-month period following each new 212-week cycle start date, as well as the growth of $1,000 invested during all other days. As you can see, the 212-week bullish six months vastly outperformed all other days until the great bull market of the 1980s and 1990s. Of equal importance, the six months following the new 212-week cycle start date also missed the bulk of most of the bear markets over the past 70-plus years, including the 1962, 1966, 1970, 1973–1974, 1981–1982, the 1987 crash, 1990, and the

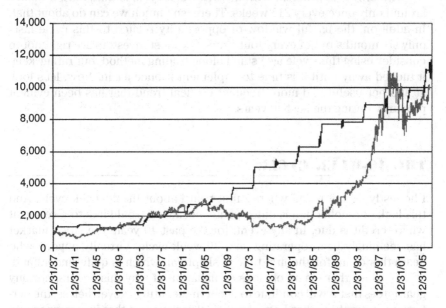

FIGURE 6.2 Growth of $1,000 invested in the Dow during bullish six months of each 212-week cycle (black line) since 1938 versus all other trading days (gray line)

TABLE 6.2   212-Week Cycle Dates

212-Week Cycle Start Dates	6-Month Exit Dates
7/4/2011	1/4/2012
7/27/2015	1/27/2016
8/19/2019	2/19/2020
9/11/2023	3/11/2024
10/4/2027	4/4/2028
10/27/2031	4/27/2032
11/19/2035	5/19/2036
12/12/2039	6/12/2040
1/4/2044	7/4/2044
1/27/2048	7/29/2048
2/19/2052	8/19/2052

2000–2003 bear markets. That's a lot of pain to miss out on and offers the kind of peace of mind that most investors crave.

Given the evidence presented here, alert investors clearly should be aware of the 212-week cycle as each new cycle rolls around. Table 6.2 displays the 212-week cycle start dates out to 2050.

The only real problem with the 212-week cycle is that, alas, it comes around only once every 212 weeks. There isn't much we can do about that. In addition, the useful window of opportunity related to this cycle lasts only six months out of every four years. So, most investors are right not to consider using this cycle as a stand-alone trading method, but rather keep it tucked away until it is time to implement it once again. Now, let's look at another useful and more frequent cyclical trend that has been evident primarily during the past 40 years.

THE 40-WEEK CYCLE

I honestly do not recall where I first heard about the 40-week cycle. And this lack of recollection is unfortunate, because I would like to give credit where credit is due. In any event, for the past 40 years the stock market has seemingly been operating on a 40-week cycle. Virtually anyone who hears this claim for the first time is skeptical, which is quite understandable because there is no obvious explanation of why this occurs, nor any guarantees that it will continue to occur in the future. Nevertheless, the performance numbers that I am about to show suggest that investors would do well to pay attention to this particular cycle.

A word of caution is in order before proceeding. Unlike most of the methods detailed in this book that can be traced back 70 or 100 years, this cycle only started to become useful in 1967. Whereas 40 years is a long test by most standards, compared to the majority of trends discussed in this book, 40 years is a relatively short test period. Likewise, that the cycle offered no real advantage prior to 1967 also begs the question, How long will it last? Still, although skepticism and doubt are understandable, a close look at the numbers offers a compelling case as to why investors would want to keep track of this key cycle. Remember that the methods detailed in this book aren't here to convince you that one is the be all and end all of stock market indicators. The goal is simply to accumulate a number of tools that will tell us the best time to be in or out of the stock market. With that in mind, the 40-week cycle could prove very useful.

For our test of the 40-week cycle, we will start at the close of trading on April 21, 1967. From that point, we will assume that the first 20 weeks (measured as 140 calendar days) is the bullish phase of the cycle and that the next 20 weeks (another 140 calendar days) is the bearish phase. As we will see in a moment, the bullish phase is actually the very bullish phase and the bearish phase is more aptly labeled the indeterminate phase. But, let's not get ahead of ourselves.

To get an idea of the potential usefulness of this particular cycle, take a look at Figure 6.3, which displays the growth of $1,000 invested in the Dow only during the bullish phase of each 40-week cycle since April 1967.

The steadily upward sloping trend of the equity curve displayed in Figure 6.3 is hard to mistake. As you can see, $1,000 invested in the Dow only during the first 20 weeks of each bullish phase would have grown to $21,308 between 1967 and 2007. Whereas the graph in Figure 6.3 is quite compelling, we still need some frame of reference to fully assess its performance and usefulness. For the sake of comparison, let's look at the action of the stock market during the bearish phase (i.e., the second 20 weeks of each 40-week cycle) in Figure 6.4.

As you can see, $1,000 invested only during each bearish phase would have shrunk to just $705 over the past 40 years. The difference in the performance of the stock market during the bullish phase versus the bearish phase could hardly be starker. Nevertheless, inspection of Figure 6.4 reveals that there have been plenty of advances during the bearish phase of the 40-week cycle, particularly in the 1980s and 1990s. Thus, investors who attempted to use this cycle as a stand-alone tool would have found themselves on the sidelines during some significant market advances over the course of these two decades. Psychologically, this can be very difficult for average investors to sit through.

Although the so-called bearish phase of the 20-week cycle has actually witnessed some pretty bullish activity since bottoming out in 1974, it

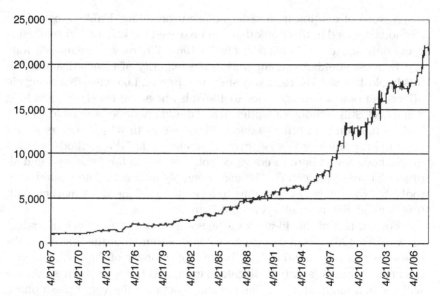

FIGURE 6.3 Growth of $1,000 invested in the Dow during the bullish 20 weeks of each 40-week cycle since April 1967

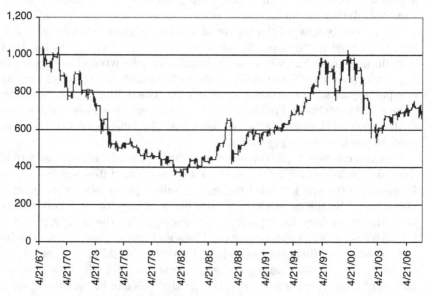

FIGURE 6.4 Growth of $1,000 invested in the Dow during the bearish 20 weeks of each 40-week cycle since April 1967

should be noted that virtually all of the major bearish activity that has occurred in the past 40 years has taken place during the bearish phase. As you can see in Figure 6.4, the market was a disaster during the bearish phase from the late 1960s into the early 1980s. Also, the 20-week bearish phase bore the brunt of the crash of 1987, the sell-off of 1998, and the sharp bear market decline of 2000–2002. So, it makes sense to focus your efforts on maximizing profitability during the bullish phase. Likewise, proceeding with great caution during the bearish phase might well prove to be a case of addition by subtraction.

Let's put some numbers to these results to get a better idea of the significance of this particular cycle:

- The average daily gain during the 20-week bullish phase was 0.000645 percent.
- The average daily gain during the 20-week bearish phase was −0.000012 percent.
- The annualized rate of return during the 20-week bullish phase was 17.7 percent.
- The annualized rate of return during the 20-week bearish phase was −0.3 percent.
- A $1,000 investment only during the bullish phase achieved a gain of 2,031 percent.
- A $1,000 investment only during the bearish phase actually lost 29.5 percent.
- Of the 53 completed bullish phases, 40 showed a profit and only 13 showed a loss.
- Of the 53 completed bearish phases, 29 showed a profit and 24 showed a loss.

Table 6.3 displays the performance during all bullish and bearish phases since 1967.

Clearly, investors should give the bullish case for the stock market the benefit of the doubt during the bullish phase of each 40-week cycle and should be cautious—though not necessarily outright bearish—during the bearish phase of each 40-week cycle. Whatever your own most aggressive approach to the stock market may be, you might consider using that approach during the bull phase and then scaling back to a more conservative or defensive approach during the bearish phase. Such an approach holds great possibilities for investors looking to maximize their long-term profitability.

TABLE 6.3 40-Week Cycle: Bullish and Bearish Phase Performance

Buy	Sell	Dow Buy	Dow Sell	Bull (%)	Bull $1,000	Buy	Sell	Dow Sell	Dow Buy	Bear (%)	Bear $1,000
4/21/67	9/8/67	883.18	907.54	2.8	1,028	1/26/68	9/8/67	907.54	865.06	(4.7)	953
1/26/68	6/14/98	865.06	913.62	5.6	1,085	11/1/68	6/14/98	913.62	948.41	3.8	989
11/1/68	3/21/69	948.41	920.00	(3.0)	1,053	8/8/69	3/21/69	920.00	824.46	(10.4)	887
8/8/69	12/26/69	824.46	797.65	(3.3)	1,019	5/15/70	12/26/69	797.65	702.22	(12.0)	781
5/15/70	10/2/70	702.22	766.16	9.1	1,111	2/19/71	10/2/70	766.16	878.56	14.7	895
2/19/71	7/9/71	878.56	901.80	2.6	1,141	11/26/71	7/9/71	901.80	816.59	(9.4)	811
11/26/71	4/14/72	816.59	967.72	18.5	1,352	9/1/72	4/14/72	967.72	970.05	0.2	813
9/1/72	1/19/73	970.05	1,026.19	5.8	1,430	6/8/73	1/19/73	1,026.19	920.00	(10.3)	728
6/8/73	10/26/73	920.00	987.06	7.3	1,534	3/15/74	10/26/73	987.06	887.83	(10.1)	655
3/15/74	8/2/74	887.83	752.58	(15.2)	1,301	12/20/74	8/2/74	752.58	598.48	(20.5)	521
12/20/74	5/9/75	598.48	850.13	42.0	1,847	9/26/75	5/9/75	850.13	818.60	(3.7)	502
9/26/75	2/13/76	818.60	958.36	17.1	2,163	7/2/76	2/13/76	958.36	999.84	4.3	523
7/2/76	11/19/76	999.84	948.80	(5.1)	2,052	4/7/77	11/19/76	948.80	918.88	(3.2)	507
4/7/77	8/26/77	918.88	855.42	(6.9)	1,911	1/13/78	8/26/77	855.42	775.73	(9.3)	460
1/13/78	6/1/78	775.73	840.70	8.4	2,071	10/20/78	6/1/78	840.70	838.01	(0.3)	458
10/20/78	3/9/78	838.01	842.86	0.6	2,083	7/27/79	3/9/78	842.86	839.76	(0.4)	457
7/27/79	12/14/79	839.76	842.75	0.4	2,090	5/2/80	12/14/79	842.75	810.92	(3.8)	439
5/2/80	9/19/80	810.92	963.74	18.8	2,484	2/6/81	9/19/80	963.74	952.30	(1.2)	434
2/6/81	6/26/81	952.30	992.87	4.3	2,590	11/13/81	6/26/81	992.87	855.88	(13.8)	374
11/13/81	4/2/82	855.88	838.57	(2.0)	2,537	8/20/82	4/2/82	838.57	869.29	3.7	388
8/20/82	1/7/83	869.29	1,076.07	23.8	3,141	5/27/83	1/7/83	1,076.07	1,216.14	13.0	438
5/27/83	10/14/83	1,216.14	1,263.52	3.9	3,263	3/2/84	10/14/83	1,263.52	1,171.48	(7.3)	406

3/2/84	1,171.48	7/20/84	1,101.37	(6.0)	3,068	7/20/84	1,101.37	12/7/84	1,163.21	5.6	429
12/7/84	1,163.21	4/26/85	1,275.18	9.6	3,363	4/26/85	1,275.18	9/13/85	1,307.68	2.5	440
9/13/85	1,307.68	1/31/86	1,570.99	20.1	4,041	1/31/86	1,570.99	6/20/86	1,879.54	19.6	527
6/20/86	1,879.54	11/7/86	1,886.53	0.4	4,056	11/7/86	1,886.53	3/27/87	2,335.80	23.8	652
3/27/87	2,335.80	8/14/87	2,685.43	15.0	4,663	8/14/87	2,685.43	12/31/87	1,938.83	(27.8)	471
12/31/87	1,938.83	5/20/88	1,952.59	0.7	4,696	5/20/88	1,952.59	10/7/88	2,150.25	10.1	518
10/7/88	2,150.25	2/24/89	2,245.54	4.4	4,904	2/24/89	2,245.54	7/14/89	2,554.82	13.8	590
7/14/89	2,554.82	12/1/89	2,745.65	7.5	5,270	12/1/89	2,745.65	4/20/90	2,695.95	(1.8)	579
4/20/90	2,695.95	9/7/90	2,619.56	(2.8)	5,121	9/7/90	2,619.56	1/25/91	2,659.42	1.5	588
1/25/91	2,659.42	6/14/91	3,000.50	12.8	5,777	6/14/91	3,000.50	11/1/91	3,056.40	1.9	599
11/1/91	3,056.40	3/20/92	3,276.40	7.2	6,193	3/20/92	3,276.40	8/7/92	3,332.18	1.7	609
8/7/92	3,332.18	12/24/92	3,326.20	(0.2)	6,182	12/24/92	3,326.20	5/14/93	3,443.00	3.5	631
5/14/93	3,443.00	10/1/93	3,581.11	4.0	6,430	10/1/93	3,581.11	2/18/94	3,887.46	8.6	685
2/18/94	3,887.46	7/7/94	3,688.42	(5.1)	6,101	7/7/94	3,688.42	11/25/94	3,708.27	0.5	688
11/25/94	3,708.27	4/13/95	4,208.18	13.5	6,923	4/13/95	4,208.18	9/1/95	4,647.54	10.4	760
9/1/95	4,647.54	1/19/96	5,184.68	11.6	7,724	1/19/96	5,184.68	6/7/96	5,697.11	9.9	835
6/7/96	5,697.11	10/26/96	6,007.02	5.4	8,144	10/26/96	6,007.02	3/14/97	6,935.46	15.5	964
3/14/97	6,935.46	8/1/97	8,194.04	18.1	9,622	8/1/97	8,194.04	12/19/97	7,756.29	(5.3)	913
12/19/97	7,756.29	5/8/98	9,055.15	16.7	11,233	5/8/98	9,055.15	9/25/98	8,028.77	(11.3)	809
9/25/98	8,028.77	2/12/99	9,274.89	15.5	12,976	2/12/99	9,274.89	7/2/99	11,139.24	20.1	972

(Continued)

151

TABLE 6.3 (Continued)

Buy	Sell	Dow Buy	Dow Sell	Bull (%)	Bull $1,000	Sell	Buy	Dow Sell	Dow Buy	Bear (%)	Bear $1,000
7/2/99	11/22/99	11,139.24	11,089.52	(0.4)	12,918	11/22/99	4/7/00	11,089.52	11,111.48	0.2	974
4/7/00	8/25/00	11,111.48	11,192.63	0.7	13,013	8/25/00	1/12/01	11,192.63	10,525.38	(6.0)	916
1/12/01	6/1/01	10,525.38	10,990.41	4.4	13,588	6/1/01	10/19/01	10,990.41	9,204.11	(16.3)	767
10/19/01	3/8/02	9,204.11	10,572.49	14.9	15,608	3/8/02	7/26/02	10,572.49	8,264.39	(21.8)	600
7/26/02	12/13/02	8,264.39	8,433.71	2.0	15,927	12/13/02	5/2/03	8,433.71	8,582.68	1.8	610
5/2/03	9/19/03	8,582.68	9,644.82	12.4	17,899	9/19/03	2/6/04	9,644.82	10,593.03	9.8	670
2/6/04	6/25/04	10,593.03	10,371.84	(2.1)	17,525	6/25/04	11/12/04	10,371.84	10,539.01	1.6	681
11/12/04	4/1/05	10,539.01	10,404.30	(1.3)	17,301	4/1/05	8/19/05	10,404.30	10,559.23	1.5	691
8/19/05	1/6/06	10,559.23	10,959.31	3.8	17,956	1/6/06	5/26/06	10,959.31	11,219.38	2.4	707
5/26/06	10/13/06	11,219.38	11,960.51	6.6	19,142	10/13/06	3/2/07	11,960.51	12,114.10	1.3	717
3/2/07	7/20/07	12,114.10	13,851.08	14.3	21,887	7/20/07	12/7/07	13,851.08	13,625.28	(1.6)	705
12/7/07	4/25/08	13,625.28				4/25/08	9/12/08				
9/12/08	1/30/09					1/30/09	6/19/09				
6/19/09	11/6/09					11/6/09	3/26/10				
3/26/10	8/13/10					8/13/10	12/31/10				
12/31/10	5/20/11					5/20/11	10/7/11				
10/7/11	2/24/12					2/24/12	7/13/12				
7/13/12	11/30/12					11/30/12	4/19/13				

THE 53-DAY CYCLE

One last cycle that I want to mention is known as the 53-day cycle. As we will see in a moment, investors would be ill advised to use this cycle as a stand-alone arbiter of what they should do in the stock market. Nevertheless, this particular cycle does become useful when it is combined with other cycles. But once again, let's not get ahead of ourselves. The 53-day cycle is just that. Every 53 calendar days a new 53-day cycle begins, with each cycle lasting exactly—you guessed it—53 calendar days. We will designate the first 27 calendar days of each new cycle as the bullish phase and the final 26 calendar days as the bearish phase. To keep this test in line with that of the 40-week cycle, we will start our test in 1967. Our first cycle begins at the close on March 22, 1967. The first bullish phase in our test lasts through April 18, 1967, and turns to the bearish phase until the next new cycle starts on May 14, 1967. The cycle then repeats from there ad infinitum.

Figure 6.5 displays the growth of $1,000 invested only during the bullish phase of each 53-day cycle since 1967. As you can see in Figure 6.5, the results are not all peaches and cream. In fact, the so-called bullish phase did not generate any real profits until 1982. The bullish phase also suffered some meaningful losses during the 2000–2002 bear market. Nevertheless,

FIGURE 6.5 Growth of $1,000 invested in the Dow only during the bullish phase of each 53-day cycle since 1967

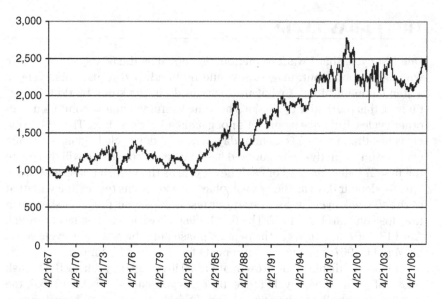

FIGURE 6.6 Growth of $1,000 invested in the Dow only during the bearish phase of each 53-day cycle since 1967

between 1967 and the end of 2007, that initial $1,000 would have grown to $6,239.

For the sake of comparison, let's consider Figure 6.6, which displays the growth of $1,000 invested only during the bearish phase of each 53-day cycle.

There are two things to note about the results in Figure 6.6. First, $1,000 invested only during the bearish phase would actually have grown to $2,402 since 1967. So, perhaps it should be referred to as the "less bullish" phase. Also, there has been an excessive amount of choppiness evident in the stock market during the bearish phases. So, although it was not exactly a great time to be completely out of the market (because the market made money overall), it was not always a great time to be in the market either because of the unpredictable performance.

To better illustrate the difference in performance between the bullish and bearish phases of the 53-day cycle, the equity curves for each are plotted together in Figure 6.7.

There are two key things to note about the comparative results displayed in Figure 6.7. First, from 1967 until just before the crash of October 1987, the bearish phase outperformed the bullish phase. Between our start date of March 22, 1967, and August 11, 1987, the Dow achieved a cumulative gain of 92 percent during the bearish phases and only 60 percent during the bullish phases. This long period of underperformance during the allegedly

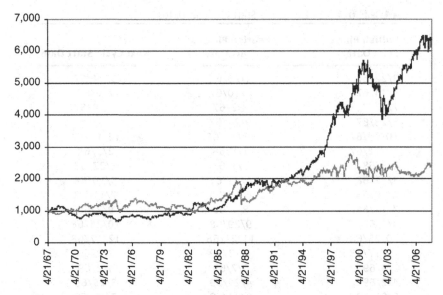

FIGURE 6.7 Growth of $1,000 invested in the Dow during the bullish phase (black line) of each 53-day cycle versus the growth of $1,000 invested in the Dow during the bearish phase (gray line) of each 53-day cycle since 1967

bullish phase is the primary reason that investors should not consider using this cycle as a stand-alone trading method.

The other thing to note, however, is the degree to which the bullish phase has outperformed the bearish phase since August 1987. From August 11, 1987, through December 31, 2007, the Dow achieved a robust cumulative gain of 296 percent during the bullish phases and a gain of only 25 percent during the bearish phases.

Table 6.4 displays the bullish and bearish cycle dates for the 53-day cycle starting in 1967 and extending into 2012.

Summary of 53-Day Cycle

The 53-day cycle is clearly less useful on a stand-alone basis than the 212-week and 40-week cycles. An investor who had strictly used only the 53-day cycle to buy and sell over the past 40 years would have ended up well behind a buy-and-hold investor. Still, the fact remains that the stock market has shown a marked propensity to perform better during the bullish phase of the 53-day cycle than during the bearish phase. As we will see in a moment, this characteristic can make this trend quite useful when used in conjunction with the other two cycles that we have already discussed.

TABLE 6.4 53-Day Cycle Start and End Dates

Bullish Phase Start Date	Bearish Phases Start Date	Next Cycle Start Date
3/22/67	4/18/67	5/14/67
5/14/67	6/10/67	7/6/67
7/6/67	8/2/67	8/28/67
8/28/67	9/24/67	10/20/67
10/20/67	11/16/67	12/12/67
12/12/67	1/8/68	2/3/68
2/3/68	3/1/68	3/27/68
3/27/68	4/23/68	5/19/68
5/19/68	6/15/68	7/11/68
7/11/68	8/7/68	9/2/68
9/2/68	9/29/68	10/25/68
10/25/68	11/21/68	12/17/68
12/17/68	1/13/69	2/8/69
2/8/69	3/7/69	4/2/69
4/2/69	4/29/69	5/25/69
5/25/69	6/21/69	7/17/69
7/17/69	8/13/69	9/8/69
9/8/69	10/5/69	10/31/69
10/31/69	11/27/69	12/23/69
12/23/69	1/19/70	2/14/70
2/14/70	3/13/70	4/8/70
4/8/70	5/5/70	5/31/70
5/31/70	6/27/70	7/23/70
7/23/70	8/19/70	9/14/70
9/14/70	10/11/70	11/6/70
11/6/70	12/3/70	12/29/70
12/29/70	1/25/71	2/20/71
2/20/71	3/19/71	4/14/71
4/14/71	5/11/71	6/6/71
6/6/71	7/3/71	7/29/71
7/29/71	8/25/71	9/20/71
9/20/71	10/17/71	11/12/71
11/12/71	12/9/71	1/4/72
1/4/72	1/31/72	2/26/72
2/26/72	3/24/72	4/19/72
4/19/72	5/16/72	6/11/72
6/11/72	7/8/72	8/3/72
8/3/72	8/30/72	9/25/72
9/25/72	10/22/72	11/17/72
11/17/72	12/14/72	1/9/73
1/9/73	2/5/73	3/3/73
3/3/73	3/30/73	4/25/73

TABLE 6.4 *(Continued)*

Bullish Phase Start Date	Bearish Phases Start Date	Next Cycle Start Date
4/25/73	5/22/73	6/17/73
6/17/73	7/14/73	8/9/73
8/9/73	9/5/73	10/1/73
10/1/73	10/28/73	11/23/73
11/23/73	12/20/73	1/15/74
1/15/74	2/11/74	3/9/74
3/9/74	4/5/74	5/1/74
5/1/74	5/28/74	6/23/74
6/23/74	7/20/74	8/15/74
8/15/74	9/11/74	10/7/74
10/7/74	11/3/74	11/29/74
11/29/74	12/26/74	1/21/75
1/21/75	2/17/75	3/15/75
3/15/75	4/11/75	5/7/75
5/7/75	6/3/75	6/29/75
6/29/75	7/26/75	8/21/75
8/21/75	9/17/75	10/13/75
10/13/75	11/9/75	12/5/75
12/5/75	1/1/76	1/27/76
1/27/76	2/23/76	3/20/76
3/20/76	4/16/76	5/12/76
5/12/76	6/8/76	7/4/76
7/4/76	7/31/76	8/26/76
8/26/76	9/22/76	10/18/76
10/18/76	11/14/76	12/10/76
12/10/76	1/6/77	2/1/77
2/1/77	2/28/77	3/26/77
3/26/77	4/22/77	5/18/77
5/18/77	6/14/77	7/10/77
7/10/77	8/6/77	9/1/77
9/1/77	9/28/77	10/24/77
10/24/77	11/20/77	12/16/77
12/16/77	1/12/78	2/7/78
2/7/78	3/6/78	4/1/78
4/1/78	4/28/78	5/24/78
5/24/78	6/20/78	7/16/78
7/16/78	8/12/78	9/7/78
9/7/78	10/4/78	10/30/78
10/30/78	11/26/78	12/22/78
12/22/78	1/18/79	2/13/79
2/13/79	3/12/79	4/7/79
4/7/79	5/4/79	5/30/79

(Continued)

TABLE 6.4 (*Continued*)

Bullish Phase Start Date	Bearish Phases Start Date	Next Cycle Start Date
5/30/79	6/26/79	7/22/79
7/22/79	8/18/79	9/13/79
9/13/79	10/10/79	11/5/79
11/5/79	12/2/79	12/28/79
12/28/79	1/24/80	2/19/80
2/19/80	3/17/80	4/12/80
4/12/80	5/9/80	6/4/80
6/4/80	7/1/80	7/27/80
7/27/80	8/23/80	9/18/80
9/18/80	10/15/80	11/10/80
11/10/80	12/7/80	1/2/81
1/2/81	1/29/81	2/24/81
2/24/81	3/23/81	4/18/81
4/18/81	5/15/81	6/10/81
6/10/81	7/7/81	8/2/81
8/2/81	8/29/81	9/24/81
9/24/81	10/21/81	11/16/81
11/16/81	12/13/81	1/8/82
1/8/82	2/4/82	3/2/82
3/2/82	3/29/82	4/24/82
4/24/82	5/21/82	6/16/82
6/16/82	7/13/82	8/8/82
8/8/82	9/4/82	9/30/82
9/30/82	10/27/82	11/22/82
11/22/82	12/19/82	1/14/83
1/14/83	2/10/83	3/8/83
3/8/83	4/4/83	4/30/83
4/30/83	5/27/83	6/22/83
6/22/83	7/19/83	8/14/83
8/14/83	9/10/83	10/6/83
10/6/83	11/2/83	11/28/83
11/28/83	12/25/83	1/20/84
1/20/84	2/16/84	3/13/84
3/13/84	4/9/84	5/5/84
5/5/84	6/1/84	6/27/84
6/27/84	7/24/84	8/19/84
8/19/84	9/15/84	10/11/84
10/11/84	11/7/84	12/3/84
12/3/84	12/30/84	1/25/85
1/25/85	2/21/85	3/19/85
3/19/85	4/15/85	5/11/85
5/11/85	6/7/85	7/3/85

TABLE 6.4 *(Continued)*

Bullish Phase Start Date	Bearish Phases Start Date	Next Cycle Start Date
7/3/85	7/30/85	8/25/85
8/25/85	9/21/85	10/17/85
10/17/85	11/13/85	12/9/85
12/9/85	1/5/86	1/31/86
1/31/86	2/27/86	3/25/86
3/25/86	4/21/86	5/17/86
5/17/86	6/13/86	7/9/86
7/9/86	8/5/86	8/31/86
8/31/86	9/27/86	10/23/86
10/23/86	11/19/86	12/15/86
12/15/86	1/11/87	2/6/87
2/6/87	3/5/87	3/31/87
3/31/87	4/27/87	5/23/87
5/23/87	6/19/87	7/15/87
7/15/87	8/11/87	9/6/87
9/6/87	10/3/87	10/29/87
10/29/87	11/25/87	12/21/87
12/21/87	1/17/88	2/12/88
2/12/88	3/10/88	4/5/88
4/5/88	5/2/88	5/28/88
5/28/88	6/24/88	7/20/88
7/20/88	8/16/88	9/11/88
9/11/88	10/8/88	11/3/88
11/3/88	11/30/88	12/26/88
12/26/88	1/22/89	2/17/89
2/17/89	3/16/89	4/11/89
4/11/89	5/8/89	6/3/89
6/3/89	6/30/89	7/26/89
7/26/89	8/22/89	9/17/89
9/17/89	10/14/89	11/9/89
11/9/89	12/6/89	1/1/90
1/1/90	1/28/90	2/23/90
2/23/90	3/22/90	4/17/90
4/17/90	5/14/90	6/9/90
6/9/90	7/6/90	8/1/90
8/1/90	8/28/90	9/23/90
9/23/90	10/20/90	11/15/90
11/15/90	12/12/90	1/7/91
1/7/91	2/3/91	3/1/91
3/1/91	3/28/91	4/23/91
4/23/91	5/20/91	6/15/91
6/15/91	7/12/91	8/7/91

(Continued)

TABLE 6.4   (*Continued*)

Bullish Phase Start Date	Bearish Phases Start Date	Next Cycle Start Date
8/7/91	9/3/91	9/29/91
9/29/91	10/26/91	11/21/91
11/21/91	12/18/91	1/13/92
1/13/92	2/9/92	3/6/92
3/6/92	4/2/92	4/28/92
4/28/92	5/25/92	6/20/92
6/20/92	7/17/92	8/12/92
8/12/92	9/8/92	10/4/92
10/4/92	10/31/92	11/26/92
11/26/92	12/23/92	1/18/93
1/18/93	2/14/93	3/12/93
3/12/93	4/8/93	5/4/93
5/4/93	5/31/93	6/26/93
6/26/93	7/23/93	8/18/93
8/18/93	9/14/93	10/10/93
10/10/93	11/6/93	12/2/93
12/2/93	12/29/93	1/24/94
1/24/94	2/20/94	3/18/94
3/18/94	4/14/94	5/10/94
5/10/94	6/6/94	7/2/94
7/2/94	7/29/94	8/24/94
8/24/94	9/20/94	10/16/94
10/16/94	11/12/94	12/8/94
12/8/94	1/4/95	1/30/95
1/30/95	2/26/95	3/24/95
3/24/95	4/20/95	5/16/95
5/16/95	6/12/95	7/8/95
7/8/95	8/4/95	8/30/95
8/30/95	9/26/95	10/22/95
10/22/95	11/18/95	12/14/95
12/14/95	1/10/96	2/5/96
2/5/96	3/3/96	3/29/96
3/29/96	4/25/96	5/21/96
5/21/96	6/17/96	7/13/96
7/13/96	8/9/96	9/4/96
9/4/96	10/1/96	10/27/96
10/27/96	11/23/96	12/19/96
12/19/96	1/15/97	2/10/97
2/10/97	3/9/97	4/4/97
4/4/97	5/1/97	5/27/97
5/27/97	6/23/97	7/19/97
7/19/97	8/15/97	9/10/97

TABLE 6.4 *(Continued)*

Bullish Phase Start Date	Bearish Phases Start Date	Next Cycle Start Date
9/10/97	10/7/97	11/2/97
11/2/97	11/29/97	12/25/97
12/25/97	1/21/98	2/16/98
2/16/98	3/15/98	4/10/98
4/10/98	5/7/98	6/2/98
6/2/98	6/29/98	7/25/98
7/25/98	8/21/98	9/16/98
9/16/98	10/13/98	11/8/98
11/8/98	12/5/98	12/31/98
12/31/98	1/27/99	2/22/99
2/22/99	3/21/99	4/16/99
4/16/99	5/13/99	6/8/99
6/8/99	7/5/99	7/31/99
7/31/99	8/27/99	9/22/99
9/22/99	10/19/99	11/14/99
11/14/99	12/11/99	1/6/00
1/6/00	2/2/00	2/28/00
2/28/00	3/26/00	4/21/00
4/21/00	5/18/00	6/13/00
6/13/00	7/10/00	8/5/00
8/5/00	9/1/00	9/27/00
9/27/00	10/24/00	11/19/00
11/19/00	12/16/00	1/11/01
1/11/01	2/7/01	3/5/01
3/5/01	4/1/01	4/27/01
4/27/01	5/24/01	6/19/01
6/19/01	7/16/01	8/11/01
8/11/01	9/7/01	10/3/01
10/3/01	10/30/01	11/25/01
11/25/01	12/22/01	1/17/02
1/17/02	2/13/02	3/11/02
3/11/02	4/7/02	5/3/02
5/3/02	5/30/02	6/25/02
6/25/02	7/22/02	8/17/02
8/17/02	9/13/02	10/9/02
10/9/02	11/5/02	12/1/02
12/1/02	12/28/02	1/23/03
1/23/03	2/19/03	3/17/03
3/17/03	4/13/03	5/9/03
5/9/03	6/5/03	7/1/03
7/1/03	7/28/03	8/23/03
8/23/03	9/19/03	10/15/03

(Continued)

TABLE 6.4 (*Continued*)

Bullish Phase Start Date	Bearish Phases Start Date	Next Cycle Start Date
10/15/03	11/11/03	12/7/03
12/7/03	1/3/04	1/29/04
1/29/04	2/25/04	3/22/04
3/22/04	4/18/04	5/14/04
5/14/04	6/10/04	7/6/04
7/6/04	8/2/04	8/28/04
8/28/04	9/24/04	10/20/04
10/20/04	11/16/04	12/12/04
12/12/04	1/8/05	2/3/05
2/3/05	3/2/05	3/28/05
3/28/05	4/24/05	5/20/05
5/20/05	6/16/05	7/12/05
7/12/05	8/8/05	9/3/05
9/3/05	9/30/05	10/26/05
10/26/05	11/22/05	12/18/05
12/18/05	1/14/06	2/9/06
2/9/06	3/8/06	4/3/06
4/3/06	4/30/06	5/26/06
5/26/06	6/22/06	7/18/06
7/18/06	8/14/06	9/9/06
9/9/06	10/6/06	11/1/06
11/1/06	11/28/06	12/24/06
12/24/06	1/20/07	2/15/07
2/15/07	3/14/07	4/9/07
4/9/07	5/6/07	6/1/07
6/1/07	6/28/07	7/24/07
7/24/07	8/20/07	9/15/07
9/15/07	10/12/07	11/7/07
11/7/07	12/4/07	12/30/07
12/30/07	1/26/08	2/21/08
2/21/08	3/19/08	4/14/08
4/14/08	5/11/08	6/6/08
6/6/08	7/3/08	7/29/08
7/29/08	8/25/08	9/20/08
9/20/08	10/17/08	11/12/08
11/12/08	12/9/08	1/4/09
1/4/09	1/31/09	2/26/09
2/26/09	3/25/09	4/20/09
4/20/09	5/17/09	6/12/09
6/12/09	7/9/09	8/4/09
8/4/09	8/31/09	9/26/09
9/26/09	10/23/09	11/18/09

TABLE 6.4 *(Continued)*

Bullish Phase Start Date	Bearish Phases Start Date	Next Cycle Start Date
11/18/09	12/15/09	1/10/10
1/10/10	2/6/10	3/4/10
3/4/10	3/31/10	4/26/10
4/26/10	5/23/10	6/18/10
6/18/10	7/15/10	8/10/10
8/10/10	9/6/10	10/2/10
10/2/10	10/29/10	11/24/10
11/24/10	12/21/10	1/16/11
1/16/11	2/12/11	3/10/11
3/10/11	4/6/11	5/2/11
5/2/11	5/29/11	6/24/11
6/24/11	7/21/11	8/16/11
8/16/11	9/12/11	10/8/11
10/8/11	11/4/11	11/30/11
11/30/11	12/27/11	1/12/12

Let's move on to the next step of combining these cycles into one comprehensive model.

COMBINING CYCLES

As we have seen so far, the powerful 212-week cycle, the equally powerful but shorter-lived 40-week cycle, and the less significant 53-day cycle have varying degrees of utility as stand-alone models. Next, we'll explore the potential to combine these models into one comprehensive model that incorporates the strengths of each. Our theory is based on the knowledge that each of the three cycles has shown at least a general propensity to identify favorable periods for the stock market and—equally important—to avoid extremely unfavorable periods. If each model does this fairly well on its own, then, if two or more of these models is bullish at one time, we might expect to see favorable market performance on a fairly regular basis. Likewise, we would expect that if all three cycles are presently in bearish phases, then the stock market is more likely to underperform. Let's put this theory to the test. Table 6.5 offers a quick review of the models we will use.

The stock market has demonstrated a propensity to rise during the bullish phase of each of the cycles we have discussed. On the other hand, the performance of the so-called bearish phases has been all over the lot.

TABLE 6.5 Summary of Repetitive Cycles of Note

Cycle	Description
212-week cycle	Bullish for 6 months after start of new cycle, then neutral until start of next cycle.
40-week cycle	Bullish for 20 weeks after start of new cycle, then theoretically bearish until start of next cycle.
53-day cycle	Bullish for 27 days after start of new cycle, then essentially neutral until start of next cycle.

Sometimes the market rises during a bearish phase, other times it declines, and on still other occasions it meanders aimlessly. In a nutshell, there is a bullish phase and an unpredictable phase for each cycle. Although it seems that we can count on the bullish phase for strong performance, we cannot make any assumptions about the market performance during the unpredictable phase. So, as we build a comprehensive model, we will look primarily to maximize our gains during overlapping bullish phases. In addition, more aggressive investors may ultimately be interested in short-selling opportunities during those times when all three cycles are bearish at the same time.

For each trading day, we will examine how many of the three cycles that we have talked about so far are presently in a bullish phase. As such, our comprehensive time cycles model (CTCM) is calculated as follows:

- If the 212-week cycle is bullish, then one point is added to the CTCM.
- If the 40-week cycle is bullish, then one point is added to the CTCM.
- If the 53-day cycle is bullish, then one point is added to the CTCM.

Following these simple rules, readings from our comprehensive model can range from 0 to 3, depending on how many cycles are bullish at the moment. So, do different CTCM readings have implications for current stock market performance? Let's analyze the results to make an objective determination.

Let's first consider the performance of the stock market when none of the three cycles is in a bullish phase. In other words, we will start by looking at stock market performance only during those times when the CTCM is equal to 0. Figure 6.8 displays the growth of $1,000 invested only when the CTCM equals 0 since April 1967.

The results depicted in Figure 6.8 are grim, as the long-term trend is unmistakably bearish. If our theory is that the stock market will perform poorly when none of the three cycles in question is bullish, Figure 6.8 seems to bear that theory out. We see a steady decline in equity over a

FIGURE 6.8 Growth of $1,000 invested in the Dow only when the CTCM equals 0 since April 1967

40-year period, with only a few rallies of any consequence along the way. Here are a few numbers to back up this fairly obvious conclusion:

- A $1,000 investment only when the CTCM equals 0 would have declined 54 percent to just $455 by December 31, 2007.
- The average daily performance when the CTCM was equal to 0 was −0.000289 percent.
- The average daily performance when the CTCM was equal to anything other than 0 was 0.000479 percent.
- When the CTCM was equal to 0, the market's annualized rate of return was −7.0 percent.
- When the CTCM was equal to anything other than 0, the market advanced at an annualized rate of return of 13.1 percent.

From these performance results it becomes clear that the stock market has shown a strong propensity to underperform when all three cycles are in bearish phases. In essence, what we have learned here is what not to do. Investors can use this knowledge by selling short, raising cash, or at the very least investing very defensively when the CTCM reads 0. Still, investors should not assume that if the CTCM is equal to 0 that the stock market is guaranteed to decline.

Figure 6.8 reveals any number of occasions when the market managed to advance for at least a short while in the face of a 0 reading for the CTCM. Nevertheless, when all three of the key cycles are simultaneously not in a bullish phase, we are definitely swimming upstream against the overall market current. So, now that we know what not to do, let's take a look at one way to use the CTCM to generate a profit in the stock market.

The simplest strategy is to be in the market whenever the CTCM is greater than 0. In other words, as long as any one of the three cycles is in a bullish phase, we will give the bullish case the benefit of the doubt and be in the market. The growth of $1,000 invested in the Dow only when the CTCM is greater than 0 appears in Figure 6.9 along with the growth of $1,000 invested in the Dow on a buy-and-hold basis.

So, $1,000 invested only when the CTCM is greater than 0 since 1967 would have grown to $33,005, and $1,000 invested in the Dow on a buy-and-hold basis during the same time would have grown to just $15,019. Clearly, an investor would have been able to gain a meaningful advantage over the stock market by paying attention to these simple, repetitive cycles. Still, the top equity curve line displayed in Figure 6.9 experienced a fair amount of volatility along the way, and did suffer a meaningful

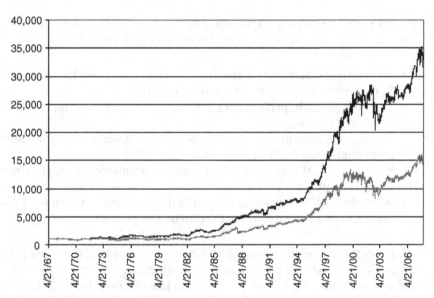

FIGURE 6.9 Growth of $1,000 invested in the Dow when the CTCM is greater than 0 (top line) versus $1,000 invested in the Dow on a buy-and-hold basis (bottom line) since March 1967

decline during the 2000–2002 bear market. Likewise, investing anytime that the CTCM is greater than 0 means that, at times, we would be in the market only with a bullish phase for the 53-day cycle, which, as we established earlier, does not appear to be the best idea. Let's add another filter to the investment process—and to better appreciate the potential usefulness of these cycles, let's look at what happens in the market when two or more cycles are in the bullish phase at the same time.

Figure 6.10 displays the growth of $1,000 invested in the Dow only during times when at least two or more of the three cycles are in a bullish phase.

The results depicted in Figure 6.10 are quite impressive. The bad news is that the overall gain drops dramatically—from $33,005 to $9,119—when we raise the requirement for being in the market from a CTCM of 1 to a CTCM of 2 or greater. Nevertheless, remember that one of our primary goals in our seasonal analyses is to attempt to identify exceptionally strong periods in the market during which we can invest aggressively without much fear of a potentially major decline. Raising the bar from one cycle being bullish to two appears to accomplish that goal.

When two or more cycles are in a bullish phase at the same time, the stock market has risen at an annualized rate of 20.0 percent. Of equal

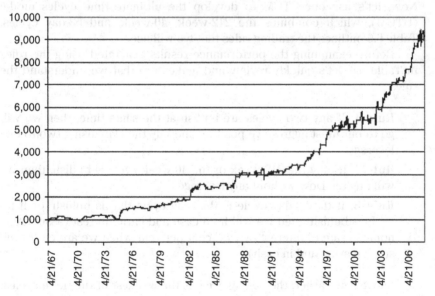

FIGURE 6.10 Growth of $1,000 invested in the Dow when two or more cycles are in a bullish phase (since 1967)

TABLE 6.6 Trading Strategy for the UTCM

Status	Strategy
CTCM = 2 or 3	Long Dow* 2
CTCM = 1 *and* bullish 212-week or 40-week cycle	Long Dow
CTCM = 0 or CTCM = 1 and bullish 53-day cycle	In cash

importance, and, as you can see in Figure 6.10, the market has demonstrated a strong propensity to advance under such bullish circumstances, with nary a major bear market decline along the way. So, now that we have identified an objective method of locating low-risk opportunities in the stock market, let's take this to the next level and see what happens when we apply some leverage during these particularly favorable times.

THE ULTIMATE TIME CYCLES MODEL

Now, let's use our CTCM to develop the ultimate time cycles model (UTCM), which combines the 212-week, 40-week, and 53-day cycles. Table 6.6 outlines the trading rules that we will use.

Before examining the performance results generated using the rules in Table 6.6, let's quickly review and make sure that we understand the rules:

Rule 1: If any two cycles are bullish at the same time, then we will go to our most aggressive position and buy the Dow using two-to-one leverage.

Rule 2: If only the 212-week or the 40-week cycle is bullish, then we will buy the Dow without any leverage.

Rule 3: If the 53-day cycle is the only cycle that is bullish, or if no cycle is bullish, then we will hold cash and earn interest (assuming a nominal rate of interest of 1 percent per year when we are out of the stock market and in cash).

As we saw earlier, the 53-day cycle is the weakest of the three cycles. Its primary strength is as a confirmation indicator for the two cycles. As a result, if it is the only one of the three cycles that is bullish at a particular time, we will simply ignore it and hold cash. The only time we will act following a bullish phase for the 53-day cycle is if one of the other cycles is also bullish. For example, if the 40-week cycle is bullish and the 212-week and 53-day cycles are not, then we will hold the Dow with no leverage. If the 53-day cycle subsequently enters a bullish phase and the 40-week cycle remains bullish, then we will hold the Dow with two-to-one leverage. From there, if the 53-day cycle went back into a bearish phase, we will hold the Dow with no leverage. Conversely, if the 212-week cycle went back into a bearish phase while the 53-day cycle remained bullish (assuming that the 40-week cycle likewise is not presently bullish), we would exit the market and return to cash.

Figure 6.11 displays the results of this strategy, which present a strong argument for the occasional use of leverage to maximize long-term profitability. Although leverage inarguably raises investors' risk, the fact remains that by using a profitable strategy, investors can exponentially increase profits by compounding money at a higher rate of return over time. The key is to use leverage only during the most favorable market periods. That is what our combination of cycles is designed to do, as displayed in Figures 6.10 and 6.11.

Despite some whipsaws and increased volatility along the way, our enhanced UTCM strategy would have seen $1,000 grow to a stunning $356,452 between December 31, 1966, and December 31, 2007, versus just $16,883

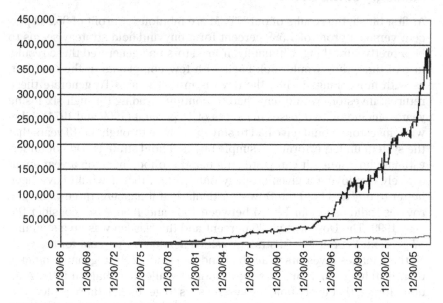

FIGURE 6.11 Growth of $1,000 invested in the Dow using UTCM since Dec. 31, 1966

using a buy-and-hold strategy. This performance is a direct result of the following:

- Taking steps to maximize profitability when the outlook is brightest (using leverage when two or more cycles are simultaneously bullish).
- Being in the market without leverage when the outlook is reasonably favorable (40-week cycle or 212-week cycle is bullish).
- Preserving capital when the outlook is not favorable (neither the 40-week cycle nor the 212-week cycle is bullish).

Table 6.7 displays the year-by-year results generated using the UTCM. Here are some performance numbers for the UTCM:

- The UTCM has shown a gain during 35 of the past 41 years.
- A buy-and-hold approach has shown a gain during 29 of the past 41 years.
- The UTCM has shown a loss during 6 of the past 41 years.
- A buy-and-hold approach has shown a loss during 12 of the past 41 years.
- The average annual gain for the UTCM was 17.0 percent.
- The average annual gain for the Dow was 8.3 percent.

Summary of the UTCM

At first blush, the results of our UTCM are fabulous: A profit of 35,542 percent versus a profit of 1,588 percent for a buy-and-hold strategy seems to be a pretty sure thing. Ultimately, if investors had generated these results in real time, they would look back with few complaints in the end. But, as with most things in life, the devil is in the details. To generate these returns, investors would have had to continue trading through six losing years—including two losses in excess of 16 percent (1969 and 1974). Likewise, investors would have had to stay the course through the 13 years that the system underperformed a simple buy-and-hold strategy. Do not underestimate how much it can grate on a person to look back on a year spent actively employing a given strategy only to find that it would have been better to buy and hold the Dow—particularly if it happens three years in a row, as it did using our UTCM between 1988 and 1990. Also, consider the year 1999. The Dow was up 25 percent and the Nasdaq was up a stunning 87 percent. Yet our UTCM strategy gained a paltry 5.7 percent for the year. Nothing makes investors want to abandon a trading strategy more quickly than watching others make a lot of money while they make a little. And, don't forget, that every time the system says to get bullish there is plenty of bearish news for investors to latch on to as a justification for not following the system just this once.

TABLE 6.7 Year-by-Year Results for UTCM versus the Buy-and-Hold Approach

Year	UTCM Percentage +(−)	Dow Percentage +(−)	System versus Dow	UTCM $1,000	Dow $,1000
1967	23.9	15.2	8.7	1,239	1,152
1968	10.4	4.3	6.1	1,367	1,201
1969	(16.4)	(15.2)	(1.2)	1,143	1,019
1970	25.3	4.8	20.5	1,432	1,068
1971	29.8	6.1	23.7	1,859	1,133
1972	21.4	14.6	6.8	2,256	1,298
1973	5.6	(16.6)	22.2	2,383	1,083
1974	(16.1)	(27.6)	11.5	2,000	784
1975	92.4	38.3	54.1	3,849	1,085
1976	8.9	17.9	(8.9)	4,193	1,279
1977	(9.6)	(17.3)	7.7	3,789	1,058
1978	9.1	(3.1)	12.3	4,135	1,025
1979	11.9	4.2	7.8	4,629	1,068
1980	26.7	14.9	11.8	5,865	1,227
1981	16.2	(9.2)	25.5	6,817	1,114
1982	34.4	19.6	14.8	9,163	1,332
1983	39.5	20.3	19.3	12,786	1,602
1984	(6.0)	(3.7)	(2.2)	12,024	1,542
1985	33.1	27.7	5.5	16,006	1,969
1986	(4.8)	22.6	(27.4)	15,233	2,413
1987	46.5	2.3	44.2	22,317	2,468
1988	3.1	11.8	(8.8)	23,006	2,760
1989	13.3	27.0	(13.6)	26,077	3,504
1990	(7.1)	(4.3)	(2.8)	24,222	3,352
1991	22.6	20.3	2.3	29,699	4,033
1992	7.0	4.2	2.8	31,781	4,202
1993	10.4	13.7	(3.4)	35,072	4,778
1994	0.7	2.1	(1.4)	35,321	4,880
1995	50.9	33.5	17.5	53,302	6,513
1996	16.9	26.0	(9.1)	62,297	8,207
1997	42.1	22.6	19.5	88,542	10,065
1998	30.8	16.1	14.7	115,776	11,686
1999	5.7	25.2	(19.5)	122,410	14,633
2000	4.3	(6.2)	10.5	127,727	13,729
2001	12.5	(7.1)	19.6	143,732	12,755
2002	15.3	(16.8)	32.0	165,675	10,617
2003	25.3	25.3	0.0	207,651	13,305
2004	10.4	3.1	7.3	229,321	13,724
2005	2.3	(0.6)	2.9	234,555	13,641
2006	33.9	16.3	17.7	314,170	15,863
2007	13.5	6.4	7.0	356,452	16,883
Average	**17.0**	**8.3**	**8.7**		

All of this points out a trading truth: A good strategy is only part of the equation. The other part of the equation is having the wherewithal and discipline to mechanically follow your approach through thick and thin. Do not make the mistake of underestimating the psychological difficulty of this task.

SUMMING UP

One of the problems that many individuals have when considering the role of seasonality in their investment plans is the simple fact that certain seasonal trends simply cannot be explained easily, if at all. Some seasonal trends make sense on a logical and intuitive basis. For example, in Chapter 3, I talked about the theory that money moves the market, and that because we know that money moves into the market on a fairly consistent basis during certain times of the month, it makes sense that the market would perform well during those times. As we saw in some detail, that was in fact the case. The seasonal trends presented in this chapter are a horse of a different color. On the one hand, the performance results for each cycle are reasonably impressive. The 212-week cycle has time and again succeeded in identifying very low-risk buying opportunities. Likewise, virtually nothing has objectively identified and modeled bullish stock market activity over the past 40 years like the 40-week cycle. Virtually all the bearish activity that has taken place in the past 40 years has occurred during the bearish 20-week phase of the 40-week cycle. Finally, the 53-day cycle, although far from perfect and certainly less effective than the 212-week and 40-week cycles, has nevertheless proved a useful tool in conjunction with the other two more dominant cycles.

The good news is that the performance results for these three cycles has been outstanding. The bad news is that absolutely no one—myself included—can explain why this has occurred. Of course, this lack of a plausible explanation leads to the even bigger question, What is the likelihood that these cycles will continue to be effective in the future? And here, too, the truth is that no one can offer ironclad guarantees.

It is left to each investor to decide what to do with the information presented in this chapter. The idea of investing all of one's investment capital on the basis of these three cycles—even in the face of the phenomenal returns generated by our UTCM—would require a tremendous leap of faith and may even be imprudent. At the other end of the spectrum, dismissing the cycles I have detailed because they cannot be explained also would be unwise. Somewhere in the middle, where these important and timely cycles are factored in along with other market indicators, seems like the place to be.

CHAPTER 7

Election Cycle Investing

M uch analysis has been done, and much information written about a purported repetitious cycle in the stock market commonly known as the "election cycle." This cycle allegedly feeds off of the four-year presidential election cycle in the United States. It is undeniable that the policies and legislation enacted by the president and administration can and do have a great deal of impact on the economy and on people's general sense of well-being. All of these influences can and do manifest themselves in the stock market. For example, if the economy is running along smoothly and the majority of investors have a strong sense of well-being, the odds are great that the stock market will move higher as a reflection of this optimistic outlook for the future. Conversely, if the economy is in the dumps and people are pessimistic about the future, whether because of specific fears or just in general, this state of affairs can ultimately manifest in the form of lower stock prices.

Some investors make the unfortunate assumption that because performance of the stock market is linked to performance of the economy, to profit from the trends in the stock market, they must correctly forecast the future direction of the economy to be on the right side of these trends. This is an extremely slippery slope for a variety of reasons. First, forecasting the future of the U.S. economy is difficult, to put it mildly. Moreover, the U.S. economy has so many moving parts to it, that it is somewhat nebulous to say that the economy is good or the economy is bad. Particularly, in the modern age of globalization, it is not uncommon for certain segments of the economy to chug along quite nicely, whereas other segments struggle. For example, in the third quarter of 2007, the gross domestic product (GDP) for the U.S. economy grew a surprisingly strong 3.9 percent, a strong performance in any era by any standards. Yet anyone involved in the housing industry at the time—be it mortgages, home building, home furnishings, appliances, you name it—was suffering through one of the worst downturns in the past 20 years. This resulted in large part from the fallout created by defaults on adjustable-rate mortgages that came home to roost in the second half of that year, as well as a natural slowdown in the housing market after many years of above-average rises in home prices. At the same time, high energy prices acted as a drag on many industries and some low-income families. So, as of the fourth quarter of 2007, if you had said that the economy was very strong (based on the large uptick in GDP) or very weak (based on declining home prices and rising energy prices), you could have made a very strong argument that you were correct. Thus, the problem with forecasting the economy is that the economy is not a homogeneous entity but an accumulation of countless working parts.

Even if you happen to be correct about the state of the economy today, there is another complicating factor in trying to relate that to the stock market, for the stock market is essentially a discounting mechanism. This means that although the state of the economy today matters, the stock market reacts as much or more on the basis of the anticipated state of economic affairs in the months ahead. Let's say that the economy is fine right now, but that a downturn is brewing 6 to 12 months down the road. If investors were to invest in stocks on the basis of an analysis of currently favorable economic trends, they could easily find themselves buying very near the high, as the market soon begins to anticipate an economic downturn and begins to decline. Likewise, major stock market bottoms typically occur when things look most bleak. The majority of investors are taken completely by surprise at a stock market bottom, as the market—in the face of seemingly unending bad economic news—suddenly begins screaming higher. People reading the business page can only scratch their heads and assume that the stock market must be wrong. But the bottom line is that the market is always right. It is investors who must adjust to the market, not the other way around. These types of experiences of "right about the economy, wrong about the stock market" can sour an individual on stocks for a long time. This, in turn, can cost them a great opportunity to increase their wealth and to preserve their capital.

Fortunately, because human nature is what it is, there are certain trends related to elections that investors can take advantage of to make money in the stock market. We will look at these trends in depth later in this chapter, but first let's survey the scene in more general terms. First, remember that one of the most important objectives for many politicians is simply to be reelected, or, at the minimum, to keep their political party in power. Thus, any necessary dirty work is most likely to be done early in a new term so as to give any new plans the maximum amount of time to work out and the maximum amount of time for voters to forget any pain associated with them. Likewise, more than anything else, the stock market hates uncertainty. Once a long-awaited piece of news is out—be it good news or bad news—the stock market will often stage a rally. What causes the market to consolidate and decline is when it is not known whether the outcome for a particular situation will be favorable or unfavorable. Thus, the stock market is more prone to consolidate when the result of an impending election is in doubt; likewise, it is prone to react favorably when the winner becomes clear, be it before an election, on election day, or after a disputed election is resolved.

THE ELECTION CYCLE: BY THE YEARS

We will define the election cycle as the 48-month period beginning on January 1 of the year after the most recent presidential election and ending on December 31 of the next presidential election year. Let's start our analysis of this cycle by looking at the historical performance of each of the four years within the presidential election cycle, to first gain an insight into any inherent underlying trends. We want to identify, in the broadest sense possible, whether the stock market has demonstrated an above-average tendency to rise or fall during a particular year in the four-year cycle. From there, we can then break things down a bit and look at some more narrowly focused slices of time that have witnessed a strong propensity to outperform.

Let's first breaks things down year by year and look at each year in terms of how it fits into the election cycle. As such, there are four distinct years in each cycle, as depicted in Table 7.1.

TABLE 7.1 The Four Years of the Election Cycle

Year	Description
Postelection	The year after a presidential election.
Midterm	Two years after the previous election year and two years before the next presidential election.
Preelection	The year prior to the next presidential election.
Election	The year in which an actual presidential election takes place.

In terms of stock market history, and as you will see in a moment, each year in this cycle has its own distinct personality. Also, some of the results are a bit surprising. Let's take a closer look at each individual year to see whether there are any unique, recurring trends that we might be able to take advantage of for an edge in our investing strategy.

The Postelection Year

As I mentioned earlier, there is a tendency for politicians to want to get any dirty work out of the way as early as possible in any term. As a result, the postelection year has garnered a reputation for not being a very good year for the stock market. In fact, when I first started following the market closely in the early 1980s, it was conventional wisdom that a post-election year was just about guaranteed to be a loser. As it turned out, this belief was based primarily on groupthink and an extrapolation of what, at the time, was the latest trend. Between 1969 and 1981, the Dow suffered four consecutive losing postelection years. This was enough at the time to convince the vast majority of investors that this was simply the way things were and that postelection years were destined to bring investors pain ad infinitum into the future. Imagine their surprise, then, when the next four postelection years—1985, 1989, 1993, and 1997—registered gains of 27.7 percent, 27.0 percent, 13.7 percent, and 22.6 percent, respectively. Anyone stuck in the mind-set that the stock market has to go down during a postelection year would likely have missed some outstanding gains. Still, as we will see in a moment, the overall performance of the stock market during postelection years has been a mixed bag. Table 7.2 displays the Dow's performance during each postelection year since 1937.

Figure 7.1 displays the growth of $1,000 invested in the Dow only during each postelection year since 1934. As you can see, there have been a number of ups and downs. In the end, it is interesting that the net result of more than 70 years of postelection year history was a net loss of $4, as $1,000 invested only during postelection years starting in 1937 would be worth $996 at the end of 2007.

Does all of this mean that investors should simply shun the stock market during postelection years? Not necessarily. As you can see in Table 7.2, on four occasions—including three since 1985—the Dow has advanced in excess of 22 percent during a postelection year. So, always remember that simply sticking your head in the sand may make you miss out on a great opportunity. Still, you can see in Figure 7.1 and Table 7.2 that the Dow's performance during postelection years has been spotty at best. Since 1934, there have been eight up postelection years and ten down postelection years.

TABLE 7.2 Dow Performance during Postelection Years

Year	Dow Percentage +(−)
1937	(32.8)
1941	(15.4)
1945	26.6
1949	12.9
1953	(3.8)
1957	(12.8)
1961	18.7
1965	10.9
1969	(15.2)
1973	(16.6)
1977	(17.3)
1981	(9.2)
1985	27.7
1989	27.0
1993	13.7
1997	22.6
2001	(7.1)
2005	(0.6)
Average	**1.6**
Median	**(2.2)**
No. up	**8**
No. down	**10**

Consider the following postelection year performance figures:

- Only 8 of the past 18 postelection years have witnessed a Dow advance.
- The average performance was a small gain of 1.6 percent; however, the median return was a loss of 2.2 percent.

Still, it is important to note that during the eight postelection years in which the Dow did post a gain, the average gain was 20 percent. So, investors would be unwise to adopt the mentality that a postelection year is certain to be bad for the stock market; doing so clearly could result in major lost opportunities. In fact, investors should pay close attention to the market early in a postelection year. If it starts higher, there is a good chance that the advance will continue.

As we saw in Chapter 5, years ending in the number 5 (e.g., 1905, 1915, 1925) have typically been strong performers. As you can see in Table 7.2, this has typically been the case even during postelection years

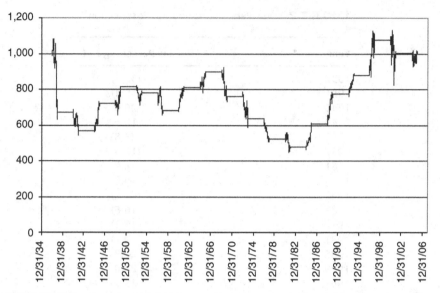

FIGURE 7.1   Growth of $1,000 invested in the Dow only during postelection years since 1934

(26.6 percent gain in 1945, 10.9 percent gain in 1965, 27.7 percent gain in 1985, and a 0.6 percent loss in 2005). Excluding these years, the postelection numbers look much worse:

- Only 5 of the past 14 postelection years that did not end in a 5 have witnessed an advance by the Dow.
- The average performance during these years was a loss of 2.5 percent and the median return was −8.2 percent (well below the annual average of roughly 9 percent).

The bottom line is that there is potential for strong gains during a postelection year. Nevertheless, some caution is in order during postelection years, particularly if the year does not end in 5.

The Midterm Year

The midterm year is often considered the rebound year. The theory is that once whatever nastiness is due to play out actually plays out during the postelection year—and often well into the postelection year—the market will bottom out and begin to rally heading into the last two years of the election cycle. Is there any truth to this? Quite a bit, as a matter of fact.

TABLE 7.3 Dow Performance during Midterm Election Years since 1934

Year	Dow Percentage +(−)
1934	4.1
1938	28.1
1942	7.6
1946	(8.1)
1950	17.6
1954	44.0
1958	34.0
1962	(10.8)
1966	(18.9)
1970	4.8
1974	(27.6)
1978	(3.1)
1982	19.6
1986	22.6
1990	(4.3)
1994	2.1
1998	16.1
2002	(16.8)
2006	16.3
Average	**6.7**
Median	**4.8**
No. up	**12**
No. down	**7**

Before delving into this theory, however, let's first look at the historical performance of the stock market solely during midterm election years.

Table 7.3 displays the yearly results for all midterm election years since 1934. Whereas the midterm year is an improvement over the typical postelection year, it is still something of a mixed bag.

Here is the summary of the midterm year by the numbers:

- Of the past 19 postelection years, 12 have witnessed an advance by the Dow and 7 witnessed a market decline.
- The average annual performance was a gain of 6.7 percent; the median return was 4.8 percent.
- If the preceding year (i.e., the postelection year) was down, the midterm election year showed a profit seven of ten times, or 70 percent of the time, with an average gain of 10 percent. Still, investors should beware of relying too heavily on this, as two of the three

losing years involved losses of 27.6 percent (in 1974) and 16.8 percent (in 2002)—multiyear bear markets can be very unforgiving.

- If the preceding year (i.e., the postelection year) was up, then the midterm election year is a coin flip, up four times and down four times. So there is no predictive value there.

As a general rule of thumb, an up postelection year offers no insight whatsoever into the potential performance for the following midterm year. Conversely, a down postelection year can be a harbinger of better days ahead. Nevertheless, investors should probably wait for some clear evidence that a new uptrend has emerged before rushing headlong into the market during a midterm year. In addition, and as you will see later in this chapter, there is a natural buying opportunity in the midterm year. For now, simply take note of the choppy nature of the annual returns generated by the Dow during midterm calendar years, as depicted in Figure 7.2.

Probably the best word to describe the performance of the Dow during midterm years is "unpredictable." Yet, ironically, it also encompasses the start of one of the most predictable trends contained in the 48-month election cycle. But, before we move on to that, let's continue on with our look at the calendar years that comprise the 48-month election cycle.

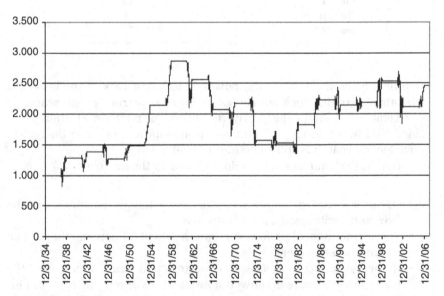

FIGURE 7.2 Growth of $1,000 invested in the Dow only during midterm election years since 1934

The Preelection Year

If you had to pick one year to be in the stock market, the preelection year would be the hands-down winner among the four years of the election cycle. As we will see in a moment, the strength and consistency of the stock market performance during this year in the election cycle is a sight to behold and is nothing short of remarkable. It is also a fairly strong testament to the idea that the powers that be will try as hard as possible to get any dirty work out of the way early in a new presidential term and to get things moving along fairly smoothly as the next presidential election appears on the horizon. The strength of the preelection year may be partly explained by the fact that the midterm election has just been completed (the midterm election occurs on the second Tuesday in November of the midterm year); thus, great uncertainty—whether the president will have a majority in Congress or whether gridlock is likely—has been removed from the marketplace. Also, remember that the stock market hates uncertainty above all else. Once a cause of uncertainty for the stock market is resolved, stock prices often follow through with a meaningful rally. Perhaps this is a factor that fuels the spectacular performance of the preelection year.

Table 7.4 displays the yearly performance of the Dow during each preelection year since 1935. The year 1939 was down for the Dow. Whether it was because Hitler invaded Poland or because the U.S. economy was struggling to rise out of the Great Depression, the Dow lost 2.9 percent. Although that is a relatively minor loss, this loss is noteworthy because 1939 is the last time the Dow registered a loss during a preelection year! As you can see in Table 7.4, the past 17 preelection years have witnessed a rise by the Dow.

Here is the summary of the preelection year by the numbers:

- The Dow advanced in 18 of 19 postelection years.
- The average performance was a gain of 15.1 percent, and the median return was 15.2 percent.

Figure 7.3 displays the growth of $1,000 from investing in the Dow only during each preelection year since 1935

Although it is hard to find things not to like about preelection years, remember that even though all but one preelection year has shown a gain on a calendar-year basis, significant fluctuations can and do take place within the calendar years themselves. Between August and October 1987, the Dow lost a stunning 36 percent. Fear ran high and dire predictions for the future were rampant. Depending on the magnitude of a given decline, along with the news of the day, investors can easily find their thinking colored to assume that this time it is different. And, of course, this time it may be different. The truth is that, just because the past 17 preelection years have

TABLE 7.4 Dow Performance during Preelection
Years since 1935

Year	Dow Percentage +(−)
1935	38.5
1939	(2.9)
1943	13.8
1947	2.2
1951	14.4
1955	20.8
1959	16.4
1963	17.0
1967	15.2
1971	6.1
1975	38.3
1979	4.2
1983	20.3
1987	2.3
1991	20.3
1995	3.5
1999	25.2
2003	25.3
2007	6.4
Average	**15.1**
Median	**15.2**
No. up	**18**
No. down	**1**

showed a gain, the next preelection year is not guaranteed to do so. Still, giving the bullish case the benefit of the doubt seems the logical thing to do.

The Election Year

Election years in the United States are almost invariably filled with political intrigue. The dominant question of the year is, Who will be the next president? Numerous candidates campaign for their political party's nomination from January into the summer. Then the two major parties hold their national conventions and each nominates a candidate. From the summer convention to the November election, the campaign heats up as the two primary candidates attempt to differentiate themselves from their opponent and ultimately win the election. In some years, the election goes down to the wire. In other years, one of the candidates is the odds-on favorite and the other candidate must somehow try to make up the distance.

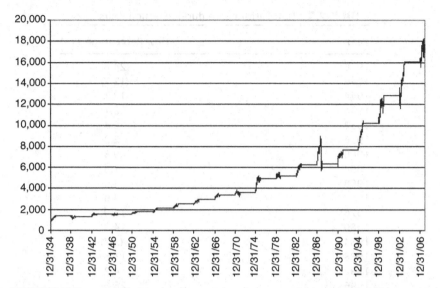

FIGURE 7.3 Growth of $1,000 invested in the Dow only during preelection years since 1935

In any event, it almost always results in great political theater. For those interested in politics, this is all very interesting. But for investors, the primary question during a presidential election year is simply, Can I make any money in the market? Fortunately, the overall answer is yes.

As we will discuss a little later, the key concern during an election year is that, if there is uncertainty about who will win the presidential election in November, the market may act poorly. The primary benefit to the stock market is that, at some point, someone will be victorious. Once that uncertainty is removed from the marketplace, the stock market typically stages an advance.

For now, consider Table 7.5, which displays the annual results for the Dow during each presidential election year since 1936.

Here is the summary of election year by the numbers:

- The Dow advanced in 13 of the past 18 election years.
- The average performance was a gain of 6.9 percent; the median return was 6.3 percent.

Figure 7.4 displays the growth of $1,000 from investing in the Dow only during each election year since 1936.

As you can see in Table 7.5 and Figure 7.4, the performance of the Dow during election years has been positive in the long run. Still, the results are far less consistent during election years than during preelection years.

TABLE 7.5 Dow Performance during Election Years

Year	Dow Percentage +(−)
1936	24.8
1940	(12.7)
1944	12.1
1948	(2.1)
1952	8.4
1956	2.3
1960	(9.3)
1964	14.6
1968	4.3
1972	14.6
1976	17.9
1980	14.9
1984	(3.7)
1988	11.8
1992	4.2
1996	26.0
2000	(6.2)
2004	3.1
Average	**6.9**
Median	**6.3**
No. up	**13**
No. down	**5**

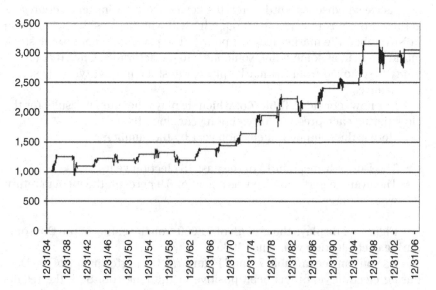

FIGURE 7.4 Growth of $1,000 invested in the Dow only during election years since 1936

In a little while we will look at a slightly narrower slice of the election year that has demonstrated a consistent tendency toward bullish action in the stock market. For now, we will simply note that election years have demonstrated a tendency toward bullish market action on the whole.

Postelection and Midterm Years Combined

Now let's look at what would happen if investors had been in the stock market only during the less favorable postelection and midterm years during the past 70 years. Figure 7.5 displays the growth of $1,000 that would have been achieved by investing in the Dow only during these two years of every four years within each election cycle starting on December 31, 1934.

There are a few important things to note about the performance in Figure 7.5. First, the good news is that investors would have made money by pursuing this strategy. The original $1,000 invested starting on December 31, 1934, would have more than doubled, growing to $2,446 by December 31, 2007. The bad news is that this works out to a very inferior annualized return of just 3.6 percent. So, this poses something of a conundrum if investors were, for some reason, bound and determined to be fully in or fully out of the stock market during these two years of each election cycle. Nevertheless, if investors were to skip these years completely, they would ultimately have underperformed a buy-and-hold approach. At the same time, if investors had invested during these years, they would have had to sit through a great deal of volatility and poor performance along the way.

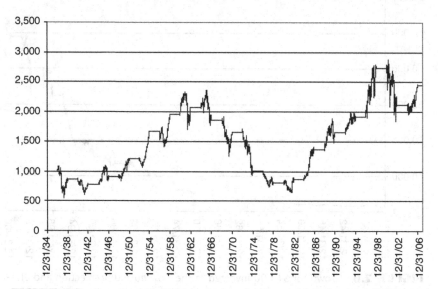

FIGURE 7.5 Growth of $1,000 invested in the Dow only during postelection and midterm election years

So, neither being always in nor always out during this two-year period is a very useful strategy. What is interesting, however, is to compare these two years to the other two years of the election cycle. So let's take a look at this.

Preelection and Election Years Combined

As we have just seen, the combined postelection and midterm years made some money over the past 70-plus years, but they were not terribly profitable and there were volatile fits and starts. This performance stands in stark contrast to the performance of the combined preelection and election years. Figure 7.6 displays the growth of $1,000 invested during the second half of each election cycle since December 31, 1934. The results are striking. Whereas there has, in fact, been some downside volatility along the way (most notably the crash of 1987), the returns have been quite the model of consistency, particularly when compared to the first two years of the election cycle that we saw in Figure 7.5.

Although $1,000 invested only during the postelection and midterm years grew to just $2,446, the same $1,000 invested during the preelection and election years grew to $52,115. This represents the difference between a total net gain of 145 percent and a total net gain of 5,111 percent—not an insignificant difference.

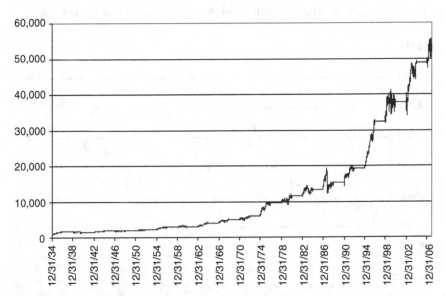

FIGURE 7.6 Growth of $1,000 invested in the Dow during preelection and election years

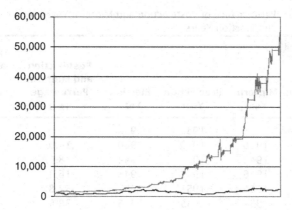

FIGURE 7.7 Comparison: Growth of $1,000 invested in the Dow during preelection and election years versus postelection and midterm years

To give you a clear idea of the magnitude of the difference between the combined postelection and midterm years and the combined preelection and election years, Figure 7.7 plots the growth of $1,000 during both periods together. The difference in the performance of these periods is compelling.

Table 7.6 lists the performance of these two periods by election cycle.

The postelection and midterm years actually outperformed the preelection and election years five of six times between 1937 and 1958. Since then, the preelection and elections years has outperformed 9 of 11 times. Some summary statistics appear in Table 7.7.

The most compelling thing in Table 7.7 is that the preelection and election years have shown a gain 17 of 18 times. The one losing period occurred 70 years ago during 1937–1938. The bottom line is that investors should be wise to give the bullish case the benefit of the doubt during the last two years of the election cycle.

We have now established that the last two years of the election cycle have a tendency to perform much better than the first two years of the election cycle. Now let's zero in to see whether we can find certain specific, repetitive patterns in the election cycle that might allow us to maximize profitability while reducing the amount of downside volatility experienced along the way.

THE ELECTION CYCLE: BY THE MONTHS

Now that we have looked at the yearly tendencies in the four-year presidential election cycle, let's zero in on stock market performance on a

188

SEASONAL STOCK MARKET TRENDS

TABLE 7.6 Performance of Postelection and Midterm Years versus Preelection and Election Years

Postelection Year	Midterm Year	Preelection Year	Election Year	Postelection and Midterm Percentage +(−)	Preelection and Election Year Percentage +(−)
		1935	1936		72.9
1937	1938	1939	1940	(14.0)	(15.3)
1941	1942	1943	1944	(8.9)	27.6
1945	1946	1947	1948	16.3	0.1
1949	1950	1951	1952	32.8	24.0
1953	1954	1955	1956	38.5	23.5
1957	1958	1959	1960	16.9	5.5
1961	1962	1963	1964	5.9	34.0
1965	1966	1967	1968	(10.1)	20.1
1969	1970	1971	1972	(11.1)	21.6
1973	1974	1975	1976	(39.6)	63.0
1977	1978	1979	1980	(19.9)	19.7
1981	1982	1983	1984	8.6	15.8
1985	1986	1987	1988	56.5	14.4
1989	1990	1991	1992	21.4	25.3
1993	1994	1995	1996	16.2	68.2
1997	1998	1999	2000	42.4	17.5
2001	2002	2003	2004	(22.7)	29.3
2005	2006	2007	2008	15.6	?
2009	2010	2011	2012		

month-by-month basis to determine whether there are specific periods in which we can anticipate superior stock market returns.

In his 1990 book *Stock Market Timing*, Dick Stoken pointed out that for the past 70 years (50 years at the time), the stock market has demonstrated a 15-month sweet spot in the four-year election cycle. To highlight

TABLE 7.7 Postelection and Midterm Years versus Preelection and Election Years

Measure	Postelection and Midterm Years	Preelection and Election Years
Average percentage +(−)	12.7	28.4
No. of times up	11	17
No. of times down	7	1

the tendency for consistency among seasonal trends, it is worth noting that since Stoken first pointed out this period, it has passed through five more cycles. All five subsequent cycles have shown a gain for the Dow during this sweet spot, with an average gain of 32.0 percent. Let's take a closer look at this most favorable election cycle period.

Zeroing In on the 15 Most Bullish Months

The 15-month period that Stoken originally highlighted begins on October 1 of the midterm election year and extends through December 31 of the pre-election year. For example, the latest cycle technically began at the close of trading on September 29, 2006 (we start at the close of the last trading day of September of each midterm election year, to include the entire first trading day of October), with the Dow at 11,679.07. The cycle ended at the close of trading on December 31, 2007, with the Dow at 13,264.82. From start to finish, the Dow registered a gain of 13.6 percent. Although this is a respectable gain, it is well below average for this period. The historical performance of the Dow during this particular time frame appears in Table 7.8.

TABLE 7.8 Dow Performance during the 15-month Favorable Period of the Election Cycle

Start Date	Start Year	End Date	End Year	Percentage +(−)
Sept. 30	1934	Dec. 31	1935	55.6
Sept. 30	1938	Dec. 31	1939	6.2
Sept. 30	1942	Dec. 31	1943	24.5
Sept. 30	1946	Dec. 31	1947	5.1
Sept. 30	1950	Dec. 31	1951	18.9
Sept. 30	1954	Dec. 31	1955	35.5
Sept. 30	1958	Dec. 31	1959	27.7
Sept. 30	1962	Dec. 31	1963	31.8
Sept. 30	1966	Dec. 31	1967	16.9
Sept. 30	1970	Dec. 31	1971	17.0
Sept. 30	1974	Dec. 31	1975	40.2
Sept. 30	1978	Dec. 31	1979	(3.1)
Sept. 30	1982	Dec. 31	1983	40.4
Sept. 30	1986	Dec. 31	1987	9.7
Sept. 30	1990	Dec. 31	1991	29.1
Sept. 30	1994	Dec. 31	1995	33.1
Sept. 30	1998	Dec. 31	1999	46.6
Sept. 30	2002	Dec. 31	2003	37.7
Sept. 30	2006	Dec. 31	2007	13.6
			Average	**25.6**

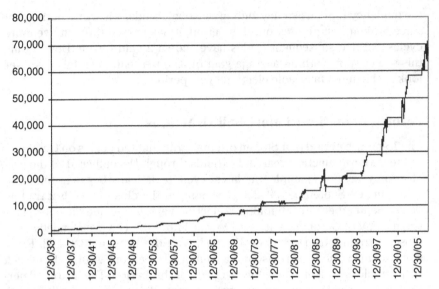

FIGURE 7.8 Growth of $1,000 invested in the Dow during 15-month midterm and preelection favorable period since Dec. 31, 1933

The results displayed in Table 7.8 are inarguably impressive. Since 1933, this 15-month period has shown a gain 18 times with only 1 loss—a 3.1 percent loss between September 30, 1978, and December 31, 1979 (it is interesting to note that the OTC Composite was up more than 13 percent during this same time). Figure 7.8 puts a face to these numbers, and the results are equally impressive.

The steady, sharp upward-sloping equity growth in Figure 7.8 is hard to dismiss. Still, in the interest of full disclosure, it should be noted that, as with any trading method, there were still moments that would try any investor's wherewithal. Most notable is that the crash of 1987 occurred during this favorable 15-month period. This involved a 36 percent decline from peak to trough between August and October 1987, including a one-day loss of 22 percent on October 19. People who remember that day—particularly if they were in the stock market that day—remember well what it feels like when a large portion of capital vanishes in a short period of time. It is interesting to note, then, that one of the most consistently bullish cycles would essentially have forced investors to ride this one out. On the brighter side, the 15-month period between October 1986 and December 1987 witnessed a net advance by the Dow, albeit a modest one of 9.7 percent. Still, if you can sit through a stock market crash and still end up making money, things can't be all bad.

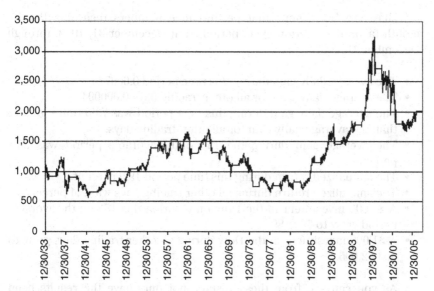

FIGURE 7.9 Growth of $1,000 invested in the Dow during all trading days not including the 15-month midterm and preelection favorable period since Dec. 31, 1933

To further appreciate the strength of the market's performance during this favorable period, let's look at market performance during all other trading days. Figure 7.9 displays the growth of $1,000 invested only during the other 33 months of the 48-month election cycle.

As you can see, there is no comparison between the results in Figure 7.8 and those in Figure 7.9. In Figure 7.9, there is a great deal of choppy and ultimately trendless market activity. Toward the far right we can see that the stock market did rally strongly during all time periods during much of the 1980s and 1990s. However, there is no implication that investors should never invest other than during the 15-month favorable period of the election cycle. This is simply a reminder that the odds are less favorable and that investors need to have a meaningful, objective reason to be in the market when this trend is not in force.

It should also be noted that, with the exception of the 36 percent decline in 1987—which lasted less than two months from start to finish—the bulk of all major bear markets have played out during the other 33 months of the election cycle. Toward the left of Figure 7.9, there are some major declines during the 1930s and early 1940s. Just past the midway point on the graph are the declines of the 1960s and the 1973–1974 bear market. Last, toward the far right of the graph, it is painfully clear that the bulk of the 2000–2002 bear market occurred during the other 33 months of the election cycle.

Here are some important performance numbers regarding the 15-month favorable election cycle period from December 31, 1933, through December 31, 2007:

- The average daily gain during this time period 0.000719.
- The average daily gain for all other trading days 0.000094.
- The average daily gain during this time period was 7.65 times greater than the average daily gain for all other trading days.
- The average gain during the 15-month favorable period was 25.6 percent.
- The annualized return during this time period 19.9 percent.
- The annualized return during all other trading days was 2.4 percent.
- A $1,000 investment in the Dow only during this 15-month favorable period grew to $68,189.
- A $1,000 investment in the Dow during all other trading days grew to just $2,005.

As you can see from these results, not only have the results been consistently profitable, but also the bulk of all stock market gains in the past 70-plus years occurred within the single 15-month period that occurs once every four years. Clearly, Dick Stoken was correct when he pegged October 1 of the midterm year as the onset of a favorable market environment.

Narrowing Down the 14 Most-Bullish Months

As any good market analyst, I felt compelled to dig deeper into the 15-month favorable election cycle to see whether there was any way to tweak things to generate better results. In the process, I found a relatively weak link in this 15-month favorable period: October of the preelection year. Table 7.9 displays the performance of the Dow during the month of October during preelection years since December 31, 1933.

Figure 7.10 displays the growth of equity during October of preelection years. The obvious villain is 1987, which witnessed a 23.2 percent decline as the crash of 1987 unfolded. Nevertheless, even without that year, the month of October during preelection years has been, at best, a neutral to slightly negative performer.

All told, the month of October during preelection years has been up nine times and down ten. This performance is far below the typical performance witnessed during the rest of Stoken's original 15-month favorable period. So, with addition by subtraction, we will remove this month from the equation and proceed using a 14-month favorable election cycle. This new 14-month period actually comprises two separate periods, as explained in Table 7.10.

TABLE 7.9 October of Preelection Years since 1935

Year	Month of October Dow Percentage +(−)
1935	5.9
1939	(0.4)
1943	(1.3)
1947	2.4
1951	(3.2)
1955	(2.5)
1959	2.4
1963	3.1
1967	(5.1)
1971	(5.4)
1975	5.3
1979	(7.2)
1983	(0.6)
1987	(23.2)
1991	1.7
1995	(0.7)
1999	3.8
2003	5.7
2007	1.1
Average	**(1.0)**
No. up	**9**
No. down	**10**

Table 7.11 displays the performance of the Dow during each new 14-month favorable election cycle period.

Figure 7.11 displays the slightly new and improved equity curve for this favorable period. The major improvements come from missing the 1979 crash (the Dow fell 10 percent in 12 trading days) and, of course, the crash of 1987.

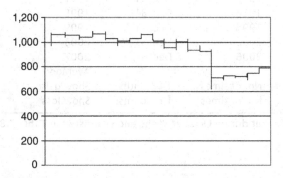

FIGURE 7.10 Growth of $1,000 during October of preelection years since 1935

TABLE 7.10 14-Month Favorable Period

14-Month Favorable Period	Description
12 months	Starting at close of last trading day during September of the midterm year and extending through the close of the last trading day during September of the preelection year.
2 months	Starting at close of last trading day of October during the preelection year and extending through close of last trading day of December during the preelection year.

TABLE 7.11 Dow Performance during the 14-Month Favorable Period

Start Date*	Start Year	End Date*	End Year	Percentage +(−)
Sept. 30	1934	Dec. 31	1935	46.9
Sept. 30	1938	Dec. 31	1939	6.7
Sept. 30	1942	Dec. 31	1943	26.2
Sept. 30	1946	Dec. 31	1947	2.6
Sept. 30	1950	Dec. 31	1951	22.9
Sept. 30	1954	Dec. 31	1955	39.0
Sept. 30	1958	Dec. 31	1959	24.7
Sept. 30	1962	Dec. 31	1963	27.9
Sept. 30	1966	Dec. 31	1967	23.1
Sept. 30	1970	Dec. 31	1971	23.7
Sept. 30	1974	Dec. 31	1975	33.2
Sept. 30	1978	Dec. 31	1979	4.3
Sept. 30	1982	Dec. 31	1983	41.3
Sept. 30	1986	Dec. 31	1987	42.9
Sept. 30	1990	Dec. 31	1991	27.0
Sept. 30	1994	Dec. 31	1995	34.1
Sept. 30	1998	Dec. 31	1999	41.2
Sept. 30	2002	Dec. 31	2003	30.3
Sept. 30	2006	Dec. 31	2007	16.7
			Average	**27.1**
	No. of times	14 months	Show gain	**19**
	No. of times	14 months	Show loss	0

*Out of the market during October of the end year listed in Table 7.8.

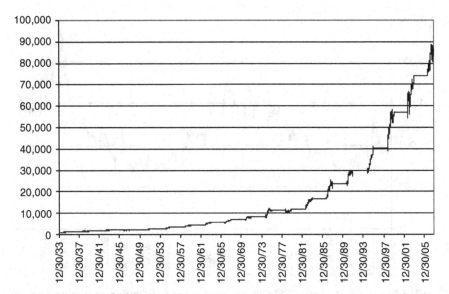

FIGURE 7.11 Growth of $1,000 invested in the Dow during 14-month midterm and preelection favorable period since Dec. 31, 1933

Once again, to fully appreciate this performance, we must compare it with something else to gain some perspective. The obvious choice is to compare it to the market's performance during the other 34 months that comprise the 48-month election cycle. That performance appears in Figure 7.12.

Here are some important performance numbers regarding the 14-month favorable election cycle period since 1933:

- The average daily gain during this period was 0.000804.
- The average daily gain for all other trading days was 0.000074.
- The average daily gain during this time period was 10.8 times greater than the average daily gain for all other trading days.
- The average gain during the 14-month favorable period was 27.1 percent.
- The annualized return during this period 22.5 percent.
- The annualized return during all other trading days was 1.9 percent.
- A $1,000 investment in the Dow only during this 14-month favorable period grew to $83,908.
- A $1,000 investment in the Dow during all other trading days grew to just $1,602.

FIGURE 7.12 Growth of $1,000 invested in the Dow during all trading days not including the 14-month midterm/preelection favorable period since Dec. 31, 1933

Although it's always great to see good performance numbers, in the real world of investing, risk management is essential. Likewise, many individuals would be uncomfortable buying and holding during a given period simply because the period has shown good performance in the past. Nevertheless, investors who desired to maximize their profitability at anytime over the past 70-plus years would have had to be in the stock market during the bulk of this 14-month favorable cycle in the greater 48-month election cycle, because this was quite frankly when most of the money was made. And, $1,000 invested in the Dow only during the favorable 14 months of every 48 would have generated a profit in excess of $86,000. Investors who skipped these months and invested only during the other 34 months of every four-year cycle over the past 74 years would have generated a profit of only $602.

As with so many other trends detailed in this book, there are two thoughts to keep firmly in mind in regard to these 14 favorable election cycle months:

1. There is no guarantee that this period will continue to outperform the rest of the months of each election cycle, let alone generate a profit.

2. Despite the previous caveat, investors might be wise to give the bullish case every benefit of the doubt during these 14 months rather than believe every word of gloom and doom that will inevitably appear in the financial press.

Adding Seven Bullish Months to the Mix

Although the 14-month favorable period that we have just discussed in detail has encompassed most of the gains made by the stock market in the past 70-plus years, it seems counterintuitive that investors should just sit out the other 34 months of each 48-month election cycle. This raises the question, Is there a second-best period in those 48 months when investors can invest confidently? As it turns out, the answer is yes. Let's first discuss the genesis of this second favorable period of the election cycle.

There are many old adages associated with investing in general and the stock market specifically, such as "go with the trend," "cut your losses," and "let your profits run." Such adages stand the test of time because there is much useful wisdom at the heart of each phrase. For example, a person who is constantly trying to fight the prevailing trend in hopes of buying a bottom or selling a top is far more likely than not to end up frustrated and well behind the market as a whole. Likewise, an investor who refuses to ever consider cutting a loss runs the risk of experiencing a catastrophic loss. Finally, investors who cannot resist the urge to take a profit rather than occasionally let their profits run are far more likely to miss out on some big profits along the way.

Another adage that applies to the stock market is "the market hates uncertainty." Whereas this is most assuredly true, it nevertheless requires a bit of explanation. The stock market is ultimately an arbiter of all things financial. In other words, the action of the stock market reflects fairly accurately the mind-set of most investors. If the outlook for the economy and corporate profitability is good, we should expect the stock market to advance. Conversely, if the outlook is less than favorable or downright negative, and if this unfavorable outlook is expected to hurt companies' earnings potential, then it is not unreasonable to expect the stock market to decline, even if only temporarily. When news comes out, it can affect the market, but that impact and how long it lasts is often unpredictable.

Sometimes bad news comes out unexpectedly and the stock market declines sharply. More times than not, that decline proves short lived—sometimes lasting days, other times weeks, and on occasion months—as investors and businesses readjust their thinking to account for the new reality. Sometimes impending bad news is anticipated and the stock market consolidates or declines in the days or weeks leading up to the announcement. Oddly, once the negative announcement is made, the stock market will at times rally as a result of that uncertainty having officially or unofficially been lifted from the marketplace. At other times, the opposite will happen. The stock market will rally in advance of some anticipated positive announcement. Then, once the announcement comes out, the stock market declines sharply. This is an example of another old adage that counsels investors to buy the rumor and sell the news. In any event, we can state with a high degree of certainty that the stock market hates uncertainty. As a corollary, we can also state that it is generally positive for the stock market when uncertainty is resolved.

Among the greatest and most unsettling uncertainties in the United States is the outcome of a presidential election. Typically, the two nominees offer different choices in terms of the policies they intend to pursue, if elected. Thus, the choice of one candidate over another can have a significant impact on the overall state of the country, in terms of not only finances but also social trends, business trends, national security, and so on. Clearly, the outcome of a presidential election amounts to the lifting of great uncertainty from the marketplace. So, does this imply that a person should wait until the day after the election and then load up on stocks, now that the uncertainty has been lifted? Not necessarily. The fact of the matter is that a presidential election with an outcome that is not well known until election day is the exception rather than the rule. On a number of occasions, the actual election has been little more than a formality, as the winner was obvious leading up to the election.

In a nutshell, what my research found was that at some point in the last seven calendar months of an election year, a great uncertainty is lifted from the market when it becomes apparent who the next president will be. If the election is shaping up as a landslide, then the uncertainty is lifted sooner; if they are counting chads in Florida, then the uncertainty will be lifted later. In most cases, the lifting of this great uncertainty has been bullish for stocks. In some cases, when perhaps the market perceives that the new president's policies may be unfavorable for corporate earnings or the economy as a whole, these other concerns may outweigh the lifting of the uncertainty.

One the whole, the last seven calendar months of the presidential election year has proved a quite favorable time for stock market investors. Specifically, we will measure the action of the Dow between the close on May 31 of each presidential election year and December 31 of that same year, for seven calendar months. Table 7.12 displays the results that have been generated during this time frame all the way back to the year 1900.

Figure 7.13 displays the growth of $1,000 invested in the Dow only during the last seven months of each election year starting in 1900. The steady upward progression in the growth of equity is unmistakable.

As you can see in Table 7.12 and Figure 7.13, stock market performance during this time frame over the past century has typically been favorable. To back up this claim, consider the following results:

- This seven-month period showed a gain 22 of 27 times, or 81.5 percent of the time.
- The average performance was a gain of 10.5 percent.

TABLE 7.12 Performance of the Dow during Last 7 Months of Presidential Election Years since 1900

Date In	Date Out	Year	Percentage +(−)
May 31	Dec. 31	1900	19.7
May 31	Dec. 31	1904	44.5
May 31	Dec. 31	1908	18.4
May 31	Dec. 31	1912	(0.2)
May 31	Dec. 31	1916	3.5
May 31	Dec. 31	1920	(21.8)
May 31	Dec. 31	1924	34.0
May 31	Dec. 31	1928	36.5
May 31	Dec. 31	1932	34.0
May 31	Dec. 31	1936	17.9
May 31	Dec. 31	1940	12.8
May 31	Dec. 31	1944	7.1
May 31	Dec. 31	1948	(7.0)
May 31	Dec. 31	1952	11.0
May 31	Dec. 31	1956	4.5
May 31	Dec. 31	1960	(1.5)
May 31	Dec. 31	1964	6.5
May 31	Dec. 31	1968	5.0
May 31	Dec. 31	1972	6.2
May 31	Dec. 31	1976	3.0
May 31	Dec. 31	1980	13.3
May 31	Dec. 31	1984	9.7
May 31	Dec. 31	1988	6.8
May 31	Dec. 31	1992	(2.8)
May 31	Dec. 31	1996	14.3
May 31	Dec. 31	2000	2.5
May 31	Dec. 31	2004	5.8
May 31	Dec. 31	2008	
	Average		**10.5**
	No. of times up		**22**
	No. of times down		**5**

- For the 22 profitable periods, the average gain was 14.4 percent.
- For the five unprofitable periods, the average loss was 6.7 percent.
- The best seven-month gain was 44.5 percent in 1904.
- In the past 50 years, the best gain was a more moderate gain of 14.3 percent in 1996.
- The worst seven-month loss was 21.8 percent in 1920.
- In the past 50 years, the worst loss was a modest decline of 2.8 percent in 1992.

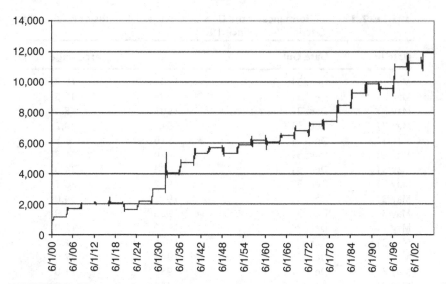

FIGURE 7.13 Growth of $1,000 invested in the Dow between May 31 and December 31 of each election year since 1900

In the past 87 years, the only three election years to show a loss during this seven-month period were the following:

- 1948 (7.0 percent), when Harry Truman defeated Thomas Dewey in a stunning upset.
- 1960 (1.5 percent), when John F. Kennedy narrowly defeated Richard Nixon.
- 1992 (2.8 percent), when Bill Clinton defeated George Bush Sr. and concerns about the economy lingered through election day.

So, given the evidence just presented, it appears that we have discovered the second most bullish phase in the 48-month election cycle. As the presidential race plays out and the winner becomes evident, a great uncertainty is removed from the marketplace and businesses as well as investors can get on with planning how they will deal with whatever changes they deem likely—or not likely—to occur as the next administration takes office or as the old administration carries on, in the case of an incumbent victory. As we have seen, this scenario plays out during the final seven months of the election year. Now let's combine our two favorable time periods in the election cycle to see what kind of results we can generate.

21 Bullish Months Combined

So far in this chapter, we have established that there are (at least) two distinct and identifiable favorable time frames within the 48-month election cycle. The 14-month period that begins on October 1 of the midterm election year and runs through December 31 of the preelection year—excluding October of the preelection year—has shown a gain 19 times in a row since 1933. The average gain in this time frame has been a well-above-average 27.7 percent. We have also seen that the last seven months of the election year has shown a strong tendency to witness a stock market advance. Since 1900, 22 of 27 election years have seen the Dow advance during the final seven months of the year. So, the next step is to consider what our results would look like if we broke each 48-month election cycle into two separate periods—the 21 favorable months, comprising the 14-month plus 7-month periods just described—versus the other, nonfavorable 27 months.

Table 7.13 lays out the favorable and nonfavorable months of each election cycle.

As you can see in Table 7.13, following the end of an election year, the status is nonfavorable for the next 21 months. Then, 21 of the 27 months remaining in that 48-month election cycle are favorable. So, what would the results look like if someone invested solely following this table? Let's take a look.

Figure 7.14 displays the growth of $1,000 invested in the Dow only during the 21 favorable months listed in Table 7.13 during each 48-month election cycle, using a starting date of December 31, 1933.

The results displayed in Figure 7.14 are quite compelling. Although the sharp upward slope of the equity curve masks that there were meaningful drawdowns along the way, the end result is difficult to quibble with. All told—and excluding any interest that could have been earned during the 27 months spent in cash every four years—$1,000 invested in the Dow only during the 21 favorable months of each election cycle would have grown to $344,142 by December 31, 2007.

As with much of the data discussed in this book, although something may seem good at face value, you still need to compare it to something else to gain some perspective. So, now let's look at how investors would have fared if they had skipped the 21 favorable months every four years and invested only during the 27 nonfavorable months of the election cycle. Figure 7.15 displays these fairly dismal results.

Had investors been unfortunate enough to invest in the Dow only during the 27 unfavorable months in each election cycle since 1933, they would have been quite displeased with the results: $1,000 invested in this manner starting on December 31, 1933, would have shrunk to just $535 by

TABLE 7.13 48-Month Election Cycle Month by Month

Month No.	Year	Month	Status
1	Postelection	January	Nonfavorable
2	Postelection	February	Nonfavorable
3	Postelection	March	Nonfavorable
4	Postelection	April	Nonfavorable
5	Postelection	May	Nonfavorable
6	Postelection	June	Nonfavorable
7	Postelection	July	Nonfavorable
8	Postelection	August	Nonfavorable
9	Postelection	September	Nonfavorable
10	Postelection	October	Nonfavorable
11	Postelection	November	Nonfavorable
12	Postelection	December	Nonfavorable
13	Midterm	January	Nonfavorable
14	Midterm	February	Nonfavorable
15	Midterm	March	Nonfavorable
16	Midterm	April	Nonfavorable
17	Midterm	May	Nonfavorable
18	Midterm	June	Nonfavorable
19	Midterm	July	Nonfavorable
20	Midterm	August	Nonfavorable
21	Midterm	September	Nonfavorable
22	Midterm	October	Favorable
23	Midterm	November	Favorable
24	Midterm	December	Favorable
25	Preelection	January	Favorable
26	Preelection	February	Favorable
27	Preelection	March	Favorable
28	Preelection	April	Favorable
29	Preelection	May	Favorable
30	Preelection	June	Favorable
31	Preelection	July	Favorable
32	Preelection	August	Favorable
33	Preelection	September	Favorable
34	Preelection	October	Nonfavorable
35	Preelection	November	Favorable
36	Preelection	December	Favorable
37	Election	January	Nonfavorable
38	Election	February	Nonfavorable
39	Election	March	Nonfavorable
40	Election	April	Nonfavorable
41	Election	May	Nonfavorable
42	Election	June	Favorable

TABLE 7.13 (Continued)

Month No.	Year	Month	Status
43	Election	July	Favorable
44	Election	August	Favorable
45	Election	September	Favorable
46	Election	October	Favorable
47	Election	November	Favorable
48	Election	December	Favorable

December 31, 2007, a loss of 46.5 percent. As always, investors should note that even within unfavorable periods, there are times when the stock market can and will rally strongly. Still, for investors looking to maximize their profitability, the results suggest that they should be invested aggressively during the 21 favorable months and should be investing much more cautiously, if at all, during the 27 unfavorable months.

Let's put some numbers to these results to gain even greater perspective on the disparity of the results. Table 7.14 displays the performance during favorable versus unfavorable periods for each election cycle since the early 1930s.

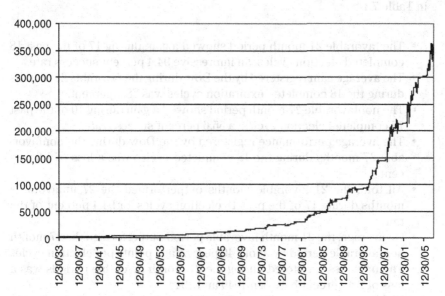

FIGURE 7.14 Growth of $1,000 invested in the Dow during the 21 favorable months of election cycle since Dec. 31, 1933

FIGURE 7.15 Growth of $1,000 invested in the Dow during the 27 nonfavorable months of election cycle since Dec. 31, 1933

Here are some facts and figures of note regarding the data that appears in Table 7.14:

- The favorable 21-month period showed a gain during 17 of the past 18 completed election cycles, an impressive 94.4 percent success rate.
- The average gain registered by the Dow during the favorable 21 months during the 18 completed expiration cycles was 38.5 percent.
- The nonfavorable 27-month period showed a gain during 10 of the past 18 completed election cycles, a 55.6 percent success rate.
- The average performance registered by the Dow during the nonfavorable 27 months during the 18 completed cycles was a loss of 1.6 percent.
- All told, the 21 favorable months outperformed the 27 unfavorable months during 17 of the past 18 election cycles, or 94.4 percent of the time.
- On average, the 21-month favorable period outperformed the 27-month nonfavorable period by about 40 percentage points per election cycle.
- The only loss registered during the 21-month favorable periods was a loss of 2.4 percent between 1940 and 1944.
- Eight times the 27-month nonfavorable period registered a net loss in excess of 14 percent.

TABLE 7.14 Election Cycle by Election Cycle (21 Favorable Months versus 27 Nonfavorable Months) since Dec. 31, 1933

Start Date	Start Year	End Date	End Year	21 Favorable Months Percentage +(−)	27 Nonfavorable months Percentage +(−)	Percentage Difference +(−)
Dec. 31	1933	Dec. 31	1936	73.1	4.0	69.1
Dec. 31	1936	Dec. 31	1940	20.4	(39.4)	59.8
Dec. 31	1940	Dec. 31	1944	35.2	(14.1)	49.2
Dec. 31	1944	Dec. 31	1948	(2.4)	22.1	(24.5)
Dec. 31	1948	Dec. 31	1952	38.5	20.6	17.8
Dec. 31	1952	Dec. 31	1956	48.5	17.8	30.7
Dec. 31	1956	Dec. 31	1960	25.6	0.4	25.2
Dec. 31	1960	Dec. 31	1964	39.3	4.2	35.1
Dec. 31	1964	Dec. 31	1968	32.2	(16.5)	48.7
Dec. 31	1968	Dec. 31	1972	34.4	(17.7)	52.1
Dec. 31	1972	Dec. 31	1976	40.3	(28.2)	68.5
Dec. 31	1976	Dec. 31	1980	20.9	(18.8)	39.8
Dec. 31	1980	Dec. 31	1984	58.6	(18.9)	77.5
Dec. 31	1984	Dec. 31	1988	56.0	17.4	38.7
Dec. 31	1988	Dec. 31	1992	26.3	23.3	2.9
Dec. 31	1992	Dec. 31	1996	56.8	27.5	29.3
Dec. 31	1996	Dec. 31	2000	48.1	15.5	32.6
Dec. 31	2000	Dec. 31	2004	41.0	(27.5)	68.6
Dec. 31	2004	Dec. 31	2008			

To reiterate, the recommendation is not that investors bury their heads in the sand and invest only during 21 of every 48 months and completely sit out the other 27 months. The recommendation is that during the 21 favorable months, investors should act aggressively to maximize profit potential and give the bullish case every benefit of the doubt, regardless of the headlines of the day. Likewise, investors might be in the stock market during the 27 nonfavorable months, but they should do so much more conservatively and cautiously, and they should consider exiting the market if the bearish evidence begins to mount.

TWO OTHER PATTERNS IN THE ELECTION CYCLE

As we have already seen, there are some powerful macroforces at work in the stock market during the 48-month election cycle. We have also detailed a simple way to know when to maximize profit potential and when to limit risk. Further study, however, reveals that there are other opportunities available to investors during the election cycle.

Specifically, we will look at one short-term trend, which lasts only about eight trading days out of every four years, and one multimonth trend that lasts for five months within each election cycle. Although these two periods differ in terms of length, and both take place during the 21 favorable months that we have already detailed, they are worth examining more closely because they can provide the confidence to trade more aggressively during times that are more likely to witness favorable stock market performance.

Midterm Election Short-Term Trade

A unique opportunity that may appeal mostly to short-term traders occurs right around the time of the midterm election. Two years after each presidential election, many states hold elections for senators or congressional representatives in districts where the incumbent's term is coming to an end. The midterm election takes place on the first Tuesday of November two years after the last presidential election. This trading opportunity is easily defined and involves only a handful of trading days.

The midterm election trade involves being in the market during the five trading days prior to the midterm election, the three trading days after the midterm election, and the day of the midterm election itself if the market is open. Prior to 1970, the stock market was closed on midterm election days. Since then, the stock market has been open on this day, so the net effect is that this time frame has gone from eight trading days to nine trading days, to include the five trading days prior, the three trading days after, and the election day itself. As we'll see in a moment, the market has demonstrated a tendency to behave favorably during this time frame.

Table 7.15 displays the percentage gain or loss achieved by the Dow during this time frame during every midterm election year starting in 1934.

Figure 7.16 displays the growth of $1,000 invested during this short-term time frame once every four years.

The results shown in Table 7.15 and Figure 7.16 are tremendously consistent. To illustrate, consider the following performance numbers:

- This pre- and postelection period has generated a profit in 17 of 19 instances, or 89.5 percent of the time.
- The average gain achieved was 3.0 percent (remember that these returns are generated in just eight or nine trading days).

TABLE 7.15	Dow Performance form 5 Days before to 3 Days after Each Midterm Election since 1934

Midterm Election Year	Midterm Election Short-Term Trade Percentage +(−)
1934	6.4
1938	4.6
1942	2.0
1946	4.0
1950	1.9
1954	2.7
1958	3.6
1962	6.3
1966	1.5
1970	2.1
1974	5.3
1978	(0.6)
1982	5.7
1986	2.4
1990	2.4
1994	(1.2)
1998	6.4
2002	2.0
2006	0.2
2010	?
Average	**3.0**
No. times up	**17**
No. times down	**2**

- The average daily gain during these pre- and postelection trading days was 0.00355 percent, or an amazing 144.3 percent on an annualized basis. Clearly, although it can be argued that we could do with fewer politicians, what we could really use is more elections!

From a practical standpoint, one thing to consider is that if investors were investing on the basis of the 21 favorable months, they would already be in the market when this short-term midterm election trading opportunity occurred. Likewise, although the returns achieved during this time frame have far surpassed average market performance, this does not amount to much of a stand-alone strategy. In other words, it would make no sense to invest only during these eight or nine days every four years and then spend the rest of the time in cash. Although the returns

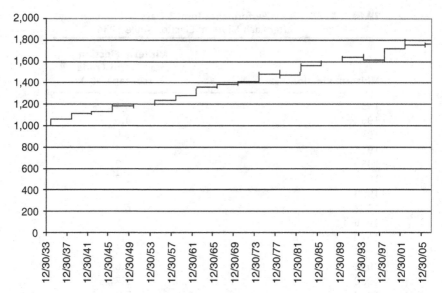

FIGURE 7.16 Growth of $1,000 invested in the Dow starting five days before and extending three days after each midterm election since 1934

are great on an annualized basis, in terms of total return investors can do far better by being in the market more often. Given these realities, one thing that aggressive investors might consider, especially if they are already in the market on these days anyway, is using leverage during these days to maximize the potential returns. This can help maximize the gains typically experienced during this bullish time while increasing risk only for a small number of trading days, which in turn can increase profitability exponentially over the long run.

March through July of a Preelection Year

Another period within the election cycle that has demonstrated a tendency toward favorable stock market performance occurs between March 1 and the end of July during preelection years. Alert readers will recognize that this period already falls within the 21 favorable months that I detailed earlier. So, what is the point of highlighting something that has already been highlighted? Again, the primary purpose of the material in this book is to give investors the knowledge regarding those periods that offer the greatest opportunity for profit. Therefore, an investor may consider investing more aggressively during this five-month period in an attempt to maximize profitability. One possibility is the use of leverage. In other words, investors might increase their exposure in the market by a factor of two to one.

TABLE 7.16 Dow Performance between the End of February and the End of July during Preelection Years since 1933

Preelection Year	Preelection: March–July Percentage +(−)
1935	23.3
1939	(2.7)
1943	4.5
1947	2.4
1951	2.3
1955	13.1
1959	11.8
1963	4.9
1967	7.7
1971	(2.3)
1975	12.5
1979	4.6
1983	7.8
1987	15.7
1991	4.9
1995	17.4
1999	14.5
2003	17.0
2007	7.7
Average	**8.8**
No. of times up	**17**
No. of times down	**2**

In this case, if the Dow advances 1 percent, the investor stands to make 2 percent, a 10 percent gain by the Dow becomes a 20 percent gain for the leveraged investor, and so on.

Table 7.16 displays the performance of the Dow (without leverage) during this favorable five-month period since 1935.

Figure 7.17 displays the growth of $1,000 invested only during this five-month period every four years.

Here are some important performance facts and figures from Table 7.14:

- This favorable 5-month period showed a gain during 17 of the last 19 completed election cycles, an impressive 89.5 percent success rate.
- The average gain registered by the Dow during this favorable 5-month period was +8.8 percent. The 17 winning periods averaged a gain of +10.1 percent. The two losing periods averaged a loss of −2.5 percent.

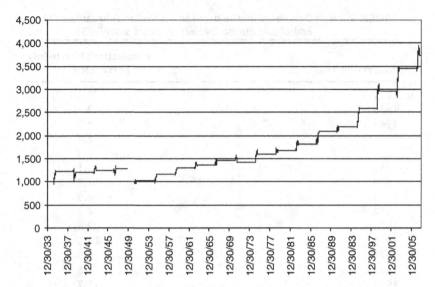

FIGURE 7.17 Growth of $1,000 invested in the Dow only between March 1 and July 31 of preelection years since 1933

- The annualized rate of return during this 5-month period was +21.6 percent.
- The annualized rate of return during all other trading days was +6.2 percent.

Figure 7.18 shows the Dow performance between February 2007 and August 2007.

THE ULTIMATE ELECTION CYCLE SYSTEM

Now that we have identified a number of different favorable and typically less favorable time periods that fall within each 48-month election cycle, let's see if there is a way to put these trends together to create a comprehensive ultimate election cycle system (UECS). Here are the rules that we will use in this test:

- If we are within five trading days before or three trading days after a midterm election, then we will buy the Dow using two-to-one leverage.
- If we are between the first trading day of March and the last trading day of July in a preelection year, then we will buy the Dow using two-to-one leverage.

INDU   7/31/07   O:13,360.66 H:13,498.53 L:13,199.79 C:13,211.99 Chg:-146.32 Cp:- ☐ Show Last

Dow Jones Industrial Average - Daily Bar Chart

+7.7%

FIGURE 7.18 Dow performance between Feb. 28, 2007, and Aug. 31, 2007

Otherwise, we will be long the Dow with no leverage between the following:

- October 1 of the midterm year and September 30 of the preelection year.
- November 1 of the preelection year and December 31 of the preelection year.
- June 1 and December 31 of the election year.
- January 1 and December 31 of a postelection year that ends in 5 (e.g., 1945, 1965, 1985, 2005).

Under any other circumstance, we will be in cash. For the purpose of this test, we will assume a nominal interest rate of 1 percent per year. Table 7.17 displays the annual results generated by the UECS.

Here are some important performance numbers from Table 7.17 regarding the UECS:

- A buy-and-hold approach showed a profit during 51 calendar years.
- The UECS showed a profit during 67 calendar years.
- A buy-and-hold approach showed a loss during 23 calendar years.

TABLE 7.17 UECS Results

Year	UECS	Buy/Hold	UECS-Buy/Hold	UECS $1,000	Buy/Hold $1000
1934	20.5	4.1	16.4	1,205	1,041
1935	59.7	38.5	21.2	1,925	1,443
1936	18.4	24.8	(6.4)	2,280	1,801
1937	1.2	(32.8)	34.0	2,307	1,210
1938	15.4	28.1	(12.6)	2,663	1,549
1939	(6.8)	(2.9)	(3.9)	2,482	1,504
1940	13.4	(12.7)	26.1	2,814	1,313
1941	1.2	(15.4)	16.6	2,848	1,111
1942	12.6	7.6	5.0	3,207	1,195
1943	20.0	13.8	6.2	3,847	1,360
1944	7.6	12.1	(4.5)	4,140	1,525
1945	26.6	26.6	0.0	5,244	1,931
1946	7.5	(8.1)	15.7	5,638	1,774
1947	1.0	2.2	(1.2)	5,695	1,813
1948	(6.6)	(2.1)	(4.5)	5,320	1,775
1949	1.1	12.9	(11.7)	5,381	2,003
1950	6.8	17.6	(10.9)	5,745	2,356
1951	20.5	14.4	6.1	6,922	2,695
1952	11.6	8.4	3.2	7,722	2,922
1953	1.0	(3.8)	4.8	7,800	2,812
1954	16.0	44.0	(27.9)	9,050	4,048
1955	39.5	20.8	18.7	12,625	4,889
1956	4.9	2.3	2.7	13,246	5,000
1957	1.0	(12.8)	13.8	13,381	4,361
1958	14.5	34.0	(19.5)	15,317	5,842
1959	26.9	16.4	10.5	19,432	6,800
1960	(1.1)	(9.3)	8.2	19,213	6,165
1961	1.0	18.7	(17.7)	19,406	7,319
1962	20.6	(10.8)	31.4	23,398	6,528
1963	18.9	17.0	1.9	27,827	7,637
1964	7.0	14.6	(7.6)	29,768	8,750
1965	10.9	10.9	0.0	33,007	9,702
1966	3.8	(18.9)	22.7	34,247	7,865
1967	30.3	15.2	15.1	44,622	9,060
1968	5.4	4.3	1.1	47,038	9,447
1969	1.0	(15.2)	16.2	47,511	8,012
1970	13.4	4.8	8.6	53,870	8,398
1971	9.3	6.1	3.2	58,888	8,911
1972	6.6	14.6	(8.0)	62,786	10,210
1973	1.0	(16.6)	17.6	63,422	8,517
1974	7.2	(27.6)	34.8	67,984	6,169
1975	46.1	38.3	7.8	99,358	8,533

TABLE 7.17 (*Continued*)

Year	UECS	Buy/Hold	UECS-Buy/Hold	UECS $1,000	Buy/Hold $1000
1976	3.4	17.9	(14.4)	102,782	10,057
1977	1.0	(17.3)	18.3	103,823	8,320
1978	(7.2)	(3.1)	(4.0)	96,383	8,058
1979	17.0	4.2	12.8	112,778	8,396
1980	13.8	14.9	(1.2)	128,313	9,650
1981	1.0	(9.2)	10.2	129,618	8,759
1982	24.0	19.6	4.4	160,751	10,476
1983	29.5	20.3	9.2	208,197	12,599
1984	10.1	(3.7)	13.9	229,268	12,128
1985	27.7	27.7	0.0	292,680	15,482
1986	10.7	22.6	(11.9)	323,890	18,978
1987	52.5	2.3	50.2	493,882	19,408
1988	7.2	11.8	(4.6)	529,503	21,707
1989	1.0	27.0	(25.9)	534,867	27,560
1990	10.7	(4.3)	15.0	592,050	26,363
1991	23.3	20.3	3.0	730,093	31,720
1992	(2.4)	4.2	(6.6)	712,465	33,044
1993	1.0	13.7	(12.7)	719,712	37,578
1994	(0.7)	2.1	(2.9)	714,406	38,383
1995	57.3	33.5	23.9	1,123,785	51,222
1996	14.8	26.0	(11.3)	1,289,567	64,547
1997	1.0	22.6	(21.6)	1,302,683	79,162
1998	25.4	16.1	9.3	1,634,075	91,906
1999	36.8	25.2	11.6	2,235,929	115,086
2000	2.9	(6.2)	9.1	2,301,693	107,976
2001	1.0	(7.1)	8.1	2,324,639	100,315
2002	15.5	(14.8)	30.3	2,684,161	85,457
2003	33.7	22.5	11.2	3,588,654	104,644
2004	6.3	3.1	3.1	3,813,755	107,938
2005	(0.6)	(0.6)	0.0	3,790,585	107,282
2006	7.7	16.3	(8.6)	4,082,259	124,756
2007	12.5	5.2	7.3	4,590,746	131,232
Average	**12.9**	**8.1**	**4.8**		

- The UECS showed a loss during only seven calendar years.
- The UECS enjoyed 16 more profitable calendar years than a buy-and-hold approach.
- The UECS showed a greater calendar-year profit than a buy-and-hold approach 47 times.
- A buy-and-hold approach showed a greater calendar-year profit than the UECS 27 times.

On a calendar year basis, the UECS beat a buy-and-hold approach 60 percent of the time; thus, investors using the UECS should not expect to beat the market every year. Also, consider the capital-preservation instincts of the UECS:

- During the 51 calendar years when the buy-and-hold approach showed a profit, the UECS outperformed the buy-and-hold approach 27 times, underperformed 22 times, and generated the same return 2 times.
- During the 23 calendar years when the buy-and-hold approach showed a loss, the UECS outperformed the buy-and-hold approach 20 times and underperformed only 3 times.
- During the 23 calendar years when the buy-and-hold approach showed a loss, the UECS showed a calendar-year gain 18 times and suffered a loss only 5 times.

This ability to weather down years for the stock market is something that can give investors a great deal of confidence when it comes to sticking to a particular investment over the long haul. This is key. For, the ultimate goal of many investors is to make money every single year and to beat the market every year in the process, the reality is that this goal is unrealistic for the vast majority of investors. The good news, however, is that by adopting a well-thought-out approach and sticking to it over the long haul, any investor can achieve the more realistic—and ultimately more useful—goal of amassing great wealth. The UECS and all of the election cycle trends detailed in this chapter may help you to achieve that goal.

SUMMING UP

Government policies, government action (or inaction, as the case may be), the economy, and the stock market are all intertwined. Government policies and actions that have a positive effect on the economy will ultimately have a positive effect on the stock market. Conversely, government policies that have a negative effect on the economy will ultimately have a negative effect on the stock market. This is not to say that the government controls the economy or the stock market. Far from it. Nevertheless, the actions of government can exert a great deal of influence over the state of the economy, and the stock market ultimately fluctuates with the overall state of economic affairs and investors' expectations for the future state of the economy. Low interest rates, low inflation, and low taxes all allow more money to be put to work in the economy and typically lead to economic growth, corporate profits, and a rising economy. All of these trends favorably influence the stock market. Conversely, high interest rates, rising inflation, and high taxes drain money from the economy and typically lead to slower economic growth at best or something far inferior at worst. Given the potential ability of government policy to influence the overall economy, and, in turn, the standard of living for millions of people, it makes a certain amount of sense that there is some correlation or interplay between key elections and the stock market. As such, it should not surprise anyone to learn that there is an almost-rhythmic nature to the stock market as presidential elections approach and recede.

In the first part of this chapter, we looked at each of the four years of each election cycle on an individual basis. What we saw was unmistakable. The postelection year and the midterm year—on a calendar basis—are middling performers at best. Since the mid-1930s, the postelection year has been up only 8 of 18 times and the midterm year has been up 12 of 19 times. Taken together, this two-year period has shown a gain during 11 of the last 18 election cycles, with an average gain of 12.7 percent. Although this does not sound too terrible at first blush, remember that over the past 100-plus years, the stock market has averaged about a 9 percent return per year. On that basis, any two-year period that does not show a gain of at least 18 to 19 percent is inferior. So, we can state that the postelection and midterm years have averaged almost one-third less than the overall long-term average.

On the flip side, the preelection and election years—both individually and collectively—have shown a strong tendency toward stock market strength. The preelection year has been the start, showing a gain during 18 of the last 19 election cycles, with an average gain of 15 percent. The election year has also tended to be strong, sporting gains during 13 of the last 18 election cycles. As a single two-year period, the preelection and election year have shown a gain 17 of 18 times, with a powerful two-year average gain in excess of 28 percent. The theory behind all of this is that politicians will do everything they can to get the economy moving in the right direction as the next major election approaches, and they will attempt to get the dirty work out of the way as early as possible in a new term. Whether this theory is actually true is somewhat irrelevant. The consistency of the trends in the stock market is what is most germane to our discussion.

After looking at things on a calendar-year basis, we narrowed things down by looking at market performance month by month. In that analysis we found several periods that have consistently captured the bulk of all stock market gains made in the past 70-plus years. Starting with research from Dick Stoken's book *Stock Market Timing*, we highlighted a 12-month and a 2-month period between the fourth quarter of the midterm election year and the end of the preelection year. When combined as a 14-month period, this time frame has seen the Dow advance 19 times without a single loss. The average cumulative gain during this period was in excess of 27 percent, and the average annualized gain was roughly 23 percent. By way of comparison, all other trading days combined generated an average annualized return of roughly 2 percent.

That was followed by a discussion of another favorable seven-month period in the election year. The premise behind this time frame is that at some point during a presidential election year, a great uncertainty—the identity of the next president—is lifted from the market place. This lifting removes a cloud from the marketplace and allows stock prices to rise. The only question is at what point in time this lifting takes place. Nevertheless, it invariably occurs some time during the last seven months of the election year. This period has seen the Dow post a gain 22 times and a loss only 5 times during the past century, with an average seven-month gain of 10.5 percent.

The next step was to combine the 14- and 7-month favorable periods to create two distinct periods in each election cycle: 21 favorable months and 27 unfavorable months. The difference in the performance of the stock market between these two periods could hardly be starker. The favorable 21-month period showed a gain during 17 of the last 18 election cycles, or 94 percent of the time, with an average gain of 38 percent. The 27 unfavorable months showed a gain during only 10 of the last 18 election cycles and registered an average loss of 1.6 percent. So, maybe it's hard to believe but true that investors could have sat out of the stock market during the same 27 months of each election cycle over the past 70-plus years—or about 56 percent of the time—and vastly outperformed a buy-and-hold approach. With the usual caveat that there is no guarantee that this trend will continue, for now investors should remain aware of where we are in terms of the 48-month election cycle and adjust their aggression or caution accordingly.

Finally, we also discussed a couple of shorter-term time frames that have shown a strong tendency toward bullish stock market price action. The first period encompasses the five trading days before and the three trading days after the midterm election. As Table 7.15 shows, this period has seen the Dow advance during 16 of the past 17 midterm elections (since 1934), with an average gain of 3 percent. The other period lasted from the end of February through the end of July of the preelection year. Although this period falls within the 21 favorable months already reviewed, it rates a special mention as a time for investors to consider pursuing particularly aggressive investment strategies. Since 1935, this period has seen the Dow register a gain 17 of 19 times, with an average gain of about 9 percent.

I closed this chapter with the UECS. It is not recommended that investors adopt this method as their sole means for determining when to be in or out of the stock market. Nevertheless, the UECS does point out clearly the potential benefits from following an objective set of trading rules and adopting a long-term mind-set.

The bottom line is simple: There is something to the repetitive nature of the election cycle. Investors would be wise to pay attention and take advantage of the periods that offer great opportunities, and to act to preserve capital when the trends are not so favorable.

CHAPTER 8

Sell in May and Go Away

W ouldn't it be something if your boss told you that you could work only about six months out of the year, say, from late fall into the middle of spring, then take the rest of the year off and still make the same money? What if your boss sweetened the pot and said that if you took the time off you would actually make more money than if you worked 12 full months every year? Wouldn't you jump at that offer? Well, your boss may not give you that opportunity, but the stock market might.

The good news is that over nearly the past 60 years, the stock market has been rewarding investors for taking some time off. And the better news is that it has involved taking the same time off every year, so there is no guesswork involved. This trend was first recognized and popularized by Yale Hirsch, of *The Stock Trader's Almanac* fame. Specifically, since about 1950, the stock market has performed immensely better between the first trading day of November and the third trading day of the following May than it has during the rest of the year. The reasons for this may be many, but I will put forward one possible explanation in particular.

After World War II ended, millions of veterans came home from the war, married, and began starting families and settling down. In many homes, the father worked and the mother stayed home to raise the kids. Millions of homes were built and countless families settled into fairly "normal" day-to-day and year-to-year routines. One of the things that often became part of this routine was the summer vacation. Because air travel was much less common in those days, at least once a year—almost invariably during the summer—Dad would pack up the car and the family would drive to some vacation destination, near or far. This ritual became part of the yearly routine for millions of families. And when the children in those families—better known as baby boomers—grew up, they carried on this tradition with their families. The tradition of the summer vacation continues unabated to this day. So, let's raise an outlandish question. If so many people take time off from all of their cares and worries—presumably including their stock market investments—during the summer, should we be surprised to find out that the stock market, in essence, takes the summer off too?

Some people will find this to be a fairly weak theory and one that should not have a direct bearing on the performance of something as expansive as the stock market. Perhaps they are correct and my vacation theory is off base. But two facts remain. First, people seem to find more ways to distract themselves during the summer months. With the kids out of school, the aforementioned vacations, outdoor activities, and so on, there is an overall tendency to devote less time to any business at hand. Second, the stock market has demonstrated an unquestionable tendency to perform more poorly in the late spring through the mid-to-late fall months than it does during the rest of the year. Is this merely a coincidence? Let's look at some results and you can decide for yourself.

NOVEMBER TO MAY

First, let's look at the aforementioned November-to-May time period that begins on November 1 of each year (technically an investor would buy at the close on October 31 of each year) and extends through the close of trading on the third trading day of the following May. We will designate this as the bullish period. The rest of the year is the bearish period. As a result, our trading rules are quite simple:

- Buy the Dow at the close of trading on the last trading day of October.
- Sell the Dow and move to cash at the close of trading on the third trading day in the month of May in the following year.
- Remain in cash until the close of the last trading day of October, then repeat.

This is another idea that was first popularized by Yale Hirsch. As with many of the methods presented in this book, this one sounds just a little too easy to be for real. But, by now, you probably recognize the value of at least considering the results first and then deciding for yourself whether you can use the method in your own investment strategy. As always, the things to look for are consistently profitable results and as little

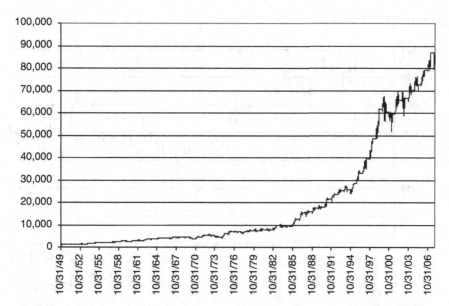

FIGURE 8.1 Growth of $1,000 invested in the Dow only between November 1 and third trading day of the following May since Oct. 31, 1949

downside volatility as possible. So, how does the November-to-May method fare? Let's take a look at the results.

Figure 8.1 displays the growth of $1,000 invested in the Dow only between the first of November each year and the third trading day of the following May, starting on October 31, 1949, through December 31, 2007.

This method is not without it's potential flaws. Figure 8.1 reveals a number of periods of downside volatility along the way. Nevertheless, by now you should understand that no method can be expected to be perfect and that the main focus should be on the size and consistency of the profit generated. On that basis, the performance in Figure 8.1 looks pretty good. Of course, we still need to compare this performance with something else to be able to assess whether the performance is of note. To accomplish this, let's look at the results generated by investing in the Dow only between the close of the third trading day of May and the last trading day of the following October. These results are displayed in Figure 8.2.

As you can see, the performance of the stock market from November to May has been vastly superior to the results generated during the remainder of the year. The numbers that follow only serve to confirm this assertion:

- The average daily gain from November to May was 0.000628 percent.
- The average daily gain during all other trading days was 0.000023 percent.

FIGURE 8.2 Growth of $1,000 invested in the Dow only between third trading day of following May and the last trading day of October since Oct. 31, 1949

- The average daily gain from November to May was 27.4 times higher than the average daily gain during all other trading days.
- The annualized rate of return during this bullish 6 months and 3 days period was 17.1 percent.
- The annualized rate of return during all other trading days was just 0.6 percent.
- A $1,000 investment only during the November-to-May bullish period from October 31, 1949, through December 31, 2007, grew to $82,666.
- A $1,000 investment during all other days in the May to October bearish period shrank to $847 during the same time.
- The Dow posted a gain during 47 of 58 November-to-May periods, 81 percent of the time.
- The Dow posted a gain during only 33 of 58 May-to-October periods, or 57 percent of the time.
- The November-to-May period outperformed the subsequent May-to-October period 45 of 58 times, or 78 percent of the time.

Table 8.1 displays the year-by-year results of both the bullish November-to-May period and the bearish May-to-October period.

TABLE 8.1	Dow Performance November 1 through Third Trading Day of May versus Fourth Trading Day of May through October 31 (through December 31, 2007)

Start Bullish	Dow	Percent- age Gain	$1,000	Start Bearish Period (May)	Dow	Percent- age Gain	$1,000	Bullish Period Percentage Gain Minus Bearish Period Percentage Gain
1949	189.54	14.1	1,141	1950	216.26	4.0	1,040	10.1
1950	225.01	16.9	1,334	1951	263.13	(0.3)	1,037	17.2
1951	262.35	(0.7)	1,325	1952	260.55	3.3	1,072	(4.0)
1952	269.23	3.3	1,369	1953	278.22	(0.9)	1,063	4.2
1953	275.81	15.3	1,578	1954	317.93	10.8	1,177	4.5
1954	352.14	20.0	1,894	1955	422.54	7.7	1,267	12.3
1955	454.87	13.0	2,140	1956	514.03	(6.6)	1,183	19.7
1956	479.85	3.7	2,219	1957	497.54	(11.4)	1,048	15.0
1957	441.04	4.6	2,320	1958	461.12	17.8	1,235	(13.3)
1958	543.22	15.2	2,674	1959	625.90	3.3	1,276	11.9
1959	646.6	(5.5)	2,526	1960	610.99	(5.0)	1,212	(0.5)
1960	580.36	18.7	2,999	1961	688.90	2.2	1,238	16.5
1961	703.92	(4.0)	2,878	1962	675.49	(12.7)	1,081	8.7
1962	589.77	21.8	3,504	1963	718.08	5.2	1,137	16.6
1963	755.23	9.5	3,835	1964	826.63	5.6	1,201	3.8
1964	873.08	6.8	4,095	1965	932.22	3.1	1,238	3.7
1965	960.82	(4.8)	3,899	1966	914.86	(11.8)	1,092	7.0
1966	807.07	11.1	4,332	1967	896.77	(1.9)	1,071	13.0
1967	879.74	4.5	4,527	1968	919.21	3.6	1,110	0.9
1968	952.39	0.7	4,558	1969	958.95	(10.7)	991	11.4
1969	855.99	(17.1)	3,779	1970	709.74	6.5	1,055	(23.5)
1970	755.61	24.1	4,688	1971	937.39	(10.5)	944	34.6
1971	839	11.3	5,216	1972	933.47	2.4	967	8.9
1972	955.52	(0.2)	5,207	1973	953.87	0.3	969	(0.5)
1973	956.58	(11.6)	4,605	1974	845.90	(21.3)	763	9.8
1974	665.52	28.6	5,920	1975	855.60	(2.3)	745	30.8
1975	836.04	18.0	6,985	1976	986.46	(2.2)	729	20.2
1976	964.93	(2.5)	6,809	1977	940.72	(13.0)	634	10.5
1977	818.35	1.3	6,897	1978	828.83	(4.4)	606	5.7
1978	792.45	8.2	7,464	1979	857.59	(4.9)	577	13.1
1979	815.7	0.1	7,469	1980	816.30	13.3	653	(13.2)
1980	924.49	5.2	7,856	1981	972.44	(12.3)	573	17.5
1981	852.55	0.2	7,874	1982	854.45	16.1	665	(15.8)
1982	991.72	22.3	9,628	1983	1,212.65	1.0	671	21.2
1983	1,225.2	(3.6)	9,285	1984	1,181.53	2.2	686	(5.8)

(Continued)

TABLE 8.1   *(Continued)*

Start Bullish	Dow	Percent-age Gain	$1,000	Start Bearish Period (May)	Dow	Percent-age Gain	$1,000	Bullish Period Percentage Gain Minus Bearish Period Percentage Gain
1984	1,207.38	3.3	9,591	1985	1,247.24	10.2	756	(6.9)
1985	1,374.31	30.5	12,519	1986	1,793.77	4.7	791	25.8
1986	1,877.71	24.5	15,588	1987	2,338.07	(14.7)	675	39.3
1987	1,993.53	2.1	15,923	1988	2,036.31	5.5	712	(3.4)
1988	2,148.65	11.4	17,739	1989	2,393.70	10.5	787	0.9
1989	2,645.08	1.9	18,081	1990	2,696.17	(9.4)	713	11.3
1990	2,442.34	20.3	21,757	1991	2,938.86	4.4	744	15.9
1991	3,069.1	9.5	23,815	1992	3,359.40	(4.0)	715	13.4
1992	3,226.3	6.9	25,460	1993	3,449.10	6.7	763	0.2
1993	3,680.59	0.5	25,578	1994	3,697.75	5.7	806	(5.2)
1994	3,908.12	11.9	28,622	1995	4,373.15	8.7	877	3.2
1995	4,755.48	15.2	32,971	1996	5,478.03	10.1	965	5.1
1996	6,029.38	19.6	39,447	1997	7,213.68	3.2	995	16.5
1997	7,442.08	22.9	48,487	1998	9,147.57	(6.1)	935	29.0
1998	8,592.1	27.5	61,823	1999	10,955.41	(2.1)	916	29.6
1999	10,729.86	(2.3)	60,384	2000	10,480.13	4.7	959	(7.0)
2000	10,971.14	(1.6)	59,424	2001	10,796.65	(15.9)	806	14.4
2001	9,075.14	10.3	65,523	2002	10,006.63	(16.1)	676	26.3
2002	8,397.03	1.6	66,573	2003	8,531.57	14.9	777	(13.3)
2003	9,801.12	5.2	70,036	2004	10,310.95	(2.7)	755	8.0
2004	10,027.47	3.6	72,531	2005	10,384.64	0.5	759	3.0
2005	10,440.07	9.2	79,202	2006	11,400.28	6.0	805	3.2
2006	12,080.73	9.6	86,811	2007	13,241.38	5.2	847	4.4
2007	13,930.01	(4.8)	82,666	2008	13,264.82		847	(4.8)

One can debate the reasons for the vast difference in performance between these two periods. One can also argue, correctly, that there is no guarantee that the difference in performance between these two periods will continue to occur ad infinitum. The only thing that cannot be debated is that the November-to-May time frame has vastly and consistently outperformed the May-to-October time frame for almost 60 years. Although investors should not necessarily take this as a sign to blindly buy and hold during this period each year, the evidence strongly suggests that astute investors should give the bullish case the benefit of the doubt from November to May.

MACD as a Filter for November to May

The *Stock Trader's Almanac* first popularized the idea of filtering the standard November-to-May time frame using an objective indicator to effectively lengthen or shorten time spent in the stock market during this favorable time based on the action of the market itself. In other words, if the market is acting well prior to November 1, this new method might get in as much as a month earlier. Likewise, if the stock market is not acting well, this new method may not enter the stock market until sometime after November 1. On the selling side of the equation, if the stock market is acting poorly, this new method may exit the stock market as early as April 1 rather than rigidly wait for the third trading day of May. Of course, if the stock market is still acting well come the third trading day of May, this new method may stay in the market until well after that time to allow us to ride the rising wave.

The Hirsch Organization picked up on some groundbreaking research by Sy Harding, in his book titled *Riding the Bear, Street Smart Report*, in which he highlighted that the use of a single popular and widely known technical indicator can greatly enhance the long-term results generated using the standard November-to-May method just detailed. The indicator that is used as a filter for both the buy and sell signals generated by the November-to-May technique is most commonly known as the MACD (typically pronounced "Mac-D"), an acronym for "moving average convergence/divergence indicator." The MACD indicator was developed by Gerald Appel, author of a number of books on trading, including *Technical Analysis: Power Tools for Active Investors*, and editor of *Systems and Forecasts*. Before looking at how the MACD can be used as a filter for the November-to-May bullish time frame, let's first learn what MACD is and how it works.

WHAT IS MACD?

For those individuals who have never encountered technical indicators, the following discussion may be a bit, well, technical. For those well versed in the art of technical analysis, the explanation will be fairly simple and straightforward. No matter. In this day and age, few people who might choose to use the MACD—or most other technical indicators for that matter—calculate the indicator values by hand. Virtually any figuring or technical-analysis software package or financial web site that allows you to create a bar graph will calculate the MACD for you. Value can also be updated fairly easily in a spreadsheet. Still, to have confidence in a given indicator, it is important to understand how it works. So, let's take a look at the calculations and applications of the MACD indicator.

The MACD indicator basically consists of two simple lines calculated using three different exponential moving averages. The interplay between these averages can be used to make an objective determination as to whether a given security or index is in an uptrend or a downtrend. The first line (typically referred to as the "MACD line") is the difference between two exponential moving averages (the typical default is 12 and 26 periods) of closing prices. The second line—usually referred to as the signal line—is an exponential moving average of the first line. When the MACD line crosses above or below the signal line, it can indicate an impending or unfolding change in trend.

The MACD user typically has control to set the day window for each moving average to whatever length he or she chooses. As you might guess, shorter-term windows lead to more frequent signals, and longer-term averages lead to less frequent signals. The key is to find the right combination to capture the type of price movement you expect.

Figure 8.3 displays the stock price fluctuations for Apple (ticker symbol: APPL). On the left-hand side of the graph is a bullish signal marked by an up arrow as the faster MACD line crosses above the slower signal line. Over the next roughly two and a half months, AAPL advanced from the mid-130s to the mid-180s. The bullish trend remained in effect until

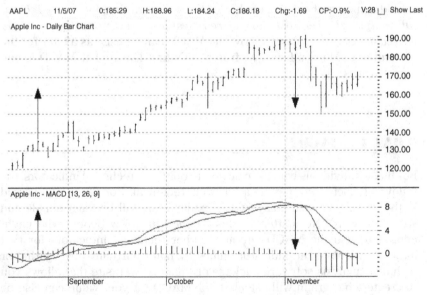

AAPL   11/5/07   O:185.29   H:188.96   L:184.24   C:186.18   Chg:-1.69   CP:-0.9%   V:28 |_| Show Last

FIGURE 8.3 Apple (AAPL) stock with MACD indicator applied

the first week of November, when the MACD line crossed back below the signal line—marked by a down arrow—thus generating a bearish signal. Within five trading days, AAPL stock had dropped back into the low 150s.

As with any indicator, there is never any guarantee that a particular bullish or bearish indication from the MACD will ultimately be followed by higher or lower prices. The primary thing to remember is that although many investors have successfully built MACD into a broader investment strategy, the use of MACD as a stand-alone signal-generating trading system is typically not recommended. With that in mind, let's look at how the MACD can be incorporated and used in combination with our November-to-May time frame.

USING MACD AS A FILTER

We will now look at how investors can use the MACD indicator to filter the standard November 1 buy signal and the standard third trading day of May sell signal to generate even more profitable trading signals. On the basis of Gerald Appel's recommendation, the Hirsch Organization suggests an 8-17-9 MACD to filter the buy signals and a 12-25-9 MACD to filter the sell signals. In other words, when looking for a buy signal we will look at the difference between the 8-day and the 17-day exponential moving averages of the Dow closing price each day. We will then look for that difference to be above or to move above its own nine-day exponential moving average. When looking for a sell signal we will look at the difference between the 12-day and the 25-day exponential moving averages of the Dow closing price each day. We will then look for that difference to be below or to move below its own nine-day exponential moving average.

Here are the official rules for combining MACD with the November-to-May method:

- Starting on October 1, a cross by the 8-17-9 MACD to the bullish side will generate a buy signal. If the 8-17-9 MACD is bullish as of October 1, then that will be our buy date. If not, we will continue to wait for the MACD to trigger an entry signal, even if that date does not occur until after the standard November 1 buy signal date.
- Starting on April 1, a cross by the 12-25-9 MACD to the bearish side will generate a sell signal. If the 12-25-9 MACD is bearish as of April 1, then that will be our sell date. If not, we will simply continue to wait for the MACD to trigger an exit signal before exiting the market, even if that date does not occur until after the standard third trading day of May sell signal date.

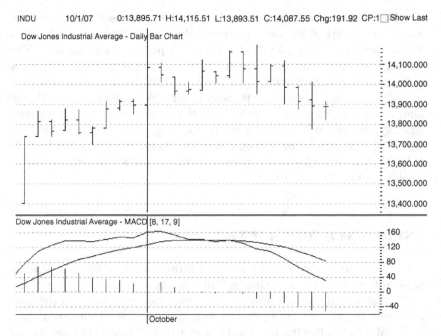

INDU   10/1/07   0:13,895.71 H:14,115.51 L:13,893.51 C:14,087.55 Chg:191.92 CP:1☐Show Last

FIGURE 8.4   Early November–May buy signal based on positive MACD

Figure 8.4 displays an example of early buy signal generated using the MACD indicator as a filter for the standard November-to-May time frame as just described. As you can see in Figure 8.4, as of October 1, the 8-17-9 MACD was bullish (i.e., the signal line was above the filter line). Thus, for 2007, the buy date for the filtered system was October 1. As a result, investors using this method would have entered the market after the October 1 buy signal rather than wait for the close of trading on October 31.

Now let's look at the sell side of the equation. Figure 8.5 displays a late sell generated using the MACD indicator as a filter for the standard November-to-May time frame that we just described. As you can see in Figure 8.5, as of the third trading day of May, the 12-25-9 MACD was still bullish. Thus, investors using this method would have waited for the signal line to drop below the filter line before exiting the market. This downside crossover occurred on May 14, 2007, thus generating a sell signal. As a result, for this particular year, the sell date for the filtered system was May 14.

Investors who choose to add this filter to their own buy and sell decision-making process need to adopt a realistic—and long-term—attitude. First, there is never any guarantee that the stock market will advance between November and May. As we saw in the previous section, this period has shown a gain 79 percent of the time since 1949. Nor is

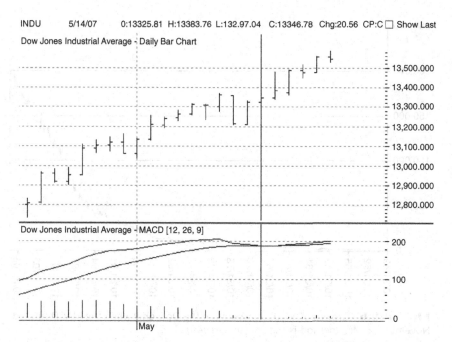

INDU   5/14/07   0:13325.81 H:13383.76 L:132.97.04 C:13346.78 Chg:20.56 CP:C ☐ Show Last

FIGURE 8.5 Late November–May sell signal based on MACD

there any guarantee that investors will not miss out on an uptrend in the stock market during the months that they are out of the market. In fact, the Dow has shown a gain 55 percent of the time between the third trading day of May and the end of October since 1949 (although the down periods are typically greater than the up periods). Likewise, there is never any guarantee from year to year that this year's filtered signals will be better than the standard approach from November 1 though the third trading day of May. Some years you may get in (or out) early and wish you had waited; other years you may get in (or out) late and wish you had done so sooner. That is just the way things work in the imperfect world of the stock market.

Nevertheless, adapting the MACD filter to use in conjunction with the standard November-to-May bullish period makes sense for two reasons:

1. On one level, adopting the MACD filter is intuitive. As we saw in Table 8.1, the stock market has inarguably shown a strong propensity to outperform from November to May. The standard approach involves the application of some very rigid rules (buy on October 31 and sell on the third trading day of May—period, no exceptions) and allows no flexibility at all given the actual price action of the stock market. Adopting the MACD as a filter allows investors to be a bit more flexible

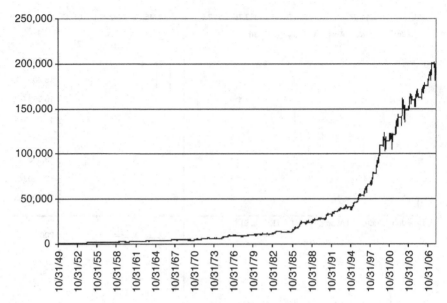

FIGURE 8.6 Growth of $1,000 invested in the Dow only when the MACD-filtered November-to-May method is bullish (since 1949)

about entering or exiting the stock market following the action of the market itself rather than essentially telling the market when it should or should not advance.

2. The performance results are displayed in Figure 8.6 and Table 8.2.

Figure 8.6 displays the growth of $1,000 invested in the Dow only when the MACD-filtered November-to-May method is bullish. As with all equity curves, there are inevitable periods of downside volatility. Figure 8.5 reveals that this one is no exception. Nevertheless, the kind of consistent equity growth that appears in Figure 8.6 is exactly the kind of real-world performance that most patient investors are looking for.

As impressive as the results displayed in Figure 8.6 are, they become even more striking when we look at the results generated when the MACD-filtered November-to-May method was not bullish. In other words, if we look at the action of the stock market during those times when this method was out of the market, we will find that investors could have missed out on a great deal of misery by moving to cash and avoiding the stock market altogether. Figure 8.7 displays the sorry results generated by being in the stock market only during those times when this timing method was on a sell signal.

TABLE 8.2 Year-by-Year Results for MACD-Filtered November-to-May Method (through Dec. 31, 2007)

Start Bullish Period (d-m-y)	Dow	Percentage Gain	$1,000	Start Bearish Period (d-m-y)	Dow	Percentage Gain	$1,000	Bullish Period Gain Minus Bearish Period Gain
31-Oct-49	189.54	12.9	1,129	22-Apr-50	213.90	7.3	1,073	5.5
14-Nov-50	229.54	13.3	1,279	10-May-51	260.07	0.1	1,074	13.2
13-Nov-51	260.41	1.9	1,304	5-Apr-52	265.44	1.4	1,089	0.5
31-Oct-52	269.23	2.1	1,330	30-Apr-53	274.75	0.2	1,091	1.9
23-Oct-53	275.34	17.1	1,559	14-May-54	322.50	13.5	1,239	3.6
5-Nov-54	366.00	16.3	1,813	29-Apr-55	425.65	7.7	1,334	8.6
21-Oct-55	458.47	13.1	2,050	9-Apr-56	518.52	(6.8)	1,243	19.9
8-Oct-56	483.38	2.8	2,107	9-May-57	496.76	(12.3)	1,090	15.1
29-Oct-57	435.76	4.9	2,210	16-May-58	457.10	17.3	1,279	(12.4)
6-Oct-58	536.29	16.7	2,579	5-May-59	625.90	1.6	1,300	15.1
6-Oct-59	636.06	(3.1)	2,499	22-Apr-60	616.32	(4.9)	1,236	1.8
7-Oct-60	586.42	16.9	2,920	21-Apr-61	685.26	2.9	1,272	14.0
9-Oct-61	705.42	(1.5)	2,876	23-Apr-62	694.61	(15.3)	1,077	13.8
10-Oct-62	588.14	22.4	3,519	1-May-63	719.67	4.3	1,123	18.1
18-Oct-63	750.60	9.6	3,858	14-Apr-64	822.95	6.3	1,194	3.3
9-Nov-64	874.57	6.6	4,112	19-May-65	932.12	2.6	1,225	4.0
26-Oct-65	956.32	(2.5)	4,007	2-May-66	931.95	(16.4)	1,024	13.9
17-Oct-66	778.89	14.3	4,579	12-May-67	890.03	(2.1)	1,003	16.4
21-Nov-67	870.95	5.5	4,830	8-May-68	918.86	3.4	1,037	2.1
14-Oct-68	949.96	0.2	4,840	21-May-69	951.78	(11.9)	914	12.1
16-Oct-69	838.77	(6.7)	4,516	15-Apr-70	782.60	(1.4)	901	(5.3)
6-Nov-70	771.97	20.8	5,454	3-May-71	932.41	(11.0)	802	31.8
29-Nov-71	829.73	15.4	6,294	24-Apr-72	957.48	(0.6)	797	16.0

(Continued)

TABLE 8.2 *(Continued)*

Start Bullish Period (d-m-y)	Dow	Percentage Gain	$1,000	Start Bearish Period (d-m-y)	Dow	Percentage Gain	$1,000	Bullish Period Gain Minus Bearish Period Gain
25-Oct.-72	951.38	(1.4)	6,204	26-Apr.-73	937.76	(11.0)	709	9.6
11-Dec.-73	834.18	0.1	6,207	26-Apr.-74	834.64	(22.4)	550	22.5
10-Oct.-74	648.08	28.2	7,959	1-May-75	830.96	0.1	551	28.1
17-Oct.-75	832.18	18.5	9,434	5-May-76	986.46	(3.4)	532	21.9
28-Oct.-76	952.63	(3.0)	9,148	27-Apr.-77	923.76	(11.4)	472	8.4
31-Oct.-77	818.35	0.5	9,190	9-May-78	822.07	(4.5)	450	5.0
14-Nov.-78	785.26	9.3	10,040	17-Apr.-79	857.93	(5.3)	426	14.6
5-Nov.-79	812.63	7.0	10,746	20-June-80	869.71	9.3	466	(2.3)
10-Oct.-80	950.68	4.7	11,253	1-May-81	995.59	(14.6)	398	19.3
14-Oct.-81	850.65	0.4	11,303	4-May-82	854.45	15.5	460	(15.1)
8-Oct.-82	986.85	23.5	13,960	13-May-83	1,218.75	2.5	471	21.0
21-Oct.-83	1,248.88	(7.3)	12,934	11-May-84	1,157.14	3.3	487	(10.6)
17-Oct.-84	1,195.89	3.9	13,433	1-May-85	1,242.05	7.0	521	(3.1)
4-Oct.-85	1,328.74	38.1	18,557	25-Apr.-86	1,835.57	(2.8)	506	40.9
6-Oct.-86	1,784.45	28.2	23,784	13-Apr.-87	2,287.07	(14.9)	431	43.1
4-Nov.-87	1,945.29	3.0	24,498	10-May-88	2,003.65	6.1	457	(3.1)
12-Oct.-88	2,126.24	11.8	27,381	8-May-89	2,376.47	9.8	502	2.0
14-Nov.-89	2,610.25	3.3	28,280	20-Apr.-90	2,695.95	(6.7)	468	10.0
22-Oct.-90	2,516.09	15.8	32,734	26-Apr.-91	2,912.38	4.8	491	11.0

17-Oct-91	3,053.00	11.3	36,429	11-May-92	3,397.58	(6.2)	460	17.5
21-Oct-92	3,187.10	6.6	38,844	26-Apr.-93	3,398.37	5.5	486	1.1
7-Oct-93	3,583.63	5.6	41,006	13-June-94	3,783.12	3.7	504	1.9
17-Oct-94	3,923.93	13.1	46,362	23-May-95	4,436.44	7.2	540	5.9
23-Oct-95	4,755.48	16.7	54,107	17-Apr.-96	5,549.93	9.2	590	7.5
17-Oct-96	6,059.20	21.9	65,323	27-May-97	7,383.41	3.6	611	18.3
18-Nov.-97	7,650.82	18.5	78,115	24-Apr.-98	9,064.62	(12.4)	535	30.9
13-Oct-98	7,938.14	39.9	109,300	13-May-99	11,107.19	(6.4)	501	46.3
20-Oct-99	10,392.36	5.1	114,887	13-Apr.-00	10,923.55	(6.0)	471	11.1
23-Oct-00	10,271.72	5.4	121,034	11-May-01	10,821.31	(17.3)	389	22.7
2-Oct-01	8,950.59	15.8	140,129	1-Apr.-02	10,362.70	(25.2)	291	41.0
2-Oct-02	7,755.61	6.0	148,544	10-Apr.-03	8,221.33	16.4	339	(10.4)
3-Oct-03	9,572.31	7.8	160,061	20-Apr.-04	10,314.50	(0.9)	336	8.7
4-Oct-04	10,216.54	1.8	163,003	1-Apr.-05	10,404.30	(0.5)	334	2.3
17-Oct-05	10,348.10	7.7	175,555	3-Apr.-06	11,144.94	4.7	350	3.0
2-Oct-06	11,670.35	14.4	200,773	14-May-07	13,346.78	5.6	370	8.8
1-Oct-07	14,087.55	(5.8)	189,048		13,264.82			

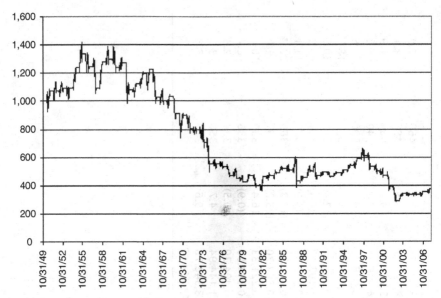

FIGURE 8.7 Growth of $1,000 invested in the Dow only when the MACD-filtered November-to-May method is bearish (since 1949)

As you can see in Figure 8.7, the performance of the stock market was, on the whole, quite dismal during bearish periods for the MACD-filtered November-to-May method. The bulk of virtually every major and minor bear market that has occurred over the past 57 years has taken place while this method was on a sell signal. All told, an initial $1,000 invested only during such bearish periods would have shrunk to just $371 by October of 2007. This stunning 62.9 percent loss of capital took place during a time when the Dow itself gained 6,037 percent on a buy-and-hold basis.

As always, it should be pointed out that Figure 8.7 reveals many occasions when the stock market was able to advance in the face of a bearish signal from this method. The market exhibited some strength during such bearish periods in the 1950s, 1980s, and 1990s. Nevertheless, one of the goals of this book is to help you train your mind to focus on the long run. The goal is not to beat the market year in and year out. The goal is to maximize profitability over the course of our investing lives. It would seem clear that this method may be of some use in achieving that goal.

Here are some important performance numbers for the MACD-filtered November-to-May method:

- The average daily gain during the MACD-filtered November-to-May period was 0.000714 percent.
- The average daily gain during all other trading days was a loss of 0.000095 percent.

- The annualized rate of return during this MACD-filtered bullish period was 19.7 percent.
- The annualized rate of return during all other trading days was −2.4 percent.
- A $1,000 investment only during the November-to-May bullish period grew to $189,048 by December 31, 2007.
- A $1,000 investment during all days not included in the November-to-May bullish period shrank to $370 during the same time
- The Dow posted a gain during 51 of the 58 completed MACD-filtered November-to-May periods, or 88 percent of the time.
- The Dow posted a gain during only 30 of the 58 completed MACD-filtered May-to-October periods, or 52 percent of the time.
- The MACD-filtered November-to-May period outperformed the subsequent MACD-filtered May-to-October period 50 of 58 times, or 86 percent of the time.

Table 8.2 displays the filtered buy and sell signals generated since 1949 using the methods just described. As you can see in Table 8.2, the net result of adding the MACD filter to the standard November-to-May time frame was that we more than doubled the gains generated using the standard November-to-May buy and sell rules.

One theme that I have touched on consistently throughout this book is, well, consistency. As I have tried to point out, no one should expect any given seasonal tendency, or combination of seasonal tendencies, to generate a profit every single year. That simply will not happen. In fact, this is why they are seasonal tendencies and not seasonal certainties.

Because long-term consistency is our key goal, then the five-year rolling rate of return is a good measure of how we are performing. Remember that the five-year rolling rate of return simply looks back over the preceding five years and tests whether a particular method made money or lost money and how much. This process is repeated every day or month or year, depending on how much data one wishes to interpret.

If we are using objective rules to identify bullish and bearish periods for the stock market, then our expectation is that the bullish periods will ultimately outperform the bearish periods over the long run. However, if we hope to stay with that method long enough to enjoy the expected long-term benefits, it is helpful if the bullish periods typically outperform the bearish period along the way. In other words, the more consistently that the bullish periods outperform the bearish periods, the more likely we are to retain the confidence needed to stay with our plan. Because of this, it makes sense to use rolling rates of return to analyze just how often, and by how much, our investment method outperforms the opposite approach to our trading method.

Table 8.3 displays the five-year rolling rates of return for the MACD-filtered November-to-May buy signals. The results in Table 8.3 compare the

TABLE 8.3 Five-Year Rolling Rates of Return

Start Year	End Year	Bullish Percentage +(−)	Bearish Percentage +(−)	Bullish Percentage Minus Bearish Percentage
1950	1955	60.5	24.4	36.1
1951	1956	60.3	15.8	44.4
1952	1957	61.6	0.2	61.4
1953	1958	66.1	17.3	48.8
1954	1959	65.5	5.0	60.5
1955	1960	37.9	(7.2)	45.1
1956	1961	42.5	2.4	40.0
1957	1962	36.5	(1.1)	37.6
1958	1963	59.2	(12.1)	71.3
1959	1964	49.6	(8.1)	57.7
1960	1965	64.5	(0.9)	65.4
1961	1966	37.2	(19.5)	56.7
1962	1967	59.2	(7.0)	66.2
1963	1968	37.3	(7.8)	45.1
1964	1969	25.5	(23.6)	49.0
1965	1970	9.8	(26.5)	36.3
1966	1971	36.1	(21.7)	57.9
1967	1972	37.5	(20.5)	58.0
1968	1973	28.4	(31.6)	60.1
1969	1974	28.3	(39.8)	68.0
1970	1975	76.2	(38.8)	115.1
1971	1976	73.0	(33.6)	106.6
1972	1977	45.4	(40.8)	86.2
1973	1978	48.1	(36.5)	84.6
1974	1979	61.8	(22.5)	84.2
1975	1980	35.0	(15.4)	50.4
1976	1981	19.3	(25.1)	44.4
1977	1982	23.6	(2.4)	26.0
1978	1983	51.9	4.7	47.2
1979	1984	28.8	14.2	14.6
1980	1985	25.0	11.8	13.2
1981	1986	64.9	27.2	37.7
1982	1987	110.4	(6.3)	116.7
1983	1988	75.5	(3.0)	78.5
1984	1989	111.7	3.1	108.6
1985	1990	110.5	(10.1)	120.6
1986	1991	76.4	(3.0)	79.4
1987	1992	53.2	7.0	46.2
1988	1993	58.6	6.3	52.3
1989	1994	49.8	0.4	49.4

(Continued)

TABLE 8.3 *(Continued)*

Start Year	End Year	Bullish Percentage +(−)	Bearish Percentage +(−)	Bullish Percentage Minus Bearish Percentage
1990	1995	63.9	15.3	48.6
1991	1996	65.3	20.1	45.2
1992	1997	81.0	32.6	48.4
1993	1998	101.1	10.1	91.0
1994	1999	166.5	(0.6)	167.2
1995	2000	147.8	(12.8)	160.6
1996	2001	123.7	(34.0)	157.7
1997	2002	112.5	(52.3)	164.8
1998	2003	90.2	(36.6)	126.7
1999	2004	46.4	(32.9)	79.3
2000	2005	41.9	(29.0)	70.9
2001	2006	45.0	(10.1)	55.2
2002	2007	43.3	26.8	16.5

five-year total return for the bullish periods to the five-year total return for the bearish periods. The goal is to see how often the bullish periods beat the bearish periods over a five-year period, as a measure of if, and by how much, the bullish periods outperform the bearish periods.

As you can see in Table 8.3, starting with the first look back in 1955, to date, there have not been any five-year periods in which the bearish periods outperformed the bullish periods as objectively identified using the MACD-filtered November-to-May method. This is a meaningful testament to the consistency of this method in identifying good times to be in, and out, of the stock market.

Given all that we have seen so far in this chapter, it seems safe to say that the adage "sell in May and go away" is actually quite well founded. We have seen so far that the November-to-May period has demonstrated a strong and consistent tendency to outperform the remaining year. In addition, by adding a relatively simple market-timing filter, we can improve the basic results by a meaningful amount. Granted, if the stock market is selling off sharply in the middle of February, it is difficult to take much comfort in the fact that the MACD-filtered November-to-May method is still bullish. But the one thing that all readers should take away from this book is the need to view any investment strategy as a long-term commitment. Investors need to recognize that there will be ups and downs along the way and that the objective execution of a winning strategy will achieve a great deal more than acting on gut feelings. The November-to-May period, filtered or not, appears to offer investors some winning guidance in the long run.

OCTOBER THROUGH JUNE FOR THE NASDAQ

So far in this book, we have focused virtually all of our analysis on the performance of the Dow. At this point, we will break from that inclination and take a look at a trend using the Nasdaq market that is similar to the Dow's November-to-May time frame. Specifically, according to the Hirsch Organization's *Stock Trader's Almanac*, the Nasdaq market has demonstrated a tendency to perform best from November through the end of the following June.

Before taking a look at some results, we need to first describe how these results were arrived at, as there was a slight change in the data used made along the way. The OTC composite index (ticker symbol: COMPQ) was first established in 1971. This index tracks the performance of all stocks listed on the Nasdaq, or over-the-counter, exchange. In 1990, the Nasdaq 100 index was established. The Nasdaq 100 (ticker symbol: NDX) is a stock market index of 100 of the largest domestic and international nonfinancial companies listed on the Nasdaq stock exchange. The Nasdaq 100 is heavily weighted toward technology stocks, which makes it difficult to use as a gauge for the overall market. This tech-heavy focus also makes the index extremely volatile compared to other indexes. Though the Nasdaq 100 will generally follow the same trend as other indexes (e.g., the Dow), it is not uncommon for it to be twice as volatile as others indexes on strong up or down days.

The primary difference between the COMPQ and the NDX for the purposes of investing is that there are any number of investment vehicles available that track the performance of the Nasdaq 100, whereas there are virtually none designed to closely replicate the performance on the OTC composite. As a result, for the purposes of calculating performance, we will use the OTC composite index from 1971 until 1990, and from there we will switch to the Nasdaq 100 index.

Figure 8.8 displays the performance of the Nasdaq 100 between November 2006 and June 2007. As you can see, from start to finish, the performance resulted in a respectable net gain of 11.6 percent, as the Nasdaq 100 advanced from 1,732 to 1,935. Nevertheless, it was by no means a straight-line advance. Along the way there were some very sharp declines in price. Most notably, the NDX suffered a 7.2 percent decline in just seven trading days from the end of February to the beginning of March. This should serve as a reminder that a longer-term perspective is important anytime you use seasonal trends to guide your investing strategy.

Figure 8.9 displays the growth of $1,000 invested in the OTC composite or Nasdaq 100 only during the months of November through the

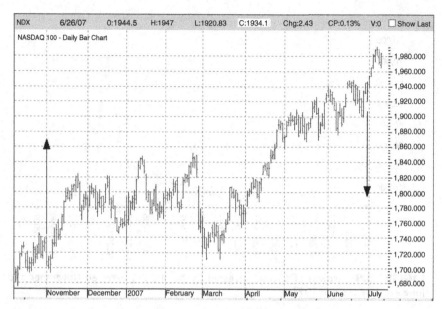

FIGURE 8.8 Nasdaq 100 (NDX): November 2006–June 2007

following June, from 1971 through 2007. As you can see from Figure 8.9, there is some good news and some bad news. The good news is that the initial $1,000 grew to a bit more than $40,000 by the end of 2007, an impressive rate of return. The bad news is that the initial $1,000 investment first ran up astronomically during the height of the late 1990s bull market, peaking just above $80,000 in March 2000. From there, the equity curve collapsed 67 percent, finally bottoming out at just less than $27,000 in February 2003. Since that time, the equity curve has increased about 37 percent. However, the gross gain remains well below the all-time peak of $80,000.

Now, despite the huge cumulative drawdown during the so-called bullish periods of the 2000–2002 bear market, the overall results generated during the bullish period over the years are far more impressive than the nowhere results that might have been generated by investing in the Nasdaq only during the months of July through October every year since 1971. The equity curve for this strategy appears in Figure 8.10. As you can see, there have been many up periods and many down periods, but there has been essentially no money made during the July-to-October period in the past 37 years. In fact, $1,000 invested in the Nasdaq during this time frame since 1971 would have grown to all of $1,006 by the end of 2007. Essentially, investors would have been far better off simply exiting the market, placing

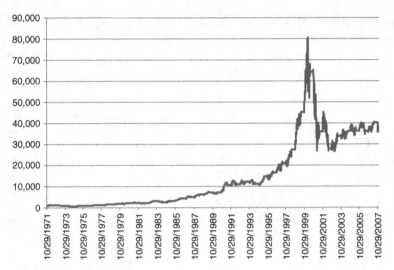

FIGURE 8.9 Growth of $1,000 invested in the Nasdaq between November and June every year since 1971

their money in cash, and earning interest rather than remain in the stock market.

So, just as with the Dow, the Nasdaq index has shown a tendency to advance between November 1 and the middle portion of the following year. Likewise, there is a tendency to perform far less well during the summer

FIGURE 8.10 Growth of $1,000 invested in the Nasdaq between July and November every year since 1971

and early fall months. Here are some performance numbers based on investing in the Nasdaq from November through June:

- The average daily gain during the November-through-June period was 0.000703 percent.
- The average daily gain during all other trading days was 0.000110 percent.
- The average daily gain between November and June was 6.4 times greater than the average daily gain during July through October.
- The annualized rate of return during this bullish eight-month period was 19.4 percent.
- The annualized rate of return during all other trading days was 2.8 percent.
- A $1,000 investment only during the November-through-June bullish period grew to $37,689 by December 31, 2007.
- A $1,000 investment during all days other than the November-through-June bullish period grew to just $1,014 during the same time.
- The Nasdaq posted a gain during 28 of the 36 completed November-through-June periods, or 78 percent of the time.
- The Nasdaq posted a gain during only 20 of the 36 completed July-through-October periods, or 56 percent of the time.
- The November-to-May period outperformed the subsequent July-through-October period 24 of 36 times, or 67 percent of the time.

Table 8.4 displays the year-by-year results of both the bullish November-through-June period and the bearish July-through-October period.

We have now established that the Nasdaq index has a tendency to rally in a manner similar to the Dow during the last two months of the year and into the middle of the following year. Not surprisingly, because the Nasdaq market is more volatile than the Dow, the swings tend to be greater—both on the upside and on the downside. This means that more money is typically made when things go as expected. It also means that the losses can be greater when things go the wrong way. So, now let's take the same MACD filter that we used earlier to filter buy and sell signals for the Dow and apply it to the Nasdaq.

Adding MACD as a Filter to the October through June Time Frame for the Nasdaq

In applying the MACD filter to the Nasdaq as we did earlier with the Dow, we will use the same 8-17-9 parameters to generate buy signals and 12-25-9 parameters to generate sell signals. Given that the Nasdaq tends to trend upward during roughly the same time frame as the Dow, and given that

TABLE 8.4 Year-to-Year Performance for Nasdaq during Bullish and Bearish Periods

Start Bearish Period	OTC	Percentage Gain	$1,000	Start Bearish Period	OTC	Percentage Gain	$1,000	Bullish Period Percentage Gain Minus Bearish Period Percentage Gain
Nov. 1971	105.10	23.8	1,238	June 1972	130.08	0.1	1,001	23.6
Nov. 1972	130.24	(22.5)	960	June 1973	100.97	9.1	1,092	(31.6)
Nov. 1973	110.16	(31.0)	662	June 1974	75.96	(14.1)	938	(16.9)
Nov. 1974	65.22	33.4	883	June 1975	87.02	(11.5)	830	45.0
Nov. 1975	76.99	17.3	1,036	June 1976	90.32	0.0	830	17.3
Nov. 1976	90.35	10.4	1,143	June 1977	99.72	(2.2)	812	12.6
Nov. 1977	97.52	23.4	1,410	June 1978	120.30	(7.6)	750	31.0
Nov. 1978	111.11	24.3	1,753	June 1979	138.13	(1.9)	736	26.2
Nov. 1979	135.52	16.4	2,041	June 1980	157.77	22.2	899	(5.8)
Nov. 1980	192.77	11.9	2,284	June 1981	215.75	(9.5)	813	21.4
Nov. 1981	195.24	(12.3)	2,004	June 1982	171.30	24.1	1,010	(36.4)
Nov. 1982	212.63	49.9	3,004	June 1983	318.69	(13.9)	870	63.7
Nov. 1983	274.55	(12.8)	2,619	June 1984	239.44	3.2	897	(16.0)
Nov. 1984	247.02	19.9	3,141	June 1985	296.19	(1.2)	886	21.1
Nov. 1985	292.54	38.6	4,354	June 1986	405.51	(11.0)	788	49.6
Nov. 1986	360.77	17.7	5,125	June 1987	424.65	(23.9)	600	41.6
Nov. 1987	323.29	22.1	6,256	June 1988	394.65	(3.1)	582	25.2
Nov. 1988	382.45	13.8	7,120	June 1989	435.29	4.7	609	9.1
Nov. 1989	455.62	1.5	7,224	June 1990	462.29	(28.7)	434	30.1
Nov. 1990	329.84							

Start using Nasdaq 100 (NDX)

Nov.				June				
Nov. 1990	172.55	47.3	10,643	June 1991	254.20	15.1	500	32.2
Nov. 1991	292.51	3.0	10,960	June 1992	301.23	9.3	546	(6.3)
Nov. 1992	329.15	11.2	12,191	June 1993	366.13	6.8	583	4.4
Nov. 1993	390.98	(7.8)	11,235	June 1994	360.30	14.6	669	(22.5)
Nov. 1994	413.05	30.3	14,634	June 1995	538.03	11.3	744	19.0
Nov. 1995	598.78	13.1	16,553	June 1996	677.30	11.0	826	2.1
Nov. 1996	751.99	27.3	21,073	June 1997	957.30	6.5	880	20.8
Nov. 1997	1,019.62	31.2	27,639	June 1998	1,337.34	4.7	922	26.4
Nov. 1998	1,400.52	64.0	45,326	June 1999	2,296.77	14.8	1,058	49.2
Nov. 1999	2,637.44	42.7	64,684	June 2000	3,763.79	(12.8)	923	55.5
Nov. 2000	3,282.30	(44.2)	36,118	June 2001	1,832.75	(25.5)	687	(18.6)
Nov. 2001	1,364.78	(23.0)	27,825	June 2002	1,051.41	(5.9)	647	(17.1)
Nov. 2002	989.54	21.4	33,790	June 2003	1,201.69	17.9	762	3.6
Nov. 2003	1,416.39	7.1	36,182	June 2004	1,516.64	(2.0)	747	9.1
Nov. 2004	1,486.72	0.5	36,347	June 2005	1,493.52	5.7	790	(5.3)
Nov. 2005	1,579.18	(0.3)	36,256	June 2006	1,575.23	10.0	869	(10.2)
Nov. 2006	1,732.54	11.6	40,474	June 2007	1,934.10	15.8	1,006	(4.1)
Nov. 2007	2,238.98	(6.9)*	37,689*		2,084.93			

*Through Dec. 31, 2007.

243

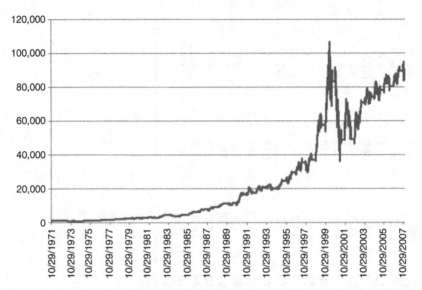

FIGURE 8.11 Growth of $1,000 invested in the Nasdaq only when MACD-filtered November–June method is bullish (since 1971)

applying the MACD filter to the Dow resulted in a meaningful improvement in performance, we would anticipate that adding the MACD filter to our November-through-June bullish period would similarly result in a significant improvement in performance results. Now let's see if that hypothesis proves true.

Figure 8.11 displays the growth of $1,000 invested in the OTC composite from 1971 until 1990 and the Nasdaq 100 from 1990 through 2007, only during those times when the MACD-filtered November-to-June method was bullish.

As you can see in Figure 8.11, using MACD to filter the November-through-June buy and sell signals resulted in a more than doubling of profitability. Remember that $1,000 invested in the Nasdaq market every October 31 and sold at the close of the following June grew to $37,689 by the end of 2007, whereas $1,000 invested using the MACD filter grew to $88,421 during the same time frame. Clearly—and as one would expect—factoring the actual trend of the market into our decision-making process greatly enhances the overall performance results.

Now let's look at what happens on the sell side. Figure 8.12 displays the growth of $1,000 invested using the OTC composite from 1971 until 1990 and using the Nasdaq 100 from 1990 through 2007, only during those times when the MACD-filtered November-to-June method was bearish.

As you can see in Figure 8.12, the performance of the Nasdaq was ultimately a big net loser during bearish periods for the MACD-filtered

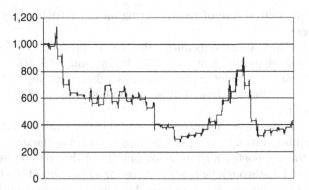

FIGURE 8.12 Growth of $1,000 invested in the Nasdaq only when MACD-filtered November-through-June trading method is bearish (since 1971)

November-to-May method. During the 1990s, the Nasdaq market enjoyed a virtually uninterrupted bull market run. Whether the MACD-filtered November-to-June method was bullish or bearish did not much matter. This period is visible in the third quadrant of Figure 8.12. During this time, the bearish equity more than quadrupled as the Nasdaq charged to sharply higher new highs. As a result, investors who had adopted this timing method to decide when to be in and out of the market would have missed major portions of the 1990 bull market. Once again, this is one of those realties that investors must face once in a while when they adopt a given investment method. No method will ever be perfect. Interestingly, despite missing out on portions of the great bull market of the 1990s, investors using this timing method over the long run would have saved themselves a great deal of money. Between 1971 and 1990, this bearish period using the Nasdaq market would have witnessed a decline in equity in excess of 70 percent. Likewise, after the market topped out in 2000, this bearish period would have witnessed a loss of roughly 67 percent. In the end, the net result of investing only during the bearish MACD-filtered November-to-June period would have been a loss of 57 percent. Remember that during this time, the OTC composite index gained 2,307 percent. So, losing money in the Nasdaq market over the past 36 years was not an easy thing to do. Here are some performance numbers:

- The average daily gain during the MACD-filtered November-through-June period was 0.000854 percent.
- The average daily gain during all other trading days was −0.000174.
- The annualized rate of return during the bullish periods was 23.9 percent.

- The annualized rate of return during all other trading days was −4.3 percent.
- A $1,000 investment only during the MACD-filtered November-through-June bullish period grew to $88,421 by December 31, 2007.
- A $1,000 investment during all days other than the MACD-filtered November-through-June bullish period shrank to $432 during the same time.
- The Nasdaq posted a gain during 30 of the 36 completed MACD-filtered November-through-June periods, or 83 percent of the time.
- The Nasdaq posted a gain during only 17 of the 36 completed MACD-filtered July-through-October periods, or 47 percent of the time.
- The MACD-filtered November-to-May period outperformed the subsequent MACD-filtered July-through-October period 26 of 36 times, or 72 percent of the time.

Table 8.5 displays the year-to-year results for the MACD-filtered November-through-June timing method using the Nasdaq market.

Trading in the Nasdaq market has always been a volatile proposition. Because of the high concentration of technology stocks built into the indexes, and the tendency of technology stocks to swoop and soar at a much faster clip than most other groups of stocks, the Nasdaq simply experiences more volatility than most other major market averages. So, if investors are going to invest in the Nasdaq market, they need to learn to live with this elevated volatility. The bad news is that when the down periods come, the losses may come fairly fast and furious. The good news is that if investors use a winning strategy consistently over a period of years, they stand a good chance of making a great deal more money than they would otherwise. The MACD-filtered November-through-June timing method is a reasonable choice of strategy for someone attempting to accomplish the goal of compounding profits to achieve a higher rate of return.

THE DEAD ZONES

So far in this book we have focused most of our attention on finding those dates and times during which the stock market has shown a propensity to perform well. But at some point it makes sense to ask the question, Are there objectively identifiable times when the market typically performs poorly? If the answer is yes, then investors may be able to enhance their long-term results simply by avoiding being in the stock market during these periods, or at least by investing more conservatively during these less favorable times. So let's look at a couple of periods that have consistently witnessed less-than-inspiring stock market performance.

TABLE 8.5 Year-to-Year Performance for Nasdaq during MACD-Filtered Bullish and Bearish Periods

Start Bearish Period (d-m-y)	OTC	Percentage Gain	$1,000	Start Bearish Period (d-m-y)	OTC	Percentage Gain +(−)	$1,000	Bullish Period Percentage Gain Minus Bearish Period Percentage Gain
4-Nov-71	105.56	24.1	1,241	7-June-72	131.00	(1.8)	982	25.9
23-Oct-72	128.66	(22.7)	959	25-June-73	99.43	(7.2)	912	(15.6)
7-Dec-73	92.32	(20.2)	765	3-July-74	73.66	(23.2)	700	3.0
7-Oct-74	56.57	47.8	1,131	11-June-75	83.60	(9.2)	636	57.0
7-Oct-75	75.88	20.8	1,366	22-July-76	91.66	(2.4)	620	23.2
19-Oct-76	89.45	13.2	1,546	27-July-77	101.25	(4.0)	596	17.2
4-Nov-77	97.21	26.6	1,958	7-June-78	123.10	(6.5)	557	33.1
6-Nov-78	115.08	19.1	2,331	3-July-79	137.03	(1.1)	550	20.2
30-Oct-79	135.48	15.5	2,693	20-June-80	156.51	26.2	695	(10.7)
9-Oct-80	197.53	11.2	2,995	4-June-81	219.68	(17.6)	573	28.8
1-Oct-81	181.09	(4.0)	2,875	7-June-82	173.84	12.5	644	(16.5)
7-Oct-82	195.59	57.4	4,527	1-June-83	307.95	(10.7)	575	68.2
3-Nov-83	274.86	(14.2)	3,886	1-June-84	235.90	5.0	604	(19.2)
15-Oct-84	247.67	17.3	4,559	3-June-85	290.59	(3.0)	585	20.4
1-Oct-85	281.77	39.4	6,356	10-June-86	392.83	(10.3)	525	49.8
1-Oct-86	352.23	20.6	7,663	30-June-87	424.67	(22.7)	406	43.3
2-Nov-87	328.33	20.1	9,204	8-July-88	394.33	(6.6)	379	26.7
29-Nov-88	368.15	22.4	11,268	13-June-89	450.73	0.7	382	21.7
9-Nov-89	454.07	1.9	11,484	11-June-90	462.79	(23.0)	294	24.9
2-Oct-90	356.38							

(Continued)

TABLE 8.5 *(Continued)*

Start Bearish Period (d-m-y)	OTC	Percentage Gain	$1,000	Start Bearish Period (d-m-y)	OTC	Percentage Gain +(-)	$1,000	Bullish Period Percentage Gain Minus Bearish Period Percentage Gain
Start using Nasdaq 100 (NDX)								
2-Oct-90	184.92	45.6	16,722	11-June-91	269.26	7.1	315	38.5
1-Oct-91	288.37	4.9	17,546	11-June-92	302.58	2.3	322	2.6
14-Oct-92	309.58	17.7	20,651	7-June-93	364.36	5.1	338	12.6
1-Oct-93	382.81	(2.8)	20,065	17-June-94	371.94	7.6	364	(10.5)
11-Oct-94	400.29	22.7	24,610	1-June-95	490.96	17.0	426	5.6
13-Oct-95	574.52	20.0	29,524	3-June-96	689.25	11.0	473	9.0
7-Oct-96	764.96	20.5	35,583	4-June-97	921.96	22.0	577	(1.4)
3-Oct-97	1,124.44	3.7	36,884	1-June-98	1,165.55	11.5	643	(7.9)
15-Oct-98	1,299.66	55.9	57,492	1-June-99	2,025.79	25.0	804	30.9
6-Oct-99	2,532.40	44.8	83,224	29-June-00	3,665.83	(14.4)	689	59.1
18-Oct-00	3,139.31	(41.4)	48,801	1-June-01	1,840.83	(37.5)	431	(3.9)
1-Oct-01	1,151.24	0.7	49,136	3-June-02	1,159.15	(26.7)	316	27.4
2-Oct-02	849.56	44.0	70,742	20-June-03	1,223.13	13.0	357	31.0
6-Oct-03	1,381.70	5.2	74,405	21-June-04	1,453.23	(0.0)	357	5.2
1-Oct-04	1,452.94	5.1	78,232	8-June-05	1,527.68	2.7	366	2.4
19-Oct-05	1,569.61	3.0	80,573	1-June-06	1,616.57	4.5	383	(1.5)
5-Oct-06	1,689.43	11.4	89,779	7-June-07	1,882.17	12.5	432	(1.1)
1-Oct-07	2,116.97	(1.5)*	88,421*					

*Through Dec. 31, 2007.

The Months of June, July, and August

As we have already discussed in detail earlier in this chapter, for much of the past half century the stock market has tended to perform best during the winter and spring months, whereas the summer months have lagged somewhat. It should be noted that this was not the case in the first half of this century. In fact, through 1964, the stock market typically showed a strong propensity to rally during June, July, and August.

Figure 8.13 displays the growth of $1,000 invested in the Dow only during these three summer months from 1900 through 1964. In other words, these results show how $1,000 would have grown had investors bought the Dow on May 31 of each year and then sold the Dow and returned to cash on August 31 of the same year. Talk about your dead zones.

From 1900 to 1923, the results are basically flat with no bullish or bearish bias of any significance. By August 1923, the initial $1,000 invested only during the summer months would have grown just 8 percent to $1,080. Then—and as you can see from about the middle of Figure 8.13—for the next 40-plus years, the summer months were typically a boom time for the stock market. By the end of 1964, the initial $1,000 would have grown to $12,607, hence the reason that "summer rally" entered the stock market lexicon. Investors became accustomed to expecting their capital to grow at some point during the summer. As you can see, through 1964 they were typically well rewarded. Then suddenly, someone pulled the plug on the much-vaunted summer rally.

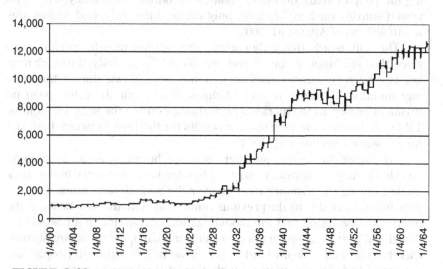

FIGURE 8.13 Growth of $1,000 invested in the Dow only during June, July, and August of every year from 1900–1964

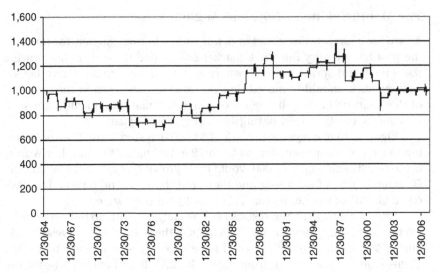

FIGURE 8.14 Growth of $1,000 invested in the Dow only during June, July, and August of every year from Dec. 31, 1964–Dec. 31, 2007

Figure 8.14 displays the growth of $1,000 invested in the Dow only during the months of June, July, and August from December 31, 1964, through December 31, 2007. Considering that a lot of sound and fury indicate nothing, the stock market essentially achieved no gain or loss whatsoever during the past 43 years during the summer months. Technically, $1,000 invested starting on May 31, 1964, only during June, July, and August was worth $996 as of August 31, 2007.

The only words that fully capture the summer months' performance since 1964 are "unpredictable" and "trendless." Technically, the stock market has been up more times than it has been down during the summer months (25 times up and 18 times down), but there has been no rhyme or reason to the market's performance during the summer months. Table 8.6 displays the year-by-year results for the Dow between June and August since December 31, 1964.

My earlier theory that summer vacations became the dominant summer theme may or may not contribute to what has taken place in the stock market during the summer months over the past 40-plus years. Another possibility is that during the previous century and into the mid-1960s, as the Industrial Revolution and the modernization of America in a post–World War II and post-Depression era continued unabated, the dominant attitude was that one had to work hard to get ahead in life. Although people may not have liked this reality very much, they at least came to accept this as a fact of life, even if grudgingly. In the mid-1960s, something of a cultural

TABLE 8.6	Percentage Gain or Loss for Dow during June, July, and August since 1965

Year	June, July & August Percentage +(−)
1965	(2.7)
1966	(10.8)
1967	5.7
1968	(0.3)
1969	(10.8)
1970	9.2
1971	(1.1)
1972	0.3
1973	(1.5)
1974	(15.4)
1975	0.4
1976	(0.2)
1977	(4.1)
1978	4.3
1979	7.9
1980	9.6
1981	(11.1)
1982	10.0
1983	1.3
1984	10.8
1985	1.4
1986	1.2
1987	16.2
1988	0.0
1989	10.4
1990	(9.1)
1991	0.5
1992	(4.1)
1993	3.5
1994	4.1
1995	3.3
1996	(0.5)
1997	4.0
1998	(15.3)
1999	2.6
2000	6.6
2001	(8.8)
2002	(12.7)

(Continued)

TABLE 8.6 *(Continued)*

Year	June, July & August Percentage +(−)
2003	6.4
2004	(0.1)
2005	0.1
2006	1.9
2007	(2.0)
No. of times up	**25**
No. of times down	**18**
Average up	**4.9**
Average down	**(6.1)**
Average all	**0.3**

revolution began to unfold, with a vast liberalization of attitudes. Granted, people's attitudes are year round, not just during the summer. But it can be argued that average people today are far more likely than earlier generations to go on a summer vacation or otherwise take some time for rest and relaxation than to say, "I can't afford to take the time off from work." Then again, perhaps all of this is irrelevant. In any event, the bottom line—which is the only thing that really matters with the stock market—is that the stock market has been a lousy place to be during the summer months over the past 40-plus years. Whether this trend will continue is unknowable. Nevertheless, the trend presents a strong argument for the adage "sell in May and go away."

Is the Summer Rally Completely Dead?

Given the results we just looked at, and the fact that the stock market has achieved essentially nothing during June, July, and August over more than four decades, one might argue that the vaunted summer rally is dead. As we saw earlier, between the mid-1920s and the mid-1960s, investors came to expect a summer rally in the stock market. Since that time, although some years have seen strong summer performance, the net result has been no new net gains for the stock market during the summer. So, is the summer rally dead? Not necessarily. Let's take a look at one particular summer time frame that has generally continued to perform well despite the overall stagnation of the stock market in the summer during the past four decades.

The time period we want to zero in on is a 12-day trading period that overlaps June and July. Our summer rally period includes the last three trading days of June plus the first nine trading days of July. To put it into a formal trading rule:

- Buy the Dow at the close of the fourth-to-last trading day of June and sell it at the close on the ninth trading day of July.

Alert readers will recognize that this period is already somewhat predisposed to be favorable, as it encompasses the bullish six-day month-end and month-beginning period detailed in Chapter 5. It also includes the typically bullish six-day period surrounding major stock market holidays (i.e., the three trading days before and the three trading days after), as July 4 falls in this 12-day period. Given this confluence of generally favorable influences on the stock market, we should not be surprised if the stock market tends to perform well during this time frame. Is that the case? Let's take a look.

Figure 8.15 displays the growth of $1,000 invested in the Dow only during the last three trading days of June and the first nine trading days of July since 1900.

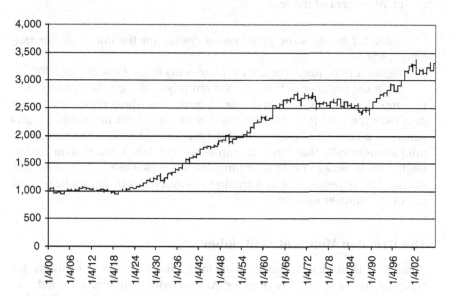

FIGURE 8.15 Growth of $1,000 invested in the Dow only during the last three trading days of June and first nine trading days of July since 1900

As you can see in Figure 8.15, late June to early July offer some respite to investors looking and hoping for a summer rally. However, the results for this period tend to run in streaks. Between 1900 and 1920, this period showed virtually no gain whatsoever. This summer rally then went on a 45-year tear through 1965. From there, the period lost money on the whole between 1965 and 1987. Since 1987, this mini summer rally has generated a total return of about 35 percent.

Here are the performance numbers for the mini summer rally of late June to early July:

- The average daily gain during the mini summer rally was 0.000965 percent.
- The average daily gain during all other trading days was 0.000218 percent.
- The average daily gain during the mini summer rally was 4.4 times greater than the average daily for all other trading days.
- The annualized rate of return during the mini summer rally was 27.5 percent.
- The annualized rate of return during all other trading days was 5.6 percent.
- The Dow posted a gain during 76 of the 108 mini-summer-rally periods, or 70 percent of the time.

Table 8.7 displays the year-by-year results for the mini summer rally since 1900.

Figure 8.16 displays the mini summer rally in the Dow during 2007.

So, is the summer rally dead? Not entirely. Although the primary summer months of June, July, and August have as a whole registered no net gain over the past four decades, alert investors could nevertheless have squeezed a little bit of profit out of the market by taking advantage of the mini summer rally that tends to unfold around July 4. Short-term traders might also be able to profit by trading the long side more aggressively during this 12-day period and then trading less aggressively during the remainder of the summer months.

The Dreaded Month of September

When people think of troubled times in the stock market, the month that typically comes to mind is October. Anyone with a cursory knowledge of stock market history typically thinks of October as the crash month. Stock market crashes of varying durations and sizes have been known to occur in October.

TABLE 8.7 Mini Summer Rally

Year	Mini Summer Rally Percentage +(−)
1900	4.8
1901	(7.6)
1902	0.6
1903	(2.6)
1904	5.0
1905	2.1
1906	(2.3)
1907	1.5
1908	4.1
1909	1.6
1910	(2.8)
1911	(0.2)
1912	(3.2)
1913	0.9
1914	1.5
1915	(0.9)
1916	(1.8)
1917	(2.4)
1918	(2.3)
1919	4.8
1920	0.8
1921	2.4
1922	2.6
1923	(1.2)
1924	2.8
1925	1.7
1926	4.1
1927	4.5
1928	(0.8)
1929	4.4
1930	3.9
1931	(6.6)
1932	4.5
1933	5.9
1934	1.7
1935	3.6
1936	1.6
1937	5.8
1938	5.4
1939	1.2
1940	1.5

(Continued)

TABLE 8.7 (Continued)

Year	Mini Summer Rally Percentage +(−)
1941	3.2
1942	6.0
1943	1.2
1944	1.3
1945	(1.3)
1946	0.8
1947	6.1
1948	0.3
1949	4.1
1950	(5.8)
1951	3.0
1952	1.7
1953	(0.2)
1954	2.4
1955	1.9
1956	4.4
1957	3.7
1958	1.1
1959	3.2
1960	(1.7)
1961	1.0
1962	10.2
1963	(1.2)
1964	2.0
1965	3.4
1966	(1.0)
1967	1.5
1968	2.1
1969	(3.5)
1970	1.4
1971	1.7
1972	(1.4)
1973	0.7
1974	(5.0)
1975	0.4
1976	0.5
1977	(2.0)
1978	2.8
1979	(0.5)
1980	2.0
1981	(4.9)

TABLE 8.7 *(Continued)*

Year	Mini Summer Rally Percentage +(−)
1982	3.2
1983	(2.0)
1984	(1.2)
1985	1.2
1986	(4.9)
1987	1.2
1988	0.2
1989	1.1
1990	4.9
1991	2.4
1992	2.3
1993	1.5
1994	1.5
1995	3.7
1996	(3.6)
1997	3.0
1998	3.5
1999	5.6
2000	2.9
2001	(0.6)
2002	(4.8)
2003	1.8
2004	(1.6)
2005	3.3
2006	(1.7)
2007	4.3
Average	**1.2**

The most memorable crash was, of course, that of 1929, a devastating blow that marked the end of the Roaring Twenties and ushered in the era of the Great Depression. Second on the list is the crash of 1987,when the Dow plummeted more than 22 percent in one day. This too was a devastating blow at the time, particularly because it took so many investors who had been enjoying a nearly nonstop five-year bull market by surprise. Other October market "crashes"—for now roughly defined as a sharp sudden decline in the stock market contained in a given month—include 1978, 1979, 1989, 1997, and 1998.

So, if September is dreaded, why are we spending so much time talking about October? Well, the purpose is to point out that, as bad as things have gotten in October, on the whole, the month of September has been

TABLE 8.8   October Crashes

Years of October Crashes
1929
1978
1979
1987
1989
1997
1998

far worse. With what we have seen so far for October, that is saying something.

A picture is worth a thousand words: Figure 8.17 displays the growth—more accurately, the destruction—of $1,000 invested in the Dow only during September every year since 1900. As you can see, the results are exceedingly grim: $1,000 invested only during September since 1900 would today be worth just $251. This represents a loss of 74.9 percent. To

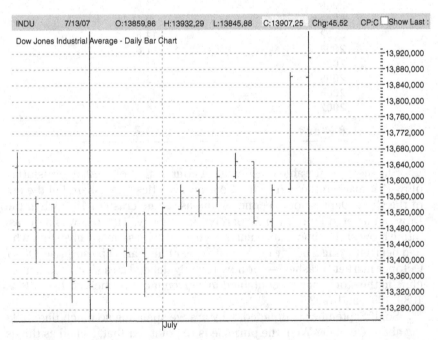

FIGURE 8.16   Mini summer rally during 2007

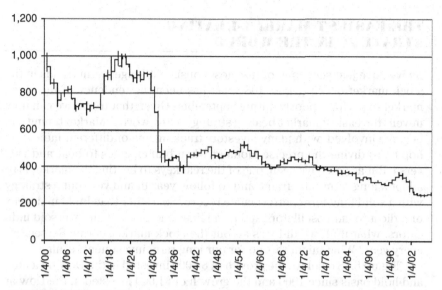

FIGURE 8.17 $1,000 invested in the Dow only during the month of September, 1900–present

illustrate this dreadful performance, consider that during the same time the Dow gained more than 19,000 percent.

Here are the unhappy performance numbers for the Dow during September over the past 108 years.

- The average daily gain during September was −0.000492 percent.
- The average daily gain during all other trading days was 0.000307 percent.
- The annualized rate of return during the month of September was −11.7 percent.
- The annualized rate of return during all other trading days was 8.0 percent.
- The Dow posted a gain during 45 of 108 months of September, or 42 percent of the time.

Clearly, September by far was the worst-performing month of the past century. Although there is no guarantee that this trend will continue into the future, investors should continue to exercise caution during this most unhappy month.

THE EASIEST MARKET-BEATING
STRATEGY IN THE WORLD

As we have just seen, one of the most consistent longer-term trends in the stock market over the past 108 years has been the tendency of the stock market to perform poorly during September. Given that trend, we can now unveil "the easiest market-beating strategy in the world." Market timing can become involved, with many investors tracking lots of different indicators hoping to divine the precise moment when bull changes to bear and vice versa. But as you have seen, one of the real keys to beating the market is to adopt a long-term time frame and to follow year in and year out a strategy with a solid long-term performance record. So, rather than build in dozens of indicators and oscillators and trend lines and overbought-oversold indicators, what if all we did was sit out the stock market during September every year? What might this do for our long-term investment results?

Figure 8.18 displays the growth of $1,000 invested in the Dow on a buy-and-hold basis since 1900 and the growth of $1,000 invested in the Dow at all times except September during the same time frame. As you can see, by applying the theory of addition by subtraction, sitting out September would have improved investors' performance exponentially.

So, $1,000 invested in the Dow on a buy-and-hold basis would have been worth $199,142 by the end of 2007. By sitting out September every

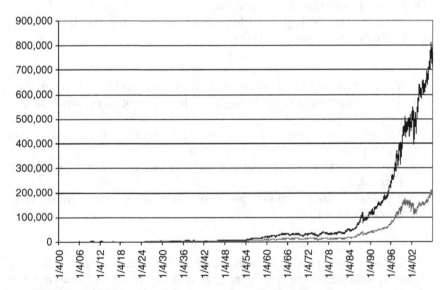

FIGURE 8.18 Buy and hold (gray line), and buy and hold minus September (black line)

year, that same $1,000 would have grown to $747,079, or 3.76 times that of the buy-and-hold strategy.

For investors who are fearful of using market timing but still wish to maximize returns, the idea of sitting out September each year offers a pretty good trade-off between simplicity and profit maximization. The two ingredients that are required of investors are (1) a long-term perspective and (2) the willingness to act on August 31 and September 30 of every year, regardless of the headlines of the day and the present outlook for the market.

OCTOBER OF YEAR 7

There is one last dead zone that I want to highlight in this chapter. In the previous section we discussed October to highlight that, although October has the reputation as being a tough month, September is the most consistent poor performer. Nevertheless, October is not always peaches and cream for investors. One phenomenon of note regarding October is the performance during Octobers of years ending in 7. Now, had you read that sentence in the first chapter of the book, you might have been tempted to disregard this as sheer coincidence. By now, hopefully, you have seen enough quirks in the stock market that tend to repeat over the long run and are willing to at least consider seasonal trends. So, is October of year 7 just one more statistical quirk, or is there information that investors need to protect themselves? Take a look at the results and judge for yourself.

As you can see in Table 8.9, the results for the Dow in Octobers of years ending in 7 have been pretty dismal. It must be said that this is a fairly small sample size; likewise, most individuals will not be comfortable acting on some trend that occurs only once every decade and lasts just one month. Still, the numbers should be enough to give you pause before investing aggressively during October of a year ending in 7. Consider the following performance results:

- The average daily gain during Octobers of years ending in 7 was −0.003141 percent.
- The average daily gain during all other trading days was 0.000281 percent.
- The annualized rate of return during Octobers of years ending in 7 was −54.7 percent.
- The annualized rate of return during all other trading days was 7.3 percent.

TABLE 8.9   October of Year 7 Performance over the Past Century

Year	Dow Close Sept. 30	Dow Close Oct. 31	Largest Intramonth Percentage Gain	Oct. Percentage +(−)	Growth of $1,000
1907	67.72	57.70	0.3	(14.8)	852
1917	83.81	74.50	0.0	(11.1)	757
1927	197.59	181.73	1.2	(8.0)	697
1937	154.57	138.17	0.0	(10.6)	623
1947	177.49	181.81	4.3	2.4	638
1957	456.30	441.04	2.0	(3.3)	617
1967	926.66	879.74	0.6	(5.1)	585
1977	847.11	818.35	0.7	(3.4)	565
1987	2,596.28	1,993.53	1.8	(23.2)	434
1997	7,945.26	7,442.08	3.0	(6.3)	407
2007	13,895.63	13,930.01	3.0	0.2	408
		Averages	**1.4**	**(8.3)**	

- The Dow posted a gain during Octobers of years ending in 7 twice and a loss nine times.
- The average gain for the month during up Octobers of years ending in 7 was 1.3 percent.
- The average loss for the month during down Octobers of years ending in 7 was 9.5 percent.
- On four occasions the performance of Octobers of years ending in 7 exceeded −10 percent for the month (1907 = −14.8 percent, 1917 = −11.1 percent, 1937 = −10.6 percent, and 1987 = −23.2 percent).
- The biggest intramonth gain during Octobers of years ending in 7 was 4.3 percent in 1947 (the month closed with a gain of 2.4 percent).

The bottom line regarding Octobers of years ending in 7 is that even when they aren't bad, they still aren't very good. And when they are bad, they are really bad.

Figure 8.19 displays the growth of $1,000 invested in the Dow only during the month of October during years ending in 7 since 1900.

As you can see in Figure 8.19, the results generated during Octobers of years ending in 7 has been nearly uniformly dreadful. To drive home the dismal performance of Octobers of years ending in 7 even further, consider the results displayed in Figure 8.20. In Figure 8.20, I have stripped away all other trading days except for Octobers of years ending in 7. In other words, the data displayed in Figure 8.20 begins on October 1, 1907 and includes every trading day through October 31, 1907. The next day of data

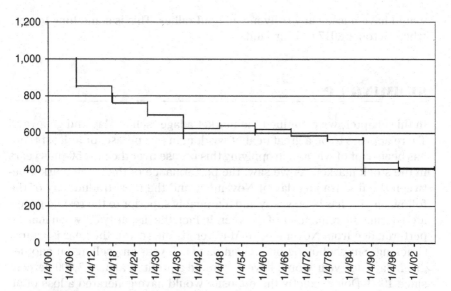

FIGURE 8.19 Growth of $1,000 invested only during Octobers of years ending in 7 every decade since 1900

considered is October 1, 1917, through October 31, 1917. Then onto 1927, 1937 and so on.

As you can see in Figure 8.20, although there were two up years for October ending in 7 during the past 107 years, there has never been much in the way of meaningful upside market activity. So, had investors decided to play it safe and completely sit out the October of years ending in 7 in each decade, they twice would have missed out on small gains but never

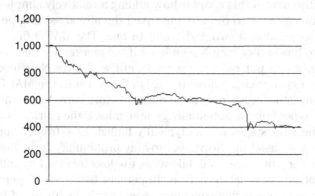

FIGURE 8.20 Growth of $1,000 during Octobers of years ending in 7 since 1900, with all other trading days stripped away

would have missed any truly meaningful rallies. This is something to note when October 2017 rolls around.

SUMMING UP

In this chapter, we examined the market adage "sell in May and go away." There appears to be a great deal of wisdom in this phrase, or at least there has been a lot of wisdom in applying this phrase over the past 50-plus years in the stock market. As we saw, the performance of the stock market between the first trading day of November and the third trading day of the following May has been vastly and inarguably superior to the results generated during the remainder of the year. In fact, the disparity between market performance from November to May versus the rest of the year is almost shocking. Simply buying on a given day each year and selling on another given day each year would have generated a profit of almost 7,000 percent since 1950. Doing exactly the opposite would have generated a loss of almost 19 percent during the same time. With the usual caveat of no guarantees, investors would be foolish to completely ignore and make no attempt to capitalize on this unmistakable trend.

Investors do not necessarily need to buy and sell mechanically on preset dates to reap some benefit from this long-established market trend. At the very least, investors should give the bullish case the benefit of the doubt between November and early May. For example, if the Dow is above a long-term moving average during this time frame, investors should consider adopting a go-with-the-trend mind-set and attempt to maximize profitability as long as the trend persists. What investors typically should not do is attempt to fade a bullish trend between November and May.

We also saw in this chapter how adding a relatively simple filter—the MACD indicator—into the mix improved the already-strong performance by a factor of almost two and a half to one. The MACD filter allows investors to buy earlier than November 1 if the market has been acting well. Likewise, it can put off a buy signal until well after November 1 if the market is experiencing a downtrend. On the sell side, the MACD filter can prompt investors either to exit the market before early May if the market is weak or to hold on for potentially greater gains if the market is acting well during the later stages of this typically bullish time frame. Applying this one filter increased the November-to-May profitability from 7,000 percent to 17,420 percent since 1950. Likewise, the loss incurred by following the inverse of this strategy grew from 16 percent to almost 63 percent. Once again, it seems clear that savvy investors should be aware of the current status of this method at all times.

We also explored in this chapter the history of mythical summer rally as well as dead zones. We learned that the summer rally existed for much of the twentieth century, but over the past 40-plus years, there has been only a small window of time between the end of June and the beginning of July with performance that could be considered a summer rally. We also saw that, on the whole, the summer months have been dead money since about 1965.

Last, we examined the performance of the stock market during September and October. We found that investors often can do themselves a great favor by being out of the market during these two months. In summary, this chapter drives home, "Yes, Virginia, there is a time to be in the stock market and a time to be out of the stock market." The information contained in this chapter gives us clear indications as to which is which.

CHAPTER 9

Putting It All Together

s you have seen throughout the previous chapters, there have been a variety of highly repetitive and consistent seasonal trends at work in the stock market over much or all of the past century. Whereas the magnitude and frequency of success for each seasonal trend vary, most of them share one thing in common—they are objectively identifiable. In other words, in almost all cases, there is little or no room for interpretation. Either a given seasonal trend is in force or it is not. Everything is black or white; there are no shades of gray. Whether or not one believes in the influence of seasonal trends, investors can come to appreciate an objective indicator that they can count on to give a buy or sell signal without any shades of gray. And as you have seen, the majority of the seasonal trends presented in this book have vastly and consistently outperformed a buy-and-hold approach for anywhere from 40 years to more than 100 years. Investors would be unwise to dismiss this type of consistency out of hand.

Despite all the favorable facts, figures, and consistently rising equity curves that I have presented throughout the previous chapters, chances are that there remains in the back of many investors' minds a certain amount of skepticism. And this is only natural. Although certain trends can be explained logically to some extent, still many others simply cannot be. As a result, the primary fear revolving around the use of seasonal trends as an investment tool is the simple fact that—as I have repeatedly mentioned throughout—there is no guarantee that these trends will continue to persist in the future. And this gives many investors reason for pause.

Yet, there is also reason for optimism that this information can be used profitably in real-world investing. In the first place, it is difficult to expect any stock market method to do more than offer 40 or 70 or 100-plus years of consistently profitable results, as have many of the methods that we have discussed. In addition, you should also remember that no one advocates for you to devote all of your investment capital to trading solely on the basis of seasonal trends. In other words, you might consider devoting some portion of your capital to seasonal-based investing and invest the rest according to whatever other fundamental or technical methods you see fit. Also, you might consider seasonal trends simply as a filter to help you to decide the level of risk exposure that you should seek at any given point in time. As we have seen throughout the previous chapters, there are times when the lack of any strong seasonally favorable trends may indicate a good opportunity to play the short side of the market, or at least move to cash. In fact, a little later in this chapter, I will show some specific methods for going short the market given a lack of favorable seasonal trends.

The primary point of this discussion is simply to dissuade you from adopting an all-or-nothing mentality in regards to seasonal trends and seasonal trading. In other words, if you find yourself saying, "I believe in seasonal trends completely," or "I have absolutely no faith whatsoever in seasonal trends," chances are that you are making a mistake. Ultimately, even the best investment methods go through down periods—and, conversely, even the worst investment methods make money at least every once in a while.

The real key to using any investment method—whether it involves a seasonal trend or something completely different—is to analyze it thoroughly enough to understand the potential pitfalls, as well as to (1) make a realistic determination regarding the likelihood of long-term success, and (2) develop a level of comfort that allows you to stick with it when the inevitable down periods come along.

Without these two key foundational pieces firmly locked away in your mind, your likelihood of using any method successfully in the long run is greatly reduced. On the other hand, once you reach a comfort level that allows you to incorporate seasonal trends into your investment plans, you open up a wide range of possibilities. The rest of this chapter will be devoted to putting together seasonal trends in ways that allow us to build several different trading models designed to generate specific buy and sell signals, without requiring any interpretation on our part. Specifically, we will build three separate models, culminating in what I unabashedly refer to as "Jay's ultimate seasonal barometer."

BUILDING SEASONAL TRADING MODELS

Throughout the course of this book I have detailed many seasonal trends, each with specific entry and exit rules. The use and application of specific rules is the key to being able to use these trends in a systematic fashion to help us identify potentially favorable—and unfavorable—times to be in or out of the stock market. Most of the methods that have been discussed don't change from year to year. Thus, it is technically possible to project these tendencies into the future and to identify in advance when the favorable days or periods should occur. There are a few methods that we have discussed that require us to wait for something to develop before we can objectively state that the indicator in question has given a definite signal. Most notably in this category there are the January indicators—most of which were developed by Yale Hirsch and popularized by *The Stock Trader's Almanac*—including the following:

- The first five days of January.
- The last five days of January.
- The month of January as a whole.

According to the rules we set up in Chapter 2, we must wait until the end of January each year before we can fully interpret these indicators.

Likewise, in Chapter 8, we discussed the use of the MACD indicator to filter buy and sell signals from the standard November-to-May method (this filtering method was developed by Sy Harding and again popularized by *The Stock Trader's Almanac*). If we use the MACD in this manner, then we cannot know in advance when the MACD-filtered November-to-May method will give a buy or a sell signal. We simply have to wait for it to occur.

Both of these sets of indicators—the January indicators and the MACD filter—have proved useful over many years in helping investors outperform the overall stock market. Nevertheless, in creating Jay's ultimate seasonal barometer, we will arbitrarily omit these two sets of indicators that require us to wait for something to happen before we can designate bullishness or bearishness. The reason is that, for our purposes, we wish to create a trading model that is as easy as possible to use. As a result, in building our trading models, we will stick to those seasonal indicators whose bullish or bearish status we can know in advance. To do this, we will create an index, or composite of indicators, that I refer to as the "known trends index" (KTI). The KTI uses only those indicators that can be identified without having to wait for something to happen. The indicators included and a description of how they fit into the overall KTI appears in Table 9.1.

For each of the indicators in Table 9.1, there are specific criteria that must exist for a given indicator to be designated as bullish (or in one case, bearish). If an indicator is presently bullish, then one point is added to the KTI (+1). If an indicator is bearish (there is only one that fits this category), then one negative point is added to the KTI (−1). In looking at all of the seasonal trends covered throughout this book, we typically find that a

TABLE 9.1 KTI Components

Method	Measure/Model Points
Days of the month	If today is trading day 1, 2, 3, 4, 9, 10, 11, 12, or the last trading day or the next-to-last trading day of the month, then +1.
November to May	If today is a trading day between November 1 and the third trading day of May, then +1.
Summer rally	If today is one of last 3 trading days of June or one of the first 9 trading days of July, then +1.
September	If today is a trading day during the month of September, then –1.
Election cycle	If today is between October 1 of a midterm election year and September 30 of a presidential preelection year, then +1. If today is between November 1 of a presidential preelection year and December 31 of a preelection year, then +1. If today is between June 1 and December 31 of a presidential election year, then +1.
March to July of preelection year	If today is between March 1 and July 31 of a presidential preelection year, then +1.
Midterm election	If today is within 5 trading days before or 3 days after a midterm election (including midterm election day itself), then +1.
40-week cycle	If today is within the most recent 20-week bullish phase, then +1.
212-week cycle	If today is within 6 months after the latest 212-week cycle buy date, then +1.
October of year 4 through March of year 6	If today is between October 1 of a year ending in 4 of the current decade and March 31 of a year ending in 6 of the current decade, then +1.
March of year 8 through September of year 9	If today is between March 1 of a year ending in 8 of the current decade and September 30 of a year ending in 9 of the current decade, then +1.
October of year 2 of even-numbered decade through December of year 5 of same decade	If today is between October 1 of a year ending in 2 of an even-numbered decade (e.g., 1902, 1922, 1942) and December 31 of a year ending in 5 of the same decade, then +1.
Holidays	If today is within 3 trading days before and 3 trading days after a major stock market holiday (excluding Martin Luther King Day), then +1.

TABLE 9.2   KTI and Stock Market Performance

KTI Reading	No. of Days	Percentage of All Days	Average Daily Dow Percentage +(−)	Annualized Percentage +(−)	Percentage of Days Up
−1	96	0.5	(0.003413)	(57.8)	35.4
0	900	4.6	(0.001113)	(24.5)	50.0
1	3,177	16.4	(0.000531)	(12.5)	48.4
2	4,766	24.6	0.000165	4.3	51.2
All days	19,413	100.0	0.000296	7.7	52.2
3	4,435	22.8	0.000428	11.4	52.7
4	3,113	16.0	0.000656	18.0	53.6
≥5	1,970	15.1	0.001378	41.5	57.2

favorable seasonal trend is generally accompanied by favorable stock market performance. Our underlying theory, then, in constructing the KTI is that we might reasonably expect that the performance of the stock market will be better when a large number of seasonal trends are presently bullish than when fewer seasonal trends are presently bullish. So with KTI, we can objectively assess the favorable seasonal trends in force at any given point in time. Our goal, then, will be to use this information to determine how aggressive we should be in our stock market investments at any given point in time.

BUILDING THE KTI

Now let's look at Table 9.1 and view the specific criteria that goes into building the KTI.

There are many rules listed in Table 9.1. This can at first be intimidating. But take heart and recognize that every trend listed in Table 9.1 can be determined in advance. So, investors could theoretically fill in multiple years of model values into a table or spreadsheet at one time. After that, it would be a simple matter of consulting that table on a daily or perhaps weekly basis to determine the present level of seasonal strength at any given point in time.

To fully appreciate the significance of various KTI readings, let's consider the values in Table 9.2. This table displays the average daily gain or loss achieved by the Dow since December 31, 1933, based on the present day's KTI reading. What you will recognize from perusing these data is that the average daily stock market performance improves uniformly as the KTI value increases.

To illustrate, let's consider the first line of data in Table 9.2, which displays the results achieved by the Dow during those trading days accompanied by a KTI reading of –1. Foremost, note that there have been only 96 such days since 1933, or roughly 0.5 percent of all trading days. Nevertheless, although these days are small in number, the overall results achieved during these days are noteworthy. As you can see in column 4 of Table 9.2, on average the Dow lost 0.003413 percent on these days. This works out to a staggering annualized loss of 57.8 percent. Also, only 35.4 percent of these –1 days showed a gain. There are two things to note at this point. First, this is stunningly awful performance. Second, the results improve as we move down Table 9.2 to higher KTI readings.

In the next two rows of Table 9.2, we find that the stock market also lost money on the whole during those trading days when the KTI readings were 0 or 1. To fully appreciate the significance of this information, remember that the Dow itself gained more than 13,100 percent between the end of 1933 and the end of 2007. The Dow lost money at an annualized rate of only 24.5 percent when the KTI stood at 0 and improved again to an annualized rate of loss of 12.5 percent when the KTI stood at 1. In all, 21.5 percent of all trading days between 1933 and 2007 were accompanied by KTI reading of 1 or less. The numbers in Table 9.2 suggest that these days would have been good times to be out of the stock market. We will drive this point home even more in a moment. For now, let's continue down the results listed in Table 9.2.

It is not until that KTI reaches 2 that the market witnesses a positive average daily gain and a positive annualized rate of return. As you can see in Table 9.2, KTI readings witnessed gains by the Dow that averaged 4.3 percent, with 51.2 percent of those trading days showing a gain. Although this is a positive return, and although the average returns continue to improve with each increase in the KTI level, this is still below the average return (7.7 percent) that buy-and-hold investors might have achieved by being invested in all trading days over the 74-year test period. To find some truly meaningful, positive results, we have to continue to higher KTI readings.

On those trading days when the KTI stood at 3, the Dow gained ground at an annualized rate of 11.4 percent, and the percentage of up days was 52.7 percent. This is the first KTI level to clearly outperform a simple buy-and-hold approach. From there the results improve significantly. KTI readings of 4—which occurred only 16 percent of the time—witnessed an average daily gain of 0.000656 percent, which works out to an extremely favorable 18.0 percent on an annualized basis. Finally, KTI reading of 5 or more—which has occurred only 15.1 percent of the time—witnessed an average daily gain of 0.001378 percent, or a spectacular 41.5 percent on an annualized basis. Also, it is interesting to note that 57.2 percent of all trading days that have been accompanied by a KTI reading of 5 or more showed a gain for the day. This is far in excess of the 51.2 percent of all trading days that showed a gain.

The results that appear in Table 9.2 are compelling and suggest that the KTI may be of great use in determining when to be more aggressive or less aggressive in the stock market. As the KTI reading reaches higher levels, the more favorable the performance of stocks has been. Clearly, investors are better off in the stock market when the KTI reads 5 or more (during which time the market rose on 57.2 percent of these trading days at an annualized rate of 41.5 percent) than when the KTI is in negative territory (during which time the market declined 64.6 percent of the time at an annualized rate of 57.8 percent).

Before moving onto the actual trading models that we will build in this chapter, let's drive home the significance of KTI readings by taking a closer look at the difference in market performance during times of extremely high versus extremely low KTI readings.

COMPARING EXTREME KTI READINGS

In Table 9.2, you can see that there have not been a lot of trading days that have witnessed a KTI reading of –1 or 0. In fact, only 996 such days of 19,413 trading days between December 31, 1933, and December 31, 2007, have witnessed such low KTI readings. We can also see that at each KTI level below 2, the market has shown an average loss. All told, there were 4,173 trading days accompanied by a KTI reading of –1, 0, or 1. In total, this represents about 21.5 percent of all trading days during the 74-year test period. The results achieved by the stock market during these times were nothing less than profoundly bearish.

Figure 9.1 displays the growth of $1,000 invested in the Dow only during those days when the KTI registered a reading of 1 or less. An initial $1,000 invested in the Dow only when the KTI read 1 or less would have shrunk to just $39—a staggering loss of 94.1 percent—by December 31, 2007. You might want to take a moment to let this piece of information sink in.

Not a lot of commentary is necessary about the results depicted in Figure 9.1. Although there were certainly meaningful advances here and there, there is no mistaking the long-term results as terrible. In short, the lesson is that investors might do well to consider avoiding the stock market when the KTI reads 1 or less. In fact—and as we will expound upon a little later—aggressive investors might consider going short during these times to take advantage of the typically bearish results in Figure 9.1.

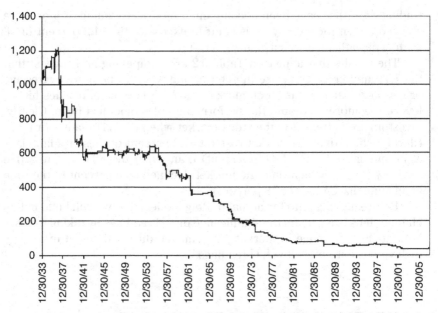

FIGURE 9.1 Growth of $1,000 invested in the Dow only when KTI is −1, 0, or +1 (Dec. 31, 1933–Dec. 31, 2007)

Now let's go to the other end of the spectrum and look at the performance of the stock market only during those times when the KTI had a reading of 5 or more. Figure 9.2 displays the growth of $1,000 invested in the Dow only during those trading days when the KTI showed a reading of 5 or more. Remember that this means that there are at least five favorable seasonal trends at work in the market at the same time. If there is any validity whatsoever to seasonality in the stock market, we would expect the stock market to perform much better when there are more favorable seasonal trends in force than when there are fewer favorable trends in force. As you can see in Figure 9.2, this theory does appear to hold up well in the real world.

As you can see in Figure 9.2, $1,000 invested in the Dow only when the KTI was at 5 or greater would have grown to more than $50,800 over the 74-year test period. Also, these results include no interest earned while out of the market, and the days in the market represent only 15 percent of all trading days since 1933. In theory, investors who adopted this model as their trading method would have been safely out of the stock market and earning interest 85 percent of the time over the past 74 years.

The difference between the results in Figures 9.1 and 9.2 could hardly be starker. In fact, there is barely any explanation required. They are, in

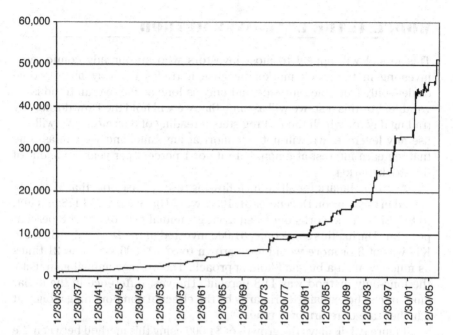

FIGURE 9.2 Growth of $1,000 invested in the Dow only when KTI is 5 or more (Dec. 31, 1933–Dec. 31, 2007)

essence, an inverse image of each other. The equity curve achieved when fewer than two of the seasonal trends in Table 9.1 were favorable is a steady, relentless decline, ultimately losing more than 96 percent of its initial value. The equity curve achieved when five or more of the seasonal trends in Table 9.1 were favorable was a steady, relentless advance, ultimately gaining 4,987 percent.

What are we to conclude from these results? In the stock market conclusions are hard to come by because the stock market keeps fluctuating day in and day out. Nevertheless, 74 years of stock market history are summed up in Table 9.2, and over that period, there is little room for debate that the stock market performs better the more seasonal bullish trends that are in force. The market results generated during the two extremes as displayed in Figures 9.1 and 9.2 seem to verify this conclusion.

From this point forward, we will operate under the assumption that the stock market is more likely to generate positive returns the higher the KTI reading and more likely to generate negative returns the lower the KTI reading. With this theory as a foundation, let's take a look at several ways that investors might go about using the seasonal trends in Table 9.1 to trade the stock market.

MODEL 1: THE LONG-ONLY METHOD

This model will appeal to most investors who are already comfortable investing in the stock market because it trades the way most people trade—only from the long side and only as long as the overall trend is favorable. For this test, we will assume that we will hold the Dow during any trading day for which the KTI registers a reading of 3 or more. We will not use any leverage, we will not sell short at any time, and we will assume that we earn interest at a nominal rate of 1 percent per year while out of the stock market.

As a benchmark for all of the following tests, please note that $1,000 invested in the Dow on December 31, 1933, would have grown 13,178 percent, to $132,781. This works out to an average annual gain of about 8 percent per year. During this same time, $1,000 invested in the Dow only when the KTI was at 3 or more would have grown to $2,792,896, or about 21 times as much as with a buy-and-hold approach. The average annual gain using the long-only method was 11.8 percent. The vast difference in the dollar amount can be explained primarily by the effect of compounding money at a higher rate of return over time.

Figure 9.3 displays the growth of $1,000 using this method between the end of 1933 and the end of 1970. Figure 9.4 displays the growth of $1,000 using this method between the end of 1970 and the end of 2007.

The results displayed in Figures 9.3 and 9.4 suggest a good deal of long-term consistency in returns. Likewise, the end result greatly outperformed a buy-and-hold approach. As another indication of long-term consistency, let's look at the performance of the system versus a buy-and-hold approach on a decade-by-decade basis. This comparison appears in Table 9.3.

TABLE 9.3   Long-Only Method versus a Buy-and-Hold Approach

Decade	Long-Only Method (%)	Buy-and-Hold (%)	Difference +(−)
1933–1939	116.5	50.4	66.1
1940–1949	118.0	33.2	84.8
1950–1959	225.6	239.5	(13.8)
1960–1969	124.6	17.8	106.8
1970–1979	169.9	4.8	165.1
1980–1989	278.8	228.3	50.5
1990–1999	280.7	317.6	(36.9)
2000–2007	108.0	15.4	92.6
Average	**177.8**	**113.4**	**64.4**

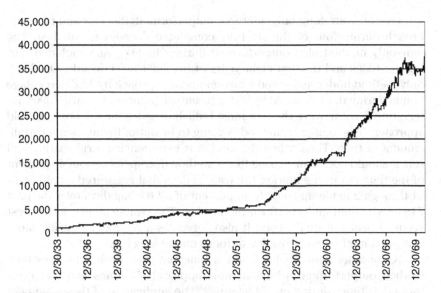

FIGURE 9.3 Growth of $1,000 invested in the Dow only when KTI is 3 or more (Dec. 31, 1933–Dec. 31, 1970)

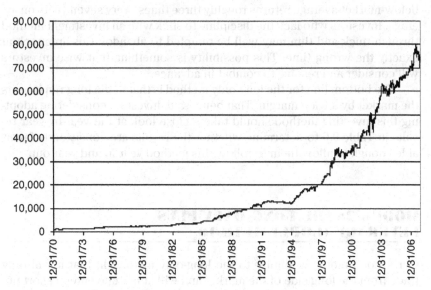

FIGURE 9.4 Growth of $1,000 invested in the Dow only when KTI is 3 or more (Dec. 31, 1970–Dec. 31, 2007)

Overall, our long-only method outperformed the buy-and-hold approach during four of the six fully completed decades in our test. The long-only method also outperformed during the six years included during the 1930s and the first eight years of the 2000–2009 decade. Our long-only method underperformed a buy-and-hold approach by 13.8 percentage points during the 1950s and by 36.9 percentage points during the 1990s. Interestingly, these were the two most bullish decades for the buy-and-hold approach. The long-only method is going to be out of the market a certain amount of time. Thus, when the market is experiencing a rip-roaring bull run, it should not be surprising that a method that spends about 46 percent of the time out of the market (all trading days that registered a reading of –1 through 2 made up roughly 46 percent of all trading days over the past 74 years) would underperform the market. The results shown in this test seem to bear out this theory. It also serves as a reminder that investors using this method must resolve to focus on the long run.

As another reality check, on a calendar-year basis, the long-only method outperformed a buy-and-hold approach 43 times and underperformed 31 times during our 74-year test. The implication of these numbers is clearly in the eye of the beholder. Although the long-term end result clearly favors the long-only method, investors looking for this method to be a holy grail run a great risk of disappointment, as they will experience below-market-average returns roughly three times every seven years on average. Investors who lack the discipline to stick with an investment method through thick and thin may well be tempted to abandon this approach at exactly the wrong time. This possibility is something that wise investors will consider and resolve to combat in advance.

The bottom line for the long-only method is that in the long run it beats the market by a wide margin. That being said, investors considering adopting this investing method should take a close look at the year-by-year results in Table 9.6 to determine whether the results are consistently favorable enough to allow them to follow this method year in and year out.

MODEL 2: THE LONG-ONLY PLUS LEVERAGE (LOPL) METHOD

Our second model is similar to the long-only method in that it will only trade from the long side of the market and will at no time enter a short position. There is, however, one important difference. Our first model would go long the Dow using no leverage anytime the KTI registered a reading of 3 or more. And the long-term results were vastly superior to those from a buy-and-hold approach. Nevertheless, as we saw earlier in this chapter, the stock market has performed far better when the KTI stands at 5 or higher (annualized rate of return of 41 percent) than at any other time. With this model, then, we will try to take advantage of that by setting up the following trading rules:

1. When the KTI is at 5 or more, we will hold the Dow using two-to-one leverage (see Chapter 1 for information on mutual funds and exchange traded funds that allow you to do this).
2. When the KTI is at 3 or 4, we will hold the Dow using no leverage.
3. When the KTI is at any level below 3, we will hold cash. We will assume a nominal interest rate of 1 percent per year.

Now let's test these rules from December 31, 1933, through December 31, 2007. Once again, let's note that, as a benchmark, $1,000 invested in the Dow on December 31, 1933, would have grown 13,178 percent, to $132,781 during this period, which works out to an average annual return of about 8 percent per year. So, how did our leveraged model perform? Quite well. Let's take a closer look at the detailed results.

An initial $1,000 invested between the end of 1933 and the end of 2007 using the rules laid out for the LOPL method grew to a fairly stunning $116,296,163, or 876 times as much as a buy-and-hold approach. At first blush, this number seems too good to be true. But on closer analysis, what it really does is emphasize the significance of compounding money at a higher rate of return. In the end, this value works out to an average annual gain of 18.4 percent versus 8.1 percent for a buy-and-hold approach.

Figure 9.5 displays the growth of $1,000 using the LOPL method between the end of 1933 and the end of 1970. Figure 9.6 displays the growth of $1,000 using this method between the end of 1970 and the end of 2007.

The results displayed in Figures 9.5 and 9.6 suggest a good deal of consistency. As discussed a moment ago, the long-term results are far in excess of a buy-and-hold approach. As we did with our original model, let's now look at the results of our LOPL method on a decade-by-decade basis compared with a buy-and-hold approach. This comparison appears in Table 9.4.

As you can see in Table 9.4, our LOPL method handily outperformed a buy-and-hold approach during each of the decades tested. On average, this model gained 242 percentage points more than a buy-and-hold strategy over the course of a decade. It is also worth noting that the worst full-decade performance occurred during the 1940s, when the LOPL method gained just 225.6 percent. Unlike our original long-only model, the LOPL method vastly outperformed a buy-and-hold approach during the two most bullish decades for the stock market as a whole—the 1950s and the 1990s. During the 1950s, the model gained more than 450 percent versus

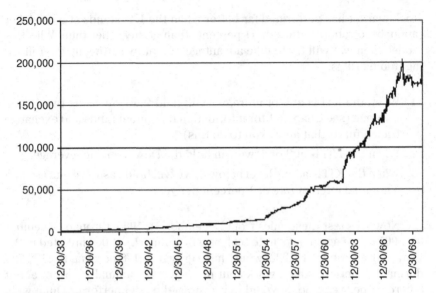

FIGURE 9.5 Growth of $1,000 invested in the Dow using LOPL
(Dec. 31, 1933–Dec. 31, 1970)

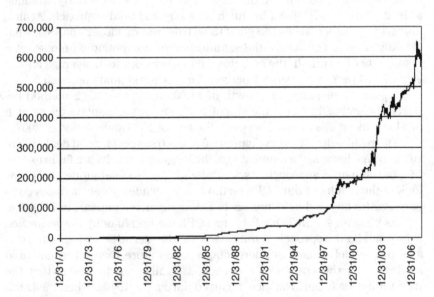

FIGURE 9.6 Growth of $1,000 invested in the Dow using LOPL
(Dec. 31, 1970–Dec. 31, 2007)

TABLE 9.4 LOPL Method versus a Buy-and-Hold Approach

Decade	LOPL Method (%)	Buy-and-Hold (%)	Difference (%)
1933–1939	194.7	50.4	144.3
1940–1949	225.6	33.2	192.4
1950–1959	451.6	239.5	212.2
1960–1969	230.8	17.8	213.0
1970–1979	347.2	4.8	342.4
1980–1989	523.2	228.3	295.5
1990–1999	656.8	317.6	339.2
2000–2007	214.6	15.4	199.3
Average	**355.6**	**113.4**	**242.3**

239 percent for the buy-and-hold approach. During the 1990s, the model gained a stunning 656 percent, more than doubling the most bullish single-decade performance for the buy and hold approach (317 percent).

All told, the LOPL method registered 65 up years and only 9 down years, versus 51 up years and 23 down years for the buy-and-hold approach. Also, the LOPL method outperformed a buy-and-hold approach during 56 of the 74 calendar years included in the test. Once again, although this sounds impressive at first, it also means that investors prone to abandon an investment method if it underperforms the overall market over a given length of time are likely to run into trouble using this method regardless of the long-term results.

For example, consider calendar year 1996. The Dow posted a fabulous 26.0 percent return for the year. The LOPL method posted a gain of just 8.9 percent. In other words, the LOPL method underperformed a simple buy-and-hold strategy by more than 17 percentage points during the year of 1996. Investors who faithfully followed this method for an entire year only to underperform the Dow by 17 percentage points are prone to feel compelled to do something other than just follow the rules. Yet having the discipline to follow the rules is a prerequisite to successfully using any strategy over time—the LOPL method is no exception.

MODEL 3: JAY'S ULTIMATE SEASONAL BAROMETER

The final version of our comprehensive seasonal investment model starts where the LOPL method leaves off. In other words, we will buy the Dow using no leverage if the KTI reading is 3 or 4, and we will buy the Dow using two-to-one leverage if the KTI reading is 5 or more. However, for Jay's ultimate seasonal barometer (JUSB) model, we will also sell short the Dow if the KTI reading is less than 2.

As we saw in Table 9.2, the Dow has lost money on the whole when the KTI reads –1, 0, or 1. In other words, in the lack of a preponderance of seasonably favorable trends, the market has shown a strong tendency to fall under its own weight. With the JUSB, we will attempt to take advantage of this. Using this information, we will set up the following trading rules:

1. When the KTI is at 5 or more, we will hold the Dow using two-to-one leverage (see Chapter 1 for information on mutual funds and exchange traded funds that allow you to do this).

2. When the KTI is at 3 or 4, we will hold the Dow using no leverage.

3. When the KTI is at 2, we will simply hold cash, earning a nominal interest rate of 1 percent per year.

4. When the KTI is at any level below 2 (i.e., –1, 0, or 1), we will hold a short position in the Dow.

Now let's test these rules from December 31, 1933, through December 31, 2007. As before, our benchmark is a growth of $1,000 to $132,781 using a buy-and-hold approach. So, how did the JUSB perform? An initial hypothetical investment of $1,000 invested following the JUSB grew to an almost unbelievable $1,535,650,131. This amount drives home the fact that profits grow exponentially over time at higher rates of return. Although the ending figure seems beyond belief, it is the result of compounding gains over 74 years at an average annual rate of 22.7 percent per year.

Figure 9.7 displays the growth of $1,000 using the JUSB method between the end of 1933 and the end of 1970. Figure 9.8 displays the growth of $1,000 using this method between the end of 1970 and the end of 2007.

Let's look at the results of the JUSB on a decade-by-decade basis versus a buy-and-hold approach. This comparison appears in Table 9.5.

As you can see in Table 9.5, the JUSB outperformed a buy-and-hold approach by large sums during each of the decades tested. On average, this model gained 426 percentage points more per decade than did a buy-and-hold approach. All told, the JUSB registered 70 up years and just 4 down years, versus 51 up years and 23 down years for the buy-and-hold approach.

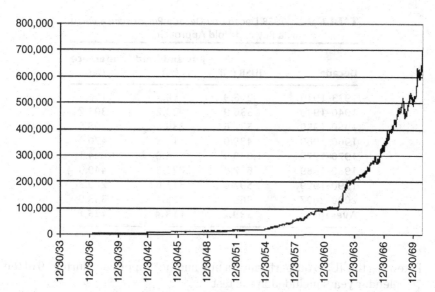

FIGURE 9.7 Growth of $1,000 invested in the Dow using JUSB
(Dec. 31, 1933–Dec. 31, 1970)

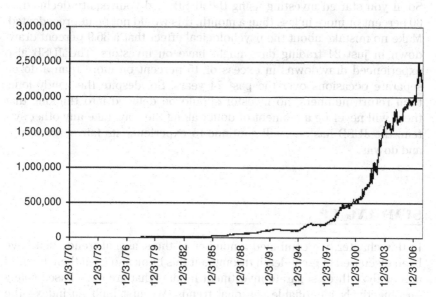

FIGURE 9.8 Growth of $1,000 invested in the Dow using JUSB
(Dec. 31, 1970–Dec. 31, 2007)

TABLE 9.5 JUSB Decade-by-Decade Performance versus a Buy-and-Hold Approach

Decade	JUSB (%)	Buy and Hold (%)	Difference (%)
1933–1939	206.9	50.4	156.5
1940–1949	336.9	33.2	303.7
1950–1959	537.6	239.5	298.5
1960–1969	488.0	17.8	470.2
1970–1979	1,098.9	4.8	1,094.1
1980–1989	677.6	228.3	449.3
1990–1999	597.6	317.6	280.3
2000–2007	369.3	15.4	353.9
Average	**539.2**	**113.4**	**425.8**

Likewise, the JUSB outperformed a buy-and-hold approach during 70 of the 74 calendar years included in the test.

It is difficult to find much to complain about in this performance. Nevertheless, it should be noted that this method experienced a maximum drawdown of 36.9 percent between March 10, 1939, and April 8, 1939. So, if you started investing using the JUSB, and your equity declined by 30 percent or more in less than a month, this would not be unprecedented. Make no mistake about the psychological effect that a 36.9 percent drawdown in just 24 trading days might have on investors. The JUSB also experienced drawdowns in excess of 15 percent on more than a dozen separate occasions over the past 74 years. So, despite the gaudy long-term return numbers, no investor should be deluded into thinking that there will never be a moment of doubt along the way. Like any other system, the JUSB has and will continue to experience its fair share of ups and downs.

SUMMING UP

In this chapter, we combined a number of the seasonal trends that have been discussed in great detail throughout this book and used them to build and analyze three separate investment models that are each based solely on objectively identifiable seasonal trends. We first built an index—the KTI—to track the number of these key seasonal trends that are favorable on any given trading day. Then, using the daily readings from the KTI, we

TABLE 9.6 Hypothetical Year-by-Year Results

Year	JUSB Method (%)	LOPL Method (%)	Long Only (%)	Buy and Hold (%)	JUSB Method Minus Buy and Hold (%)	JUSB Method $1,000	LOPL Method $1,000	Long Only $1,000	Buy and Hold $1,000
1934	8.1	20.4	14.5	4.1	4.0	1,081	1,204	1,145	1,041
1935	35.8	43.3	29.0	38.5	(2.8)	1,468	1,726	1,477	1,443
1936	12.7	17.6	15.0	24.8	(12.1)	1,655	2,029	1,698	1,801
1937	38.5	7.1	7.1	(32.4)	70.9	2,291	2,173	1,818	1,217
1938	50.0	44.2	20.2	27.3	22.7	3,438	3,135	2,185	1,549
1939	(10.7)	(6.0)	(0.9)	(2.9)	(7.8)	3,069	2,947	2,165	1,504
1940	39.2	7.9	8.3	(12.7)	52.0	4,273	3,181	2,344	1,313
1941	18.4	1.2	1.2	(15.4)	33.8	5,059	3,220	2,373	1,111
1942	16.4	24.9	21.2	7.6	8.8	5,891	4,023	2,876	1,195
1943	22.3	22.3	13.3	13.8	8.5	7,206	4,921	3,259	1,360
1944	11.1	13.8	11.3	12.1	(1.0)	8,006	5,597	3,628	1,525
1945	25.1	29.7	14.0	26.6	(1.5)	10,018	7,261	4,135	1,931
1946	6.2	5.3	(0.1)	(8.1)	14.4	10,644	7,643	4,131	1,774
1947	6.5	5.7	0.1	2.2	4.3	11,337	8,081	4,136	1,813
1948	15.5	11.8	6.0	(2.1)	17.7	13,097	9,033	4,384	1,775
1949	2.4	6.2	7.6	12.9	(10.5)	13,408	9,593	4,719	2,003
1950	1.8	4.9	3.8	17.6	(15.8)	13,656	10,066	4,898	2,356
1951	29.7	24.3	11.1	14.4	15.4	17,715	12,510	5,442	2,695
1952	8.7	10.2	8.3	8.4	0.3	19,254	13,790	5,892	2,922
1953	3.2	(0.2)	(0.2)	(3.8)	7.0	19,880	13,759	5,879	2,812
1954	18.4	31.4	18.6	44.0	(25.6)	23,538	18,079	6,973	4,048
1955	40.8	39.4	23.7	20.8	20.1	33,153	25,210	8,624	4,889
1956	26.5	13.8	16.3	2.3	24.2	41,940	28,692	10,033	5,000
1957	29.7	9.7	9.7	(12.8)	42.5	54,399	31,466	11,003	4,361

(Continued)

TABLE 9.6 (Continued)

Year	JUSB Method (%)	LOPL Method (%)	Long Only (%)	Buy and Hold (%)	JUSB Method Minus Buy and Hold (%)	JUSB Method $1,000	LOPL Method $1,000	Long Only $1,000	Buy and Hold $1,000
1958	22.2	30.0	22.6	34.0	(11.8)	66,470	40,900	13,489	5,842
1959	28.7	29.4	13.9	16.4	12.3	85,534	52,921	15,365	6,800
1960	13.2	2.7	1.5	(9.3)	22.6	96,846	54,358	15,602	6,165
1961	5.1	10.2	10.2	18.7	(13.6)	101,807	59,900	17,192	7,319
1962	64.2	27.2	11.0	(10.8)	75.0	167,187	76,179	19,087	6,528
1963	24.8	24.8	15.3	17.0	7.8	208,671	95,081	22,012	7,637
1964	7.5	9.4	8.7	14.6	(7.0)	224,413	104,017	23,929	8,750
1965	26.5	28.0	16.2	10.9	15.7	283,965	133,162	27,796	9,702
1966	11.5	(3.0)	(2.6)	(18.9)	30.4	316,638	129,232	27,066	7,865
1967	35.3	31.5	22.7	15.2	20.1	428,510	169,880	33,216	9,060
1968	11.2	9.4	7.9	4.3	7.0	476,632	185,831	35,846	9,447
1969	5.5	(5.8)	(3.7)	(15.2)	20.7	502,909	175,078	34,506	8,012
1970	40.6	13.1	11.2	4.8	35.8	707,130	198,099	38,373	8,398
1971	38.7	28.2	14.1	6.1	32.6	981,027	254,027	43,787	8,911
1972	17.2	15.9	14.4	14.6	2.6	1,150,037	294,502	50,108	10,210
1973	(4.3)	(2.9)	(2.9)	(16.6)	12.3	1,100,741	286,105	48,679	8,517
1974	33.7	(2.3)	(1.4)	(27.6)	61.3	1,471,584	279,597	47,996	6,169
1975	91.3	90.9	40.8	38.3	53.0	2,815,240	533,675	67,558	8,533
1976	30.3	24.3	21.8	17.9	12.4	3,667,246	663,341	82,275	10,057
1977	19.0	0.3	0.3	(17.3)	36.3	4,365,694	665,360	82,525	8,320
1978	9.6	0.2	1.6	(3.1)	12.8	4,785,723	666,662	83,821	8,058
1979	26.0	17.4	11.5	4.2	21.8	6,029,421	782,973	93,474	8,396
1980	8.3	4.5	1.0	14.9	(6.6)	6,530,955	818,007	94,397	9,650
1981	17.1	1.4	1.4	(9.2)	26.3	7,645,085	829,860	95,765	8,759

Year									
1982	11.9	19.4	14.0	19.6	(7.7)	8,551,955	990,578	109,138	10,476
1983	46.4	45.4	26.5	20.3	26.1	12,519,531	1,440,540	138,042	12,599
1984	1.7	3.5	(2.8)	(3.7)	5.4	12,732,785	1,490,977	134,129	12,128
1985	29.4	27.2	24.5	27.7	1.8	16,480,025	1,896,723	166,932	15,482
1986	4.9	10.0	9.1	22.6	(17.7)	17,287,815	2,086,363	182,202	18,978
1987	82.3	53.3	34.6	2.3	80.0	31,516,846	3,198,884	245,299	19,408
1988	25.6	27.8	23.6	11.8	13.8	39,587,545	4,089,237	303,299	21,707
1989	18.4	19.4	16.7	27.0	(8.5)	46,883,845	4,883,970	354,045	27,560
1990	28.2	11.4	11.4	(4.3)	32.6	60,111,334	5,442,487	394,533	26,363
1991	28.8	31.7	16.4	20.3	8.5	77,449,927	7,166,900	459,131	31,720
1992	15.8	9.9	9.0	4.2	11.7	89,711,866	7,879,976	500,548	33,044
1993	(12.1)	(2.2)	(2.2)	13.7	(25.9)	78,815,286	7,702,768	489,292	37,578
1994	(2.9)	(0.1)	(2.5)	2.1	(5.0)	76,536,311	7,695,509	476,918	38,383
1995	74.1	74.1	35.8	33.5	40.6	133,216,099	13,394,501	647,772	51,222
1996	3.0	8.9	9.1	26.0	(23.0)	137,209,919	14,590,868	706,742	64,547
1997	13.5	13.4	13.4	22.6	(9.1)	155,733,314	16,545,829	801,434	79,162
1998	45.6	53.4	38.8	16.1	29.5	226,718,504	25,377,528	1,112,364	91,906
1999	44.3	45.6	21.2	25.2	19.1	327,213,258	36,960,573	1,347,972	115,086
2000	13.9	(0.0)	(1.0)	20.1	20.1	372,789,546	36,950,986	1,334,658	107,976
2001	34.1	17.7	17.7	(7.1)	41.2	499,997,652	43,504,836	1,571,381	100,315
2002	36.2	14.9	15.6	(16.8)	53.0	681,029,605	49,980,406	1,816,234	83,500
2003	68.7	68.7	29.0	25.3	43.4	1,149,043,048	84,327,667	2,343,603	104,644
2004	9.7	7.9	4.9	3.1	6.6	1,260,923,455	90,972,713	2,458,400	107,938
2005	1.1	1.1	1.2	(0.6)	1.7	1,274,961,191	91,985,504	2,488,546	107,282
2006	9.3	10.5	8.9	16.3	(7.0)	1,393,673,487	101,660,882	2,709,100	124,756
2007	10.2	14.4	3.5	6.4	3.8	1,535,650,131	116,296,163	2,803,150	132,781
	22.7	**18.4**	**11.8**	**8.1**	**14.6**				

measured the effect of investing using different degrees of aggressiveness. As one might expect when using a well-founded approach, which has a positive expectation for profit over a long period of time, the more aggressive the investor, the greater the rate of return, as profits compound over time at a higher rate. Of course, the more aggressive the investor, the greater the risk and the greater the volatility of those returns. Thus, investors must carefully consider how much risk and volatility of return can reasonably be expected from a given trading method. Investors must also consider just how much risk they are willing to tolerate before embarking on any particular investment campaign.

The first model that we looked at in this chapter—the long-only method—buys and holds the Dow only during those trading days when the KTI stands at a reading of 3 or higher and simply holds cash earning interest the rest of the time. This method handily outperformed a buy-and-hold approach, with an average annual gain of 11.8 percent versus 8.1 percent for the buy-and-hold approach. The worst drawdown experienced using this method was a decline of 24.2 percent between February and April 1938. Since the start of the 1940s, the worst drawdown using this method was 16.6 percent.

The second model that we looked at in this chapter—the LOPL method—buys and holds the Dow using two-to-one leverage during those trading days when the KTI stands at 5 or higher and holds the Dow using no leverage when the KTI stands at 3 or 4. This method holds cash earning interest when the KTI is at any level below 3. This method greatly outperformed a buy-and-hold approach, with an average annual gain of 18.4 percent versus 8.1 percent for the buy-and-hold approach. The one note of caution is that this method did experience a 36.9 percent drawdown in less than a month back in 1939. Since that time, the greatest drawdown from a peak in equity has been 18.6 percent. It should also be noted that drawdowns in excess of 10 percent are not uncommon.

The third model that we looked at in the chapter—the JUSB—follows the same rules as the LOPL method, but it also will go short the Dow if the KTI stands at –1, 0, or 1. The hypothetical average annual gain achieved by this method was an impressive 22.7 percent, vastly outperforming the 8.1 percent average annual return for the buy-and-hold approach. The one note of caution is that, like the LOPL method, this method also experienced a 36.9 percent drawdown in less than one month back in 1939. Since that time, the largest drawdown was a 23.2 percent decline in equity between September 1992 and November 1994. In general, drawdowns in excess of 15 percent are not uncommon.

Table 9.6 displays the hypothetical year-by-year results achieved by the various models that we have discussed in this chapter.

As I have stated several times, it is completely understandable that some individuals will view the prospect of investing using seasonal trends with skepticism. Still, looking past the doubts to closely examine the actual results displayed in all of the tables and figures herein, it seems fair to ask whether investors who dismiss seasonal stock markets out of hand are doing themselves a serious disfavor. I leave you to ponder your own answer to this question.

Index

Printed in the United States
By Bookmasters